Communications in Computer and Information Science 2770

Series Editors

Rationale
The CCIS series is devoted to the publication of proceedings of computer science conferences. Its aim is to efficiently disseminate original research results in informatics in printed and electronic form. While the focus is on publication of peer-reviewed full papers presenting mature work, inclusion of reviewed short papers reporting on work in progress is welcome, too. Besides globally relevant meetings with internationally representative program committees guaranteeing a strict peer-reviewing and paper selection process, conferences run by societies or of high regional or national relevance are also considered for publication.

Topics
The topical scope of CCIS spans the entire spectrum of informatics ranging from foundational topics in the theory of computing to information and communications science and technology and a broad variety of interdisciplinary application fields.

Information for Volume Editors and Authors
Publication in CCIS is free of charge. No royalties are paid, however, we offer registered conference participants temporary free access to the online version of the conference proceedings on SpringerLink (http://link.springer.com) by means of an http referrer from the conference website and/or a number of complimentary printed copies, as specified in the official acceptance email of the event.

CCIS proceedings can be published in time for distribution at conferences or as post-proceedings, and delivered in the form of printed books and/or electronically as USBs and/or e-content licenses for accessing proceedings at SpringerLink. Furthermore, CCIS proceedings are included in the CCIS electronic book series hosted in the SpringerLink digital library at http://link.springer.com/bookseries/7899. Conferences publishing in CCIS are allowed to use our online conference service (Meteor) for managing the whole proceedings lifecycle (from submission and reviewing to preparing for publication) free of charge.

Publication process
The language of publication is exclusively English. Authors publishing in CCIS have to sign the Springer CCIS copyright transfer form, however, they are free to use their material published in CCIS for substantially changed, more elaborate subsequent publications elsewhere. For the preparation of the camera-ready papers/files, authors have to strictly adhere to the Springer CCIS Authors' Instructions and are strongly encouraged to use the CCIS LaTeX style files or templates.

Abstracting/Indexing
CCIS is abstracted/indexed in DBLP, Google Scholar, EI-Compendex, Mathematical Reviews, SCImago, Scopus. CCIS volumes are also submitted for the inclusion in ISI Proceedings.

How to start
To start the evaluation of your proposal for inclusion in the CCIS series, please send an e-mail to ccis@springer.com

Liezel Nel · Tanya Stott · André Calitz
Editors

ICT Education

54th Annual Conference of the Southern African Computer Lecturers' Association, SACLA 2025
Bloemfontein, South Africa, July 30 – August 1, 2025
Revised Selected Papers

Springer

Editors
Liezel Nel
Department of Computer Science
and Informatics
University of the Free State
Bloemfontein, South Africa

Tanya Stott
Department of Computer Science
and Informatics
University of the Free State
Bloemfontein, South Africa

André Calitz
Department of Computing Sciences
Nelson Mandela University
Gqeberha, South Africa

ISSN 1865-0929 ISSN 1865-0937 (electronic)
Communications in Computer and Information Science
ISBN 978-3-032-12456-2 ISBN 978-3-032-12457-9 (eBook)
https://doi.org/10.1007/978-3-032-12457-9

This Springer imprint is published by the registered company Springer Nature Switzerland AG
The registered company address is: Gewerbestrasse 11, 6330 Cham, Switzerland

Preface

The 54th Annual Conference of the Southern African Computer Lecturers' Association (SACLA) was held from July 30 to August 1, 2025, in Bloemfontein, South Africa, hosted by the University of the Free State. As in previous years, SACLA provided a vital platform for academics and researchers in Computer Science (CS), Information Systems (IS), and Information Technology (IT) education to share ideas, present research, and strengthen collaborations across institutions.

The theme of SACLA 2025 was *"Innovation in CS, IS, & IT Education: Navigating the Next Frontier."* This theme reflects the drive to explore novel approaches to curriculum design, digital pedagogy, and the responsible integration of emerging technologies, particularly generative artificial intelligence, into teaching and learning. The conference also encouraged reflection on evolving challenges in higher education and the search for innovative solutions to support student success.

A total of 37 papers were submitted to SACLA 2025. Each submission underwent a rigorous double-blind peer review process, with at least three reviews per paper. Authors were required to respond to reviewer feedback with detailed rebuttals and change logs, thereby contributing to the quality and integrity of the final contributions. Following this process, nine revised and extended papers were selected for inclusion in this Springer CCIS volume, representing 24.3% of the overall submissions. These papers were contributed by authors from various institutions across Southern Africa, with more than 60% of the contributions in this volume emanating from collaborations between multiple institutions. This highlights the strong culture of partnership and shared scholarship that characterizes the SACLA community.

As part of the conference, SACLA 2025 recognized excellence in research through the presentation of Best Paper Awards across three tracks.

- The *Best Paper in Information Systems* was awarded to Carolien van den Berg (University of the Western Cape) and Belinda Verster (Cape Peninsula University of Technology) for their paper *"Quintuple Helix, the Informal Economy and Sustainable-Smart Innovations: Lessons to be Learned from a Transdisciplinary Student Project."*
- The *Best Paper in Computer Science* was awarded to Marc Levin, Herman Kandjimi, and Aslam Safla (University of Cape Town; Namibia University of Science and Technology) for their paper *"Leveraging Abstract Syntax Trees to Generate Instructive Hints in Programming."*
- The *Best Paper in Informatics*, which also received the *Overall Best Paper Award*, was awarded to Rouxan C. Fouché (University of the Free State) for the paper *"Beyond Language Barriers: Programme-Specific Effects of English Medium Instruction in South African Computer Science Education."*

The *Best Reviewer Award* was presented to Mark Brand (Nelson Mandela University) in recognition of his high-quality and timely reviews.

The Program Committee for SACLA 2025 consisted of 36 members, including both local and international scholars. Their expertise, constructive feedback, and dedication to the review process were central to ensuring the quality of this volume. We gratefully acknowledge their contribution, as well as the efforts of additional reviewers who supported the process.

We extend our sincere thanks to all authors for their submissions, to the reviewers and session chairs for their service, and to the delegates for their active participation. Special appreciation is due to the organizing team at the University of the Free State for their commitment in hosting the event, and to Springer for their continued support in publishing this volume.

September 2025

Liezel Nel
Tanya Stott
André Calitz

Organization

Executive Committee

Conference Chair

Bennie Botha	University of the Free State, South Africa

Conference Program Chair

Liezel Nel	University of the Free State, South Africa

SACLA President

Estelle Taylor	North-West University (Potchefstroom Campus), South Africa

Program Committee Chairs (Technical Committee)

André Calitz	Nelson Mandela University, South Africa
Liezel Nel	University of the Free State, South Africa
Tanya Stott	University of the Free State, South Africa

Program Committee

Shirley Atkinson	University of Exeter, UK
Shaun Bangay	Deakin University, Australia
Lynette Barnard	Nelson Mandela University, South Africa
Carl Boel	Ghent University, Belgium
Benjamin Botha	University of the Free State, South Africa
Mark Brand	Nelson Mandela University, South Africa
Alan Chalmers	University of Warwick, UK
Rouxan Fouché	University of the Free State, South Africa
Lynn Futcher	Nelson Mandela University, South Africa
Patricia Gouws	University of South Africa, South Africa

Sponsors

We would like to thank our generous sponsors (BBD Software, Oracle Academy, Micro-zone, IBM, SAS, IITPSA, Cengage, and the UFS's Department of Computer Science & Informatics) for their contribution to SACLA 2025.

bbd
bbdsoftware.com

ORACLE
Academy

MICROZONE

IBM

sas

IITPSA
Institute of Information Technology Professionals South Africa

Cengage

UNIVERSITY OF THE FREE STATE
UNIVERSITEIT VAN DIE VRYSTAAT
YUNIVESITHI YA FREISTATA
UFS
NATURAL AND AGRICULTURAL SCIENCES
COMPUTER SCIENCE AND INFORMATICS

Contents

A Phenomenographic Evaluation Approach for Inclusive UX Design Thinking Education 1
Rennie Naidoo

Contextualization, Assessment, and Generative AI in an Online Environment: An Experiment with a Hypothetical Case Study in Enterprise Architecture 17
Wesley Moonsamy and Hugo Lotriet

Leveraging Abstract Syntax Trees To Generate Instructive Hints In Programming 33
Marc Levin, Herman Kandjimi, and Aslam Safla

Beyond Language Barriers: Programme-Specific Effects of English Medium Instruction in South African Computer Science Education 51
Rouxan C. Fouché

A Framework for Integrated Project and Context-Based ICT Education 69
Jacqui Muller and Japie Greeff

Development of the GE-ARCS-E Model to Evaluate the Impact of Gamification on Programming Students' Motivation and Engagement 84
Marisa Venter and Lizette de Wet

Quintuple Helix, the Informal Economy and Sustainable-Smart Innovations: Lessons to Be Learned from a Transdisciplinary Student Project 102
Carolien van den Berg and Belinda Verster

Evaluating AI-Generated C# Code in Computing Education: Implications for Academic Integrity 119
Adewuyi Adetayo Adegbite and Eduan Kotzé

Overcoming Debugging Challenges: Expert Strategies for Novice Programmers 137
Tipson Maleti and Liezel Nel

Author Index 153

A Phenomenographic Evaluation Approach for Inclusive UX Design Thinking Education

Rennie Naidoo(✉)

Department of Information Systems, School of Business Sciences, University of the Witwatersrand, Braamfontein, South Africa
rennie.naidoo@wits.ac.za

Abstract. As computing education attracts increasingly diverse students, the need for adaptive and inclusive teaching approaches has become critical. Traditional pedagogical models often rely on standardized frameworks and evaluation methods that overlook the diversity of student experiences and learning styles, particularly in complex fields like UX design. This study employs a phenomenographic approach to evaluate and understand the range of student conceptions of UX design thinking in an undergraduate systems analysis and design course. Through the UX design thinking module, students engage with user-centered tools such as personas, customer journeys, and empathy maps. Analysis of student feedback reveals four experiential conceptions during the course—*skepticism, adjustment, practical utility, and user-centeredness*—showcasing the spectrum from surface-level understanding to deeper appreciation of UX principles. Findings demonstrate the effectiveness of phenomenography in capturing diverse learning experiences, underscoring its value as an evaluation tool for creating more inclusive and responsive UX design education. Future research should explore the effectiveness of the phenomenographic educational evaluation approach in fostering empathetic student development and enhancing inclusive teaching practices in computing education.

Keywords: Computing education · Empathy maps · Evaluation · UX · Inclusive education · Phenomenographic analysis

1 Introduction

The importance of UX design thinking in helping deepen students' understanding of user needs and behaviours about digital technology has been increasingly recognized, with computing scholars advocating for the integration of UX knowledge and skills into the curricula [1–3]. However, teaching UX design thinking effectively to ensure the successful design of digital applications and tools remains a major challenge [4–6]. Many students struggle to create designs that resonate with users due to a lack of real-life experience and empathy cultivation [7]. UX mapping skills, such as creating personas, customer journey maps, and empathy maps, are essential tools that foster UX design thinking among students [8, 9]. These maps help students understand user needs,

L. Nel et al. (Eds.): SACLA 2025, CCIS 2770, pp. 1–16, 2026.
https://doi.org/10.1007/978-3-032-12457-9_1

visualize user journeys, and cultivate empathy, which are critical for developing user-centered designs. By introducing the importance of empathy in UX design thinking and systematically analyzing and addressing user-related challenges, students can generate innovative user-centered solutions. UX design thinking focuses on creating and evaluating technologies tailored to human users, prioritizing usability and user satisfaction [10, 11]. By applying design thinking principles, UX mapping tools have the potential to enable students to apply their theoretical knowledge to practical problems, ultimately enhancing their ability to design user-centered solutions.

However, evaluating the effectiveness of UX design thinking in computing education is crucial to ensure that students truly benefit from this approach. Educational evaluation is generally viewed as the systematic investigation and assessment of the extent to which educational objectives are being realized [12]. In other studies, it is viewed as the information necessary for decision-making to improve educational programs [13]. According to Nevo [13], a commonly accepted definition is "the merit or worth of educational programs." Notwithstanding the different standpoints, all these definitions share both descriptive and judgmental components and aim to provide valuable insights into evaluating and continuously improving educational practices and outcomes. Traditional pedagogical approaches often rely on uniform conceptual frameworks and conventional evaluation methods [2, 14, 15]. These evaluation methods assume homogeneity in student understanding, resulting in standardized instructional materials and activities that do not account for individual learning differences [5, 16, 17]. Critics argue that this educator-centered approach prioritizes comprehensive syllabus coverage over student inclusion and engagement, potentially hindering student development [18, 19]. Such a standardized educational model overlooks the rich diversity of student experiences and conceptual variations in student understanding, leading to a one-size-fits-all strategy that may not effectively meet diverse educational needs [1, 20].

In South Africa, where this study is situated, and increasingly on a global scale, computing educational programs are attracting a highly diverse student body with varied cultural, basic educational, and socio-economic backgrounds [21–23]. This diversity enriches the learning environment but presents unique pedagogical challenges in diverse educational settings, particularly in teaching UX [6, 24]. Another dimension of this diversity challenge arises from the fact that systems analysis and design courses, including UX, are taught to students from various disciplines, including computer science, informatics, information systems, software engineering, information sciences, and even the humanities. These students bring different perspectives, foundational knowledge, and learning styles to the classroom, further complicating the task of delivering effective UX education. Addressing differences in student understanding requires a teaching approach that is both adaptive and inclusive, capable of bridging diverse starting points to improve teaching and learning outcomes [25, 26]. Jones and Asensio [27] have proposed that course designers use phenomenography to evaluate and align teaching approaches with diverse student learning experiences. The phenomenographic approach offers a student-centered evaluation approach as it emphasizes the qualitatively different ways students experience and conceptualize knowledge, shifting focus from basic UX principles and technocentric perspectives to deeper empathetic understanding and offers a valuable lens to understand and address these differences [28, 29].

The purpose of this paper is to report on a novel phenomenographic evaluation approach for assessing diverse student conceptions of UX design thinking in computing education with the use of UX mapping skills. This evaluation is based on evidence collected from student feedback using a phenomenographic approach as part of an undergraduate systems analysis and design course. It does so by addressing the following questions:

How do students from diverse backgrounds conceive and experience the learning process of UX mapping tools within the framework of design thinking principles, and what qualitative variations exist in their understanding and application of these tools? And how can educational interventions be continuously improved to better align with students' evolving conceptualizations of learning design thinking principles and UX mapping skills?

This paper is structured as follows. First, we examine UX mapping tools and their pedagogical applications within UX design thinking education, highlighting their role in fostering user-centered learning. Next, we outline the phenomenographic evaluation approach used to capture diverse student conceptions and experiences with UX design thinking. This is followed by a detailed analysis of the qualitative data collected, identifying distinct variations in student perspectives. Finally, we present recommendations for refining UX design thinking teaching strategies to address student diversity and promote inclusive practices, offering insights for advancing qualitive evaluation approaches in computing education research.

2 Literature Review

UX maps are visual tools employed by educators, designers, and product teams to chart and analyze the complex interactions between users and digital-enabled products and services. These tools help in identifying key interactions, pain points, and opportunities for improvement, ensuring better UX designs that strive for a seamless and intuitive user experience [30, 31]. User journey maps, experience maps, and service blueprints are integral components of the UX mapping toolkit, each serving a distinct purpose in user-centered design [20, 32]. The literature defines user or customer journey maps as detailed visualizations that trace the path a user follows to achieve a specific goal within a product or service, from initial contact through various interactions to the final outcome. According to Rosenbaum et al. [9], they are instrumental in highlighting the user's emotions, expectations, and experiences at each stage, allowing designers to pinpoint opportunities for enhancing usability and end-user satisfaction. Experience maps offer a broader perspective, capturing the entirety of a user's interactions with a product or service within a given context [33]. Unlike journey maps that focus on a specific task or goal, experience maps consider the user's overall experience, including external influences and actions not directly related to the product.

On the other hand, service blueprints go beyond the front-end user experience to reveal the behind-the-scenes processes and interactions that make it possible [30]. These blueprints map out the relationship between different service components, including user actions, touchpoints, front-end and back-end activities, and the roles of various service agents. By illustrating both the visible user journey and the invisible organizational processes, service blueprints enable teams to identify inefficiencies, redundancies, and gaps in service delivery, leading to improved operational efficiency and user satisfaction. According to Ferreira et al. [34], empathy maps can complement journey maps and service blueprints by providing a foundational understanding of the user's emotional and cognitive states. Empathy maps are used in UX design and research to gain deeper insights into users' thoughts, feelings, experiences, and needs. By capturing what users say in interviews or surveys, what they think about their needs and challenges, what actions they take in specific contexts, and how they feel about their experiences, empathy maps help designers identify and understand user pain points, desires, and motivations [31].

The fictional characters of personas are also created based on research to represent the different user types that might use an IS-based product or service [33]. Personas humanize the design process, enabling developers and designers to empathize with the users for whom they are creating IS-based solutions [35]. By encapsulating key characteristics, needs, goals, and observed behavior patterns of a target user group, personas make abstract data about potential users tangible and accessible. This method also allows for a greater understanding of user needs, enhancing the decision-making process in system development projects. Furthermore, personas encourage a user-centered approach to design thinking and problem-solving.

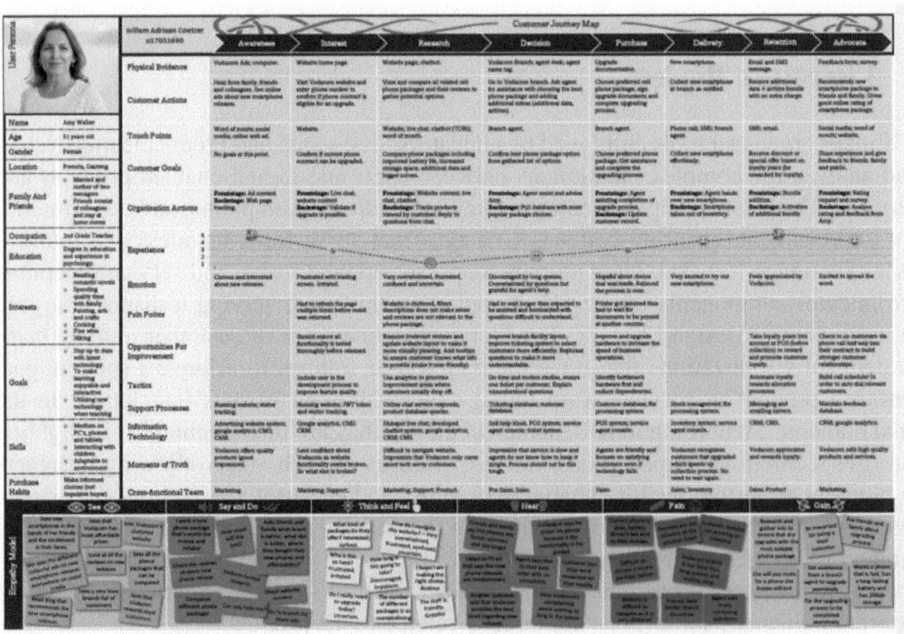

Fig. 1. A Main Student Deliverable – Integrated UX Maps.

Figure 1 illustrates a student's adeptness at weaving together the various UX mapping tools. This integration of a persona, customer journey map, and empathy map allows students to not only visualize the users' external actions and interactions but also to internalize their thoughts, feelings, and motivations [31]. Such an approach is critical for preparing students for their capstone learning projects and for their future roles as UX designers, where they will be expected to apply a similar level of analysis, synthesis, and empathetic insight to real-world projects [26]. User-centeredness is at the heart of the design thinking process in the classroom, where the focus is on helping students create solutions that genuinely meet the needs and preferences of users. In UX design education, this principle comes to life through continuous user research and feedback, which are integral parts of classroom activities. Tools like personas and user journey maps enable students to consistently keep the user at the forefront of their design process. By prioritizing user needs throughout their projects, students learn to design products that are not only functional, but also enjoyable and ethical to use, ensuring that their classroom experience mirrors real-world design challenges.

3 The Integrated UX Map Assignment

This UX design thinking module places a strong emphasis on user-centered design thinking techniques, an approach that is increasingly vital for harnessing the potential of recent technology trends [1]. One of the goals of the module was to foster ludic engagement, encouraging students to interact with learning materials and design processes in a playful, exploratory, and deeply engaging manner [19]. A key deliverable was the development of an integrated poster that encompasses three critical elements of UX design: (1) persona model, (2) customer journey map, and (3) empathy map. These maps together not only allowed students to empathize with target users but also to map out the entire experience of these users as they interact with an IS-based service or product. By integrating UX theoretical knowledge with practical application in the creation of these UX maps, students are likely to gain a holistic view of UX design, preparing them to create more empathetic and effective IS solutions.

Individual students were requested to develop a single integrated UX poster independently that combined a persona model, a customer journey map, and an empathy map (See Fig. 1). Students were informed that their poster should serve as an essential tool for a design team to enhance the user experience for any trending application that aligned with a relevant United Nations (UN) Sustainable Development Goal relevant to the South African context. For the assignment, each student was also tasked with creating a detailed persona model as a component of their integrated UX poster. As part of their integrated UX poster, students were required to create an empathy map that provided deep insights into the user's experiences. Students were asked to leverage tools like Google and Google Scholar to conduct further research on the abovementioned maps and techniques. Students were also told to consider software like Visio or PowerPoint to design their poster and submit it as a single A4 or A3 PDF file. Students were encouraged to provide feedback on their experience of developing the persona, customer journey map, and empathy map, focusing on the ease or difficulty of the task, the perceived usefulness of these tools, and their applicability in creating user-centered designs. The classroom training component of this module was structured to provide students with a comprehensive understanding of UX design tools, emphasizing their practical application. The training was also designed to equip students with the necessary skills to develop integrated posters featuring persona models, customer journey maps, and empathy maps.

The module utilized a selection of seminal readings and templates that guide students through the intricacies of UX mapping tools. These resources were carefully chosen to enrich student understanding and practical application of these tools. The service blueprinting reading introduced students to the concept of service blueprinting, a technique crucial for service innovation. It provided a detailed framework for visualizing service processes, customer interactions, and the various touchpoints that characterize a customer's experience. The resource by Rosenbaum et al. [9] offers a step-by-step guide to creating detailed and realistic customer journey maps. It emphasized the importance of ensuring that the maps reflect the true journey of the customer. Ferreira et al. [34] shows how empathy mapping can be applied to understanding user needs and perspectives. This reading provides guidance on the methodology of creating empathy maps, outlining the different elements that need to be considered. It also guides students on how to effectively synthesize user research into a visual format that highlights the user's emotional and cognitive experience.

Alongside these readings, the module provides students with templates for creating persona models, customer journey maps, and empathy maps. These templates served as practical tools, helping students structure their work and ensure that all essential components of the UX mapping tools were effectively captured. The templates were also designed to be flexible, allowing for creativity and innovation while maintaining a clear and organized approach to mapping user experiences. Together, these readings and templates form a comprehensive toolkit, empowering students to excel in the creation of user-centered design solutions.

4 Research Design

This study explored the diverse experiences and understandings of undergraduate IS students learning design thinking and UX mapping skills, utilizing a phenomenographic research approach. Phenomenography is a research approach aimed at understanding the qualitatively different ways in which people experience, understand, and conceptualize various phenomena and aspects of the world around them. The phenomenographic approach is suitable for this study because, like design thinking, it aligns with constructivist epistemologies, emphasizing the subjective interpretation of reality and focusing on understanding the diverse ways students experience and conceptualize UX design thinking [36]. This qualitative approach allows for a deeper exploration of student perspectives, ensuring that the curriculum is designed to meet the varied needs and experiences of learners.

Figure 2 presents a conceptual diagram representing the relationship between the researcher, the students, the object of study (UX mapping skills), and the phenomenon. It illustrates how the educator and students interact with and experience the learning phenomenon in the context of UX education. It emphasizes the subject's experiences and conceptualization of the phenomenon and the researcher's role in analyzing the relation between the subject and the phenomenon. Phenomenography adopts a second-order perspective, focusing not on the phenomenon as such (first-order perspective) but on student experiences and conceptions [37].

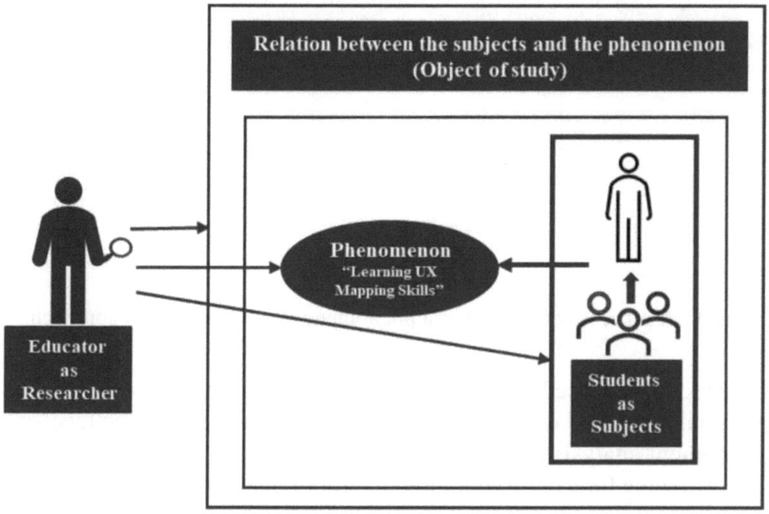

Fig. 2. The relational aspects of a UX phenomenographic study.

The aim of the research is to understand and describe these experiences from the participant's point of view without the researcher superimposing their interpretations [38, 39]. In this way, the researcher brackets their understanding and focus on the subject's interpretation of the phenomenon. By emphasizing the relationship between the individual and the phenomenon, phenomenography provides an understanding that is contextually bound and dependent on this interaction. For example, students with a strong technical background might initially struggle to appreciate the value of personas in design, whereas students with a background in marketing or psychology might readily appreciate the role of empathy maps in understanding user needs.

Figure 3 shows that the research used course feedback surveys, focusing on student interactions with the assigned UX mapping tools. The analysis involved identifying descriptive categories that capture the range of students' experiences and understandings. To obtain these variations in students' conceptions, the research employed a combination of thematic analysis and content analysis [40, 41]. The qualitative survey responses were read multiple times to extract meaning units, which were then clustered into categories based on similarities and differences in conceptions. The emerging categories were refined through comparison and contrast, resulting in the final four outcome spaces presented in Table 1.

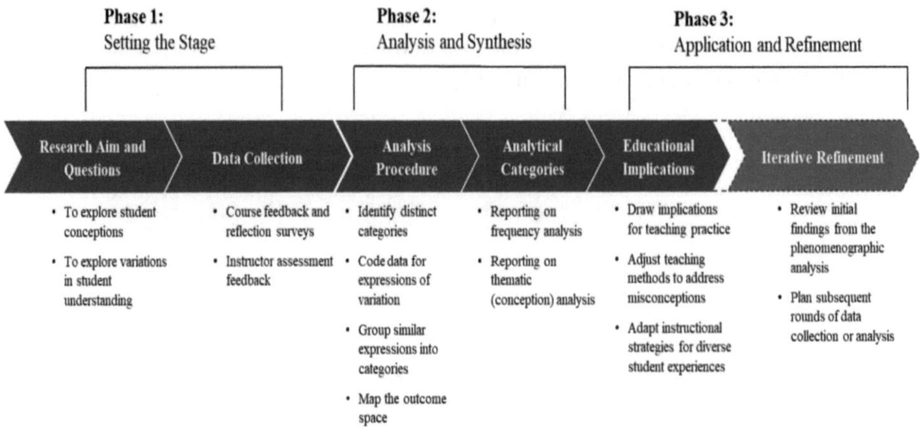

Fig. 3. A process perspective of a phenomenographic evaluation approach.

These methods were used in a complementary manner: thematic analysis focused on identifying, analyzing, and reporting patterns (conceptions) within the feedback survey data, while content analysis was used to systematically quantify the presence of these conceptions, allowing for a more structured interpretation of the data. These conceptions were then organized into an outcome space illustrating the spectrum of perspectives on UX mapping skills. For example, the outcome space of this study included categories such as "skeptical" and the "practical utility" conceptions of UX mapping skills.

5 Results

Near the end of the project, students were surveyed concerning their experience with using customer journey maps, personas and empathy maps in a software design project. The qualitative feedback collected aimed to understand the practicality and effectiveness of these UX tools in a real-world project setting. The questions were designed to gauge students' willingness to incorporate these methods into future projects. The analysis of student feedback on the assignment revealed four key conceptions, shown in Table 1, each underpinned by specific student experiences and perspectives.

Table 1. Content Analysis of Student Conceptions

Conception	Frequency Analysis
Practical Utility	1, 3, 4, 5, 6, 7, 8, 9, 10, 11, 12, 13, 14, 15, 16, 17, 18, 19, 20, 21, 22, 23, 24, 25, 26, 27, 28, 29, 30, 31, 32, 33, 34, 35, 36, 37
User centeredness	4, 5, 6, 7, 10, 12, 13, 14, 15, 16, 17, 19, 20, 21, 24, 25, 26, 30, 31, 32, 34, 36, 37
Adjustment	1, 3, 8, 9, 11, 17, 18, 21, 23, 26, 27, 28, 29, 33, 35
Skepticism	2, 22, 38

The content analysis of student conceptions (Table 1) reveals a range of experiential categories reflecting diverse engagement levels with UX design thinking principles. The most prevalent conception, Practical Utility, was cited by 37 students, indicating a strong recognition of the functional benefits of UX mapping tools. User-centeredness was the next most common conception, identified by 24 students. Fifteen students reported the conception of Adjustment. Finally, Skepticism was noted among four students. The overlapping of conceptions suggests that students do not fit neatly into single categories but exhibit a blend of conceptions that reflect different facets of their learning journey.

In the first conception—practical utility—many students expressed a recognition of the practical benefits these tools offer. Student 5's reflection that personas and empathy maps *"can be very useful to determine what the needs and wants of users of a specific app are and can help to improve the design of the app. I think I could use them to help create the user interface of a project I am working on as they give a good idea of what the end user wants from a specific app or website."* suggests an appreciation of these tools in linking theory to practice. Student 10 echoed this sentiment, finding simplicity and utility *"once I genuinely understood the concept of each of them,"* speaking to the moment where conceptual understanding translates into practical application. When expanding on the utility of employing personas and empathy maps in software design projects, Student 10 also provided an affirmative stance, underscoring the value these tools bring to understanding users: *"Yes, it does give more insight into the customer."* This affirmation reflects a broader recognition of the importance of deep customer insights in the design process. The functional relevance of these tools in UX design was further reinforced by Student 18, who believed in their usefulness *"in terms of finding more about what your target is when creating an application."* Collectively, these reflections capture the instrumental value that students ascribe to UX tools within the software design process.

Another prominent conception in Table 1 is the student commitment to user-centeredness. This conception is rooted in the recognition of deeply understanding and prioritizing the needs, preferences, and experiences of users in the design process. Student 18's reflection offers a compelling insight into the necessity of a user-centric approach, noting, *"I believe they can be useful in terms of finding more about what your target is when creating an application."* This feedback from the student highlights the perceived importance of UX tools in identifying and understanding the target audience for an application, suggesting that these tools are crucial for developing user-centric software solutions. Similarly, Student 34 also acknowledged how these tools allow designers to *"step into the role of their customer"*, highlighting the empathetic orientation required for user-centered design. Student 40's insight that these tools *"can help identify what exactly the user needs"* also exemplifies the application of these tools in developing practical solutions. This conception reflects a consensus on the value of UX mapping tools in providing deeper insights into user needs, thereby facilitating the development of more tailored and user-aligned design solutions.

The third conception, identified as adjustment, is where students report experiencing initial difficulties before reaching a level of comfort with the UX mapping tools. For instance, student 9 articulated the initial challenges with the process as *"difficult to get started, but once I understood the topic, it was easier"*, which underscores the adaptation and transformative learning journey from confusion to clarity. When expanding on the potential use of UX mapping tools in software design projects, the same student articulated a compelling rationale for embracing these tools: *"Definitely, as I believe that as designers, we sometimes think about the project more than the user, which causes major problems and can lead to a failed project."* This finding highlights a keen awareness among students of the pitfalls of overlooking user perspectives, asserting that neglecting user insights can significantly jeopardize project success. Similarly, the assistance from course materials was crucial, as Student 27 found *"it very easy to develop the models with the help I received from the < course id > notes."* The time investment to understand the necessary components was highlighted by Student 33, who mentioned that designing the diagrams *"just took some time to do and understand what needs to be in them."* These insights reveal the shift from an initial state of perplexity to one of competence, reflecting the dynamic nature of learning and adaptation.

Albeit the least prevalent conception among the participants, this conception encapsulates a critical viewpoint questioning the real-world applicability of UX tools, especially for undergraduate students who have no work experience. Student 22 highlighted the challenges encountered as a novice: *"I found developing this assignment to be very difficult because it was hard to understand.... I have never heard of a persona model or empathy map prior to the assignment, so I don't have an in-depth understanding of it or have actually seen the results that they bring. That being said, they seem to be useful."* Further complicating their experience is the acknowledgement of unfamiliarity and a lack of clarity on how these models translate into actionable insights, thereby casting doubt on their usefulness. Student 38's feedback accentuated this conception of skepticism, mentioning, *"I'm not certain of the usefulness of these posters in real-world scenarios, but I'm not a diagram person, so my usefulness might not be the same as another person's."* This student articulates a personal disconnect with diagrammatic tools and questions their applicability, an uncertainty that is perhaps intensified by a lack of exposure to real-world software projects.

In phenomenographic research, the conceptions of individuals can be complex and multidimensional. For example, when considering the range of student responses to the utility of UX mapping, it was evident that conceptions do not exist in isolation but often intersect and influence one another. For instance, Student 10's affirmative stance on the value of UX tools for gaining *"more insight into the customer"* reflects not just an appreciation for the practical utility of these tools but also touches upon the conception of user-centeredness. Similarly, the reservations expressed by some students about the real-world applicability of these tools underscores an intersection between the steep learning curve with UX and skepticism about their educational value. These qualitative differences highlight the spectrum of learning experiences among students, from many who achieve a deeper appreciation of UX mapping tools in their work to some who remain at a more surface level of understanding and application [56].

6 Discussion

Addressing variations in student conceptions, particularly in systems analysis and design courses, is crucial for students from diverse cultural and educational backgrounds. As noted by Rose et al. [38], recognizing and accommodating diverse conceptions in the classroom in response to the insights gained from a phenomenographic analysis can foster an inclusive learning environment. This approach signals to students that their unique perspectives and backgrounds are valued and that education is accessible to everyone, not just those with a specific set of prior experiences.

The phenomenographic results in Fig. 4 reveal a spectrum of student conceptions regarding the learning of UX design thinking principles in our empirical setting, ranging from skepticism to a deep understanding of user-centeredness. Initially, some students exhibited skepticism, likely due to their unfamiliarity with or doubts about the relevance of UX design thinking and mapping tools. Others encountered challenges as they adjusted to these new concepts but gradually began to integrate them into their approach. A significant portion of students recognized the practical utility of UX tools, seeing their value in addressing real-world design problems. The most advanced group seem to fully embrace the principles of user-centered design, focusing on understanding and prioritizing the needs and emotions of users throughout the design process.

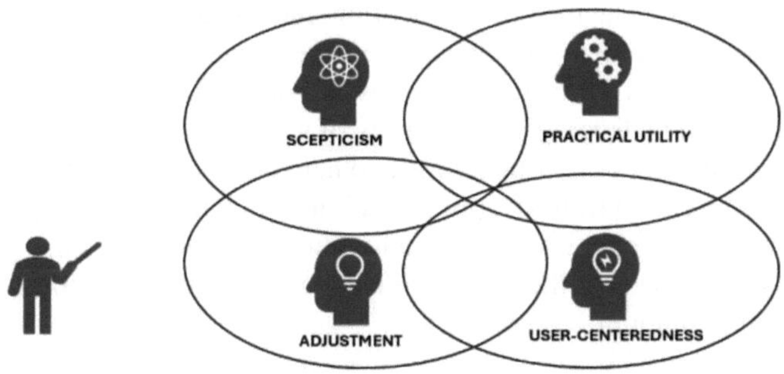

Fig. 4. Overlapping student conceptions of UX design thinking.

The findings highlighted several areas for continuous improvement in teaching UX design thinking principles. For example, given the skepticism some students hold regarding the practical relevance of UX tools, instructors could design assignments that directly tie the use of personas and empathy maps to real-world scenarios. Moreover, engaging in building a user interface prototype or capstone learning project by partnering with local businesses or community organizations to work on actual design challenges could bridge the gap between theory and practice, making the educational experience more tangible and directly applicable.

The importance of user-centered design principles also emerged as a significant conception. Educators can develop curriculum content that places a strong emphasis on understanding and prioritizing user needs. This could include case studies of successful and failed projects, highlighting the role of user-centered design in their outcomes, and exercises that require students to critically engage with user feedback and iterate on design prototypes.

To address the critical engagement with UX mapping tools, instructors can incorporate reflective practice assignments where students critically evaluate the utility of personas and empathy maps in various stages of the design process. Encouraging students to document their learning journey, the challenges faced, and how they overcame them or altered their approach can also foster a deeper understanding of the value of these tools. Considering the spectrum of understanding and experiences among students, peer learning sessions can be valuable. Facilitating peer learning sessions can help students who struggle with these concepts to learn from those who have effectively applied them, promoting a collaborative environment. This can help students who are skeptical or find the concepts challenging to see practical examples of how their peers have successfully applied these tools. Acknowledging the role of external aids, as mentioned by one student, instructors can curate a list of online resources, templates, and tools that students can use to facilitate the creation of personas and empathy maps. Incorporating software or digital platforms specifically designed for UX design into the curriculum can also provide hands-on experience with the tools professionals use in the field.

The exploration of student experiences and understandings of UX mapping principles and tools through a phenomenographic lens underscores the diverse conceptions students hold towards systems application development [26]. The insights derived from this analysis, complemented by a detailed assessment of student submissions, have informed a series of targeted improvement strategies aimed at enhancing the pedagogical approach to teaching UX design within systems analysis and design courses.

This approach can be leveraged in a variety of systems analysis and design courses, such as process modeling, object modeling, and network modeling, to enhance teaching methods, curriculum content, and overall educational outcomes. Tailoring course content and teaching strategies to address these variations helps bridge knowledge gaps, ensuring that all students, regardless of their background, can grasp the core concepts necessary for success in their computing careers [38].

The ability to work effectively in diverse teams is a critical skill in today's global workforce, particularly in the computing field. Experiencing diversity in educational backgrounds within the classroom prepares students for the collaborative and multicultural nature of modern workplaces. Finally, actively seeking qualitative feedback and analyzing student conceptions using a phenomenographic approach to evaluation can create a feedback loop for continuous course improvement.

7 Conclusion, Limitations, and Future Research

The paper set out to evaluate how the integration of design thinking principles and UX mapping tools (such as personas, customer journey maps, and empathy maps) enabled students to engage in more insightful and user-centered design work in an empirical setting of a final-year undergraduate course. The phenomenographic analysis uncovered a spectrum of conceptions among students, from seeing UX tools as challenging yet enriching learning experiences to viewing them as essential instruments for deepening empathy with users [31]. This range of understanding underscores the importance of addressing these conceptual variations to enhance educational effectiveness.

This study's contribution to the computing evaluation education literature is twofold. First, this study illustrates that a phenomenographic inquiry can be instrumental in identifying the range of conceptions students hold about UX design thinking [38]. The novelty of this approach also lies in the application of phenomenographic findings to inform teaching practice. By uncovering the qualitative differences in students' conceptions of UX mapping tools, this research provides valuable evaluation insights for instructors. The study shows how these insights can be used to guide the development of instructional activities that are more closely aligned with students' conceptions, thereby continuously improving learning effectiveness. Second, by examining the varied ways students understand and engage with UX mapping tools, our research not only highlights the diversity of student perspectives but also underscores the importance of creating inclusive educational environments that cater to this diversity [42]. This approach not only enriches the learning experience by recognizing and valuing the varied perspectives and backgrounds of students but also prepares them to create UX designs that are accessible and meaningful across different user groups.

One limitation of the phenomenographic evaluation inquiry into the variations in how students experience and understand key concepts in systems analysis and design courses is that it might not fully capture the depth and breadth of conceptual variations or the richness of the learning experiences among students. Future research should consider conducting comparative studies that explore the outcomes of computing education through the lens of phenomenographic inquiry alongside experiential learning and other pedagogical approaches. This would help in understanding the spectrum of learning experiences among IS students and how these experiences influence their conceptual grasp of the subject matter.

While the phenomenographic approach offers deep insights into the qualitative variations in students' learning experiences, its reliance on detailed individual interviews can be challenging to implement in large classroom environments. This limits its scalability in courses with several hundred students. To address this, future implementations could incorporate a quantitative survey-based approach that captures structured reflections on students' engagement with UX tools [43]. As computing education increasingly integrates intelligent technologies, future research could explore the potential of AI-powered assessment tools to scale phenomenographic evaluations [44]. Such approaches can make evaluations more feasible at scale and ensure teaching strategies can be continuously informed by diverse student feedback.

Additionally, this study focused predominantly on the educational outcomes within the context of a specific computing module in UX design thinking. While this focus has yielded valuable insights into teaching and learning dynamics in this area, it leaves open questions regarding the applicability and effectiveness of identified strategies across other course specializations including more technical courses [26]. Future research could explore how variations in student conceptions influence learning in areas such as cybersecurity, data analytics, or cloud computing within computing education. This would help us understand whether and how teaching strategies should be adapted to the specific content and challenges of these specialized areas.

Moreover, this study does not fully address how other aspects of diversity, such as cultural, socio-economic, and gender differences, impact learning in computing education. Future research should extend the investigation to these areas of diversity to uncover deeper insights into inclusive pedagogy and its effects on student engagement and achievement, potentially transforming computing education pedagogy for the better. As contemporary educational challenges increasingly demand a focus on social cohesiveness, integrating empathy into UX design allows students to develop user-centered solutions that resonate with diverse user needs and experiences. However, much like in broader educational discourse, it is essential to approach virtues such as user-centeredness critically. In conclusion, efforts that seek to critically examine concepts such as user-centeredness will be crucial in the continuous improvement of computing education, ensuring it remains responsive to the evolving needs of diverse student cohorts and the demands of the rapidly evolving global digital space. Finally, as UX design thinking continues to evolve and gain prominence, this study urges computing educators to thoughtfully integrate phenomenographic evaluation into the curricula to foster continuous improvement and inclusiveness.

Disclosure of Interests. The author has no competing interests to declare that are relevant to the content of this article.

References

1. Avis, J.: Socio-technical imaginary of the fourth industrial revolution and its implications for vocational education and training: a literature review. J. Vocat. Educ. Train., 1–27 (2018). https://doi.org/10.1080/13636820.2018.1498907
2. Pratt, J.A., Keys, A., Wirkus, T.: Preparing Information systems graduates for a complex society: aligning is curricula with liberal education learning outcomes, vol. 25 (2014)
3. Topi, H., et al.: MSIS 2016: global competency model for graduate degree programs in information systems. Commun. Assoc. Inf. Syst. **40**, MSIS-i-MSIS-107 (2017). https://doi.org/10.17705/1CAIS.04018
4. Getto, G., Potts, L., Salvo, M.J., Gossett, K.: Teaching UX: designing programs to train the next generation of UX experts. In: Proceedings of the 31st ACM International Conference on Design of Communication, pp. 65–70. ACM, Greenville, North Carolina, USA (2013). https://doi.org/10.1145/2507065.2507082
5. Gray, C.M., Parsons, P., Toombs, A.L., Rasche, N., Vorvoreanu, M.: Designing an aesthetic learner experience: ux, instructional design, and design pedagogy. Inter. J. Designs Learn. **11**, 41–58 (2019). https://doi.org/10.14434/ijdl.v11i1.26065
6. Vorvoreanu, M., Gray, C.M., Parsons, P., Rasche, N.: Advancing UX education: a model for integrated studio pedagogy. In: Proceedings of the 2017 CHI Conference on Human Factors in Computing Systems, pp. 1441–1446. ACM, Denver, Colorado, USA (2017). https://doi.org/10.1145/3025453.3025726
7. Bialystok, L., Kukar, P.: Authenticity and empathy in education. Theory Res. Educ. **16**, 23–39 (2018). https://doi.org/10.1177/1477878517746647
8. Micheaux, A., Bosio, B.: Customer journey mapping as a new way to teach data-driven marketing as a service. J. Mark. Educ. **41**, 127–140 (2019). https://doi.org/10.1177/0273475318812551
9. Rosenbaum, M.S., Otalora, M.L., Ramírez, G.C.: How to create a realistic customer journey map. Bus. Horiz. **60**, 143–150 (2017). https://doi.org/10.1016/j.bushor.2016.09.010

10. Hewett, T.T., et al.: ACM SIGCHI curricula for human–computer interaction. ACM (1992)
11. Leidig, P., Salmela, H.: IS2020—A Competency Model for Undergraduate Programs in Information Systems. ACM, New York (2021). https://doi.org/10.1145/3460863
12. Stake, R.: Responsive evaluation. In: Kellaghan, T., Stufflebeam, D.L. (eds.) International Handbook of Educational Evaluation, pp. 63–68. Springer, Dordrecht (2003). https://doi.org/10.1007/978-94-010-0309-4_5
13. Nevo, D.: The conceptualization of educational evaluation: an analytical review of the literature. Rev. Educ. Res. **53**, 117–128 (1983). https://doi.org/10.3102/00346543053001117
14. Payne, S.L., Flynn, J., Whitfield, J.M.: Capstone business course assessment: exploring student readiness perspectives. J. Educ. Bus. **83**, 141–146 (2008). https://doi.org/10.3200/JOEB.83.3.141-146
15. Santana-Mancilla, P.C., Rodriguez-Ortiz, M.A., Garcia-Ruiz, M.A., Gaytan-Lugo, L.S., Fajardo-Flores, S.B., Contreras-Castillo, J.: Teaching HCI skills in higher education through game design: a study of students' perceptions. Informatics **6**, 22 (2019). https://doi.org/10.3390/informatics6020022
16. Churchill, E.F., Bowser, A., Preece, J.: Teaching and learning human–computer interaction: past, present, and future. Interactions **20**, 44–53 (2013)
17. Patil, M.S., Desai, P., Vijayalakshmi, M., Raikar, M.M., Battur, S., Parikshit, H., Joshi, G.H.: UX design to promote undergraduate projects to products: case study. In: 2016 IEEE 4th International Conference on MOOCs, Innovation and Technology in Education (MITE), pp. 302–307. IEEE, Madurai, India (2016). https://doi.org/10.1109/MITE.2016.066
18. Kang, J., Girouard, A.: Impact of UX internships on human-computer interaction graduate students: a qualitative analysis of internship reports. ACM Trans. Comput. Educ. **22**, 1–25 (2022). https://doi.org/10.1145/3517132
19. MacDonald, C.M., Rozaklis, L.: Assessing the implementation of authentic, client-facing student projects in user experience (UX) education: insights from multiple stakeholders. Proc. Associat. Inform. Sci. Technol. **54**, 268–278 (2017). https://doi.org/10.1002/pra2.2017.14505401030
20. Altay, B.: User-centered design through learner-centered instruction. Teach. High. Educ. **19**, 138–155 (2014). https://doi.org/10.1080/13562517.2013.827646
21. Chen, L., Pratt, J.A., Cole, C.B.: Factors influencing students' major and career selection in systems development: an empirical study. J. Comput. Inf. Syst. **56**, 313–320 (2016). https://doi.org/10.1080/08874417.2016.1164005
22. Holvikivi, J.: Culture and cognition in information technology education. Eur. J. Eng. Educ. **32**, 73–82 (2007)
23. Wegener, R., Menschner, P., Leimeister, J.M.: Design and evaluation of a didactical service blueprinting method for large scale lectures. In: Proceedings of the International Conference on Information Systems, Orlando, Florida, USA, pp. 1–17 (2012)
24. Shah, V., Kumar, A., Smart, K.: Moving forward by looking backward: embracing pedagogical principles to develop an innovative msis program. J. Inf. Syst. Educ. **29**, 139–156 (2018)
25. Bruce, C., Edwards, S., Lupton, M.: Six Frames for Information literacy education: a conceptual framework for interpreting the relationships between theory and practice. Innov. Teach. Learn. Inf. Comput. Sci. 5, 1–18 (2006). https://doi.org/10.11120/ital.2006.05010002
26. Gull, H., Saeed, S., Iqbal, S.Z., Saqib, M., Bamarouf, Y.A., Alqahtani, M.A.: Reflections on teaching human–computer interaction course to undergraduate students. In: 2018 International Conference on Computational Science and Computational Intelligence (CSCI), pp. 659–662. IEEE, Las Vegas, NV, USA (2018). https://doi.org/10.1109/CSCI46756.2018.00132
27. Jones, C., Asensio, M.: Experiences of assessment: using phenomenography for evaluation. J. Comput. Assist. Learn. **17**, 314–321 (2001). https://doi.org/10.1046/j.0266-4909.2001.00186.x

28. Han, F., Ellis, R.A.: Using phenomenography to tackle key challenges in science education. Front. Psychol. **10**, 1414 (2019). https://doi.org/10.3389/fpsyg.2019.01414
29. Yates, C., Partridge, H., Bruce, C.: Exploring information experiences through phenomenography. Libr. Inf. Res. 36, 96–119 (2012). https://doi.org/10.29173/lirg496
30. Bitner, M.J., Ostrom, A.L., Morgan, F.N.: Service blueprinting: a practical technique for service innovation. Calif. Manage. Rev. **50**, 66–94 (2008). https://doi.org/10.2307/41166446
31. Ferreira, B.M., Barbosa, S.D.J., Conte, T.: PATHY: using empathy with personas to design applications that meet the users' needs. In: Kurosu, M. (ed.) Human–Computer Interaction. Theory, Design, Development and Practice, pp. 153–165. Springer, Cham (2016). https://doi.org/10.1007/978-3-319-39510-4_15
32. Avdiji, H., Elikan, D., Missonier, S., Pigneur, Y.: A design theory for visual inquiry tools. J. Assoc. Inf. Syst. 21, 695–734 (2020). https://doi.org/10.17705/1jais.00617
33. Bradley, C., Oliveira, L., Birrell, S., Cain, R.: A new perspective on personas and customer journey maps: proposing systemic UX. Int. J. Hum.-Comput. Stud. **148**, 102583 (2021). https://doi.org/10.1016/j.ijhcs.2021.102583
34. Ferreira, B., Silva, W., Oliveira, E., Conte, T.: Designing personas with empathy map. In: Proceedings of the 27th International Conference on Software Engineering and Knowledge Engineering, 1 July (2015). https://doi.org/10.18293/SEKE2015-152
35. Cooper, A.: The inmates are running the asylum. Springer (1999)
36. Gottlieb, M., Wagner, E., Wagner, A., Chan, T.: Applying design thinking principles to curricular development in medical education. AEM Educ. Train. **1**, 21–26 (2017). https://doi.org/10.1002/aet2.10003
37. Marton, F.: Phenomenography: A research approach to investigating different understandings of reality. In: Qualitative Research in Education, pp. 141–161. Routledge (2004)
38. Rose, E., Le Heron, J., Sofat, I.: Student understandings of information systems design, learning and teaching: a phenomenography Approach. J. Inf. Syst. Educ. **16**, 183–195 (2005)
39. Richardson, J.T.E.: The Concepts and Methods of Phenomenographic Research. Rev. Educ. Res. **69**, 53–82 (1999)
40. Krippendorff, K.: Content analysis: an introduction to its methodology. Sage (2018)
41. Braun, V., Clarke, V.: Using thematic analysis in psychology. Qual. Res. Psychol. **3**, 77–101 (2006)
42. Collins, A., Azmat, F., Rentschler, R.: 'Bringing everyone on the same journey': revisiting inclusion in higher education. Stud. High. Educ. **44**, 1475–1487 (2019). https://doi.org/10.1080/03075079.2018.1450852
43. Hoffelinck, M., Detroz, P., Verpoorten, D.: Students' experience of comparison-based learning in self-assessment: a phenomenographic study in higher education. High. Educ. Res. Dev. 1–17 (2025). https://doi.org/10.1080/07294360.2025.2463521
44. Giri, A.: Revolutionizing student evaluation: the power of ai-powered assessment. In: Improving Student Assessment With Emerging AI Tools, pp. 333–362. IGI Global Scientific Publishing (2025)

Contextualization, Assessment, and Generative AI in an Online Environment: An Experiment with a Hypothetical Case Study in Enterprise Architecture

Wesley Moonsamy[1](✉) and Hugo Lotriet[2]

[1] University of Pretoria, Hatfield 0002, Pretoria, South Africa
wesley.moonsamy@up.ac.za

[2] University of South Africa, Roodepoort 1709, Florida Park, South Africa

Abstract. Contextualization of questions has been suggested to deal with the capabilities of generative AI in an online environment. For this paper we experimented with contextualization to observe how generative AI (in this instance ChatGPT) deals with different elements of contextualization. The experiment used a hypothetical case study for a tailored course in Enterprise Architecture at post-graduate level and looked at contextualization along two axes: (1) Contextualized questioning, and (2) providing different learner contexts in the form of personas to ChatGPT and seeing whether ChatGPT adapted its responses. The contextualized questioning aspects used three different assessments. For the first assessment, individual questions on Enterprise Architecture were asked. For the second and third assessments the case study was used. In the second assessment a general essay that addresses certain elements of Enterprise Architecture was requested, while in the third assessment structured questions on the case study were asked. Responses for each of the assessments were independently marked by the authors, with marking results compared and discussed. The experiment found differences in the quality of responses generated by ChatGPT related to contextualization and degree of structuring in the questions, and in the responses provided to the different personas. Differences in responses to the personas were however not contextualized. It was observed that ChatGPT produced higher quality answers to individually structured questions but fared poorly when prompted for an essay. Educators should therefore contextualize and structure questions in the form of case studies which stimulate learner creativity and critical thinking skills.

Keywords: Generative AI · ChatGPT · essay assessments · creativity and critical thinking skills · Enterprise Architecture · contextualized essay

1 Introduction

Artificial Intelligence (AI) open language applications have become a significant technological disruptor in most areas of application. Although there are numerous AI chatbots available, the frontrunner for the moment is ChatGPT [1, 2]. This may well change in the future, depending on the quality of the language models used by emerging applications [1].

L. Nel et al. (Eds.): SACLA 2025, CCIS 2770, pp. 17–32, 2026.
https://doi.org/10.1007/978-3-032-12457-9_2

Education, and especially online education has been particularly concerned about the rise of ChatGPT (and other open language AI applications), as the technology has the potential to severely disrupt normal ("traditional") tuition practices. This is welcomed by some [3]. However, there are concerns related to especially assessment practices where AI through its similarities to human (i.e. "expert") intelligence [3] could lead to various practical, legal and ethical issues [3, 4]. Examples include bias, copyright, plagiarism, privacy, security and repeatability [3, 5]. In similar settings, ChatGPT can introduce source code plagiarism thereby undermining assessments involving programming [6].The result may be that academic integrity is undermined [7] and that learning effectively does not take place and that creative and critical thinking skills are stifled [3].

Essay writing in applied areas of scholarship such as science, is a beneficial method of assessment as it helps to develop students critical thinking abilities [8]. Nevertheless, ChatGPT now offers challenges to this form of assessment, especially online, as it is capable of writing essays that simulate the writing of students in applied sciences such as business, quite well, having demonstrated its ability to pass exams at MBA level and having for instance better language skills than non-native English speakers [3]. This obviously provides students with an opportunity for cheating, however as Geerling et al. [9] point out, this is not the first opportunity for cheating by means of technology, and educators need to find ways of dealing with this in assessment. (They also point out that ChatGPT is not the only present threat – there are various applications from the large IT corporations that pose similar threats.) However, as ChatGPT is quite new, this means that guidelines for educators and lecturers on how to deal with assessment of essays under these circumstances need to be established.

This paper contributes in this regard. It uses a (mind-experiment) case study situated in Enterprise Architecture (EA). EA was selected as both authors have an interest in teaching this subject in an online environment. EA is a good (typical) example of a subject, where essay writing is prevalent at Honours level (NQF 8[1]), with the students having to typically discuss (critically) the conceptual principles of EA, then apply these to case studies or similar. In this case study we prompted ChatGPT to provide responses to a typical essay assignment related to a fictional case study, after which the responses provided by ChatGPT were evaluated using a marking rubric created based on Bloom's Taxonomy learning objectives.

The paper is set out as follows: We first present a literature review that considers essay writing as a form of assessment and its typical pedagogical considerations, as well as the current understanding in literature on the potential impact of ChatGPT on essay writing. We then discuss our case study method and present the case study that was used for the purpose of this study. Results from the case study are presented and discussed, and some recommendations are made on guidelines for educators on essay writing, considering ChatGPT and its potential impact.

[1] National Qualifications Framework Level 8.

2 Literature Review

2.1 Essay Writing as an Assessment and ChatGPT

Sweeney [10] argues that uniqueness, creativity and work that cannot be easily imitated are critically important to higher education assessments which can include essays. Malik et al. [11] supplement this notion by discussing the importance of innovation and critical thinking in essay writing. Malik et al. and Sweeney [10, 11] are also of the view that generative AI including tools such as ChatGPT have the potential to stifle these key learning objectives. These skills which are meant to be developed during essay writing may no longer mature as pointed out by Dwivedi et al. [3] who pose the question on whether any assessment that relies on the generation of texts should still be considered significant in assessing the cognitive abilities of students. One of the strengths of generative AI technologies such as ChatGPT is their ability to produce long texts that simulate human writing [7]. Choi et al. [12] for instance found that ChatGPT has better abilities at generating essays than for instance answering Multiple Choice questions. It is also considered to be strong in simulating critical and higher order thinking [13]. One should however keep in mind that there are still shortcomings in the application – for example it does produce incorrect information, it is biased, and it struggles to deal with subtle complexities of language [2, 7]. Furthermore, ChatGPT does not produce novel insights [2].

As an aside, it should be noted that ChatGPT can assist in aspects related to essay writing other than the generation of texts. Some of these include improving skills related to writing, finding information on specific topics and providing feedback to students [1, 13].

Various aspects relating to ChatGPT, and essay writing have been investigated. For instance, AlAfnan et al. [4] examined the impact of ChatGPT on submissions made by different groups of students (for instance business, communications, and composition). Chaka [1] compared various available AI applications in terms of the accuracy and quality of the responses provided by these applications. Gregorcic and Pendrill [5] attempted (unsuccessfully) to enter into a Socratic dialogue with it to engage with the erroneous and contradictory responses (in Physics) generated by the chatbot. Choi et al. [12] considered essay writing performance in relation to answering of other types of questions in Law exams. Geerling et al. [9] assessed its ability to perform in the Test of Understanding in College Economics (which it passed). ChatGPT can generate arguments and essays that meet specifications set by users [3]. Its language use is good, and its structuring of essays is considered good, albeit formulaic [12].

There are nevertheless significant issues related to the texts that ChatGPT can generate. These include the propensity towards plagiarism and the use of generic and "superficial" language in responses (which indicate a lack of interpretation of fine distinctions in arguments in the texts used by the tool) [1]. Furthermore, the information used to train the model is not recent, its responses are biased [1] and it can generate wrong, uneven and inconsistent responses [5, 12], it has inadequate ways of dealing with ambiguity and it is sensitive to the exact phrasing of user prompts [1]. Furthermore, in essays where application is important, it often could identify applicable concepts and principles, but failed to effectively apply theoretical concepts to "facts" [12]. In open-ended questions it struggled with identifying issues [12]. It also struggled to maintain a core focus [12]. ChatGPT has issues when confronted with poorly formulated assignments. Furthermore, because it is essentially a "black box" its outcomes are not based on a transparent process, which creates issues.

2.2 Dealing with ChatGPT in an Educational Context

Various approaches have been considered and implemented, which include banning ChatGPT, changes in teaching approaches, and use of technology to regulate and detect use of ChatGPT [14, 15]. Lo [13] indicates that this leads mainly to three types of strategies. These are modification of the assessment tasks, detection technologies related to AI writing, and institutional measures (such as ethics education, and policies related to AI use).

There are already a significant number of recommendations and guidelines on how to deal with ChatGPT related to student writing assignments that have been published within the past year. These relate broadly to two categories, i.e. technical, and educational. Each of these categories can further be divided into two sub-categories, i.e. changes to dealing with assignment content, and changing processes and structures related to the assignment. The various examples of recommendations and the categories and sub-categories are presented in Table 1.

Of these recommendations, from a massified low resource perspective, it could be argued that the recommendations related to changing of processes and structures, will probably lead to better results, however the resource implications are significant and may not be attainable (both for technical and educational recommendations). Similarly, it is recommended that universities implement the bigger systemic recommendations, however these will only yield benefits on medium- to long term and cannot be relied on to solve the direct issues experienced by lecturers at assignment level.

This leaves the options of looking at ways in which to influence the content of essays in ways that would make use of ChatGPT more challenging. The technical recommendations can be implemented with integrity software, but these will probably not solve all problems, as issues and challenges have been reported. However, it should be noted that AI develops rapidly, and this may negate any responses by implementing technical solutions [3].

The most promising route for immediate benefits therefore seems to be one where educators work with the educational content and implement educational content solutions to force students to engage in human ways with the assignment that would be more difficult for ChatGPT to emulate.

We have therefore for the purpose of this study taken these recommendations and did an exploratory study to see what the effects would be on ChatGPT if we changed approaches to essay writing to incorporate some of the suggested recommendations. Specifically, we explored whether the incorporation of elements of contextualization and personalization would impact on the responses elicited from ChatGPT.

We developed a (theoretical) case study with a "normal" essay for enterprise architecture. We used this as a baseline to understand what ChatGPT does and how it presents.

Table 1. Technical and educational approaches to dealing with assignment content.

Technical	Educational
Can be determined by educator	
Dealing with assignment content: Require proper referencing and citations [16] Verify references [13] Check against software [4] Embed multi-media resources in assessment questions [13]. Embed images in assessment questions [9]	Dealing with assessment content: Avoid theory-based essays [4] Ask questions that require personalization of responses [4, 9] Structure required responses to be more critical, creative, and imaginative [4, 9, 16] Ask questions that relate to higher cognitive skills [9]. Ensure that assessments are meaningful in ways that cannot be imitated [9] Ensure that responses require contextual awareness [16]
Requires institutional changes	
Changing processes and structures related to the assignment: Establish policies and procedures for the use of AI in assignments [13]	Changing processes and structures related to the assessment: Use ChatGPT responses for class discussions [4] Combine writing with oral responses [3] Use alternative assessment formats (e.g. podcasts, debates, interviews) [3] Employ non-digital assessment [13] Learners should submit drafts of essays [13, 16] Do interactive assessments [16] Do student awareness and training related to the ethical use of AI in their studies [13]

We then implemented some of the content-related changes and compared the ChatGPT response to see whether any of the recommendations have an impact.

3 Research Methodology

A qualitative approach utilising an assessment and rubric was selected for this study. A similar approach was used by other researchers when evaluating ChatGPT's performance on a medical licensing examination [17]. In that research ChatGPT passed the examination at the level of a third-year student (NQF 7). In this research, ChatGPT was tested at NQF 8 level to determine ChatGPT's performance on a continuous assessment-based set of questions. The research experiment has been illustrated in Fig. 1.

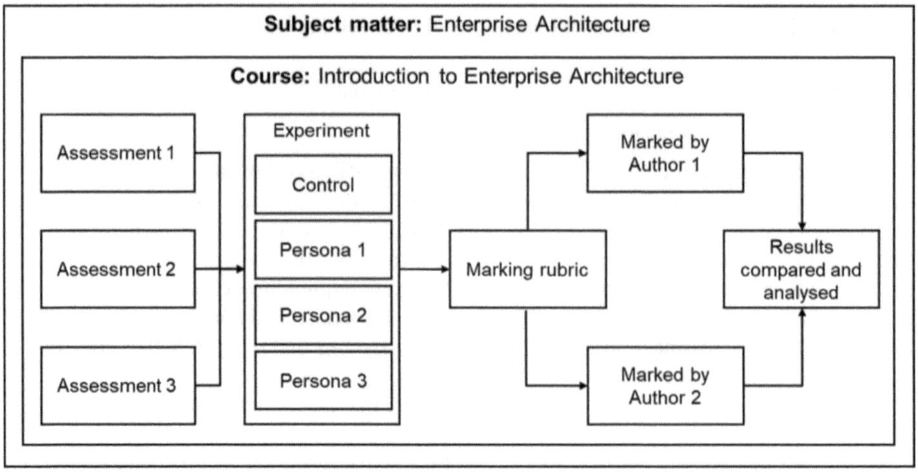

Fig. 1. The research experiment.

3.1 Research Protocol

An experiment was conducted by having four conversations with ChatGPT via three personas and one control. The conversations were used to ask ChatGPT to construct answers to one assessment which was tested in three different ways. The answers to the assessment were then marked using a rubric based on appropriate Bloom's taxonomy learning objectives. The details of the research protocol are explained in the sections that follow.

3.2 Subject Matter

EA is a method that organizations use to understand and alleviate complexities that arise from digital transformation scenarios [18]. It is also used by organizations to understand their business processes, resources and technology [19]. EA was selected as the subject of the study as it can be assessed by using open ended questions or case studies as will be explained later.

EA is normally done by an Enterprise Architect. The role of an Enterprise Architect is constantly developing yet the terms EA and Enterprise Architect are still weakly understood [20]. Betterteam [21] describes an Enterprise Architect as a person who determines the course and creates the approach of the operations of the organization. The Enterprise Architect also optimises the technology infrastructure and business operations.

Thönssen and von Dewitz [20] list nine skills that relate to The Open Group Architecture Framework (TOGAF). Three common job profiles were investigated during this research. Their skills were mapped against the nine TOGAF related skills presented in Table 2.

It is assumed that subsets of professionals who perform any of the three job profiles described in Table 2 may want to transition into an EA role. This may require them to learn the required skills by taking an appropriate EA course.

Table 2. EA skills grouped into common job roles.

Job role	EA skills aligned with job role	TOGAF based EA skills
Business analyst	1, 2, 3, 4	1. Business modelling 2. Business process design 3. Role design 4. Organization design 5. Data design 6. Application design 7. Systems integration 8. IT industry standards 9. Services design
Data analyst	5, 7, 8	
Solutions architect	4, 5, 6, 7, 8, 9	

Source: Adapted from Thönssen and von Dewitz [20]

3.3 Course Outline

A hypothetical course "Introduction to Enterprise Architecture" was formulated as part of this research. Going forward it will be referred to as "the course". To formulate the course, three popular EA courses offered by accredited institutions were examined to determine their course outlines. These were considered when formulating the courses objectives. The details of the investigated EA courses are presented in Table 3.

Table 3. Summary of investigated EA courses and their outlines.

Course name	Summarized course outlines
EA Bootcamp [22]	Defining EA, the problems we're using EA to solve, other approaches to the problems, and the contributions EA can make, EA challenges in the external business environment and an outline of the EA development process.
Applied Business Architecture [23]	Introduction, Strategic Planning and Business Architecture, engaging stakeholders and Eliciting Concerns, Business Modelling and Capability Mapping.
Enterprise Architect Training [24]	Architecture and Architects, Architecture Frameworks, Applications Architecture, Infrastructure Architecture and Architecture Management.

Once these EA courses were examined, a set of course objectives and related outcomes for the course were developed. They are listed in Table 4.

Table 4. Objectives and related outcomes for the course.

Course objective	Outcomes
Defining EA	Describe Enterprise Architecture, name and describe a few Enterprise Architecture Frameworks (EAFs).
Solving business challenges using EA	Learn how to solve business problems within a domain using EA principles, evaluation and selection of an appropriate EAF.
Stakeholder management	Identify relevant stakeholders and uncover the stakeholder's concerns.
Capability identification and mapping	Identify the capabilities of the organization by department.
Strategic planning	Plan for the implementation of a project and design the future state of the organization.

3.4 The Assessment

Continuous assessment is an assessment strategy used in multiple disciplines [25] that allows students to be periodically tested formally or informally throughout the course. It is believed that the average scores of these assessments would be more dependable than a single formal assessment at the end of this course [26, 27]. Open Distance eLearning (OdeL) universities such as the University of South Africa use continuous assessment for several qualifications. This experiment was conducted using continuous assessment in the form of an assessment.

Three assessments were created for this experiment, each worth 50 marks. The first assessment comprised ten open-ended questions. The second assessment was presented as a case study where ChatGPT was expected to provide an essay. Assessment 3 combined the case study from assessment 2 but ChatGPT was guided by a set of related closed ended questions. This assessment was a "deconstructed" case study. The three assessments have been presented in Appendix 1, 2 and 3.

3.5 Marking Rubric

An adaptable marking rubric was created based on the course outcomes as well as the thinking skills discussed earlier. The marking rubric was used to assess all three responses across the four personas. The adapted marking rubric [28] can be accessed from supplementary material [29]. Once the assessments and the rubrics were created, the personas for the experiments were created.

3.6 Personas

For the purposes of this research, three personas (based on the three job roles presented in Table 2) were created. These are a (1) Business analyst, (2) Data analyst and a (3) Solutions architect. These job roles were presented in Table 2. Four new ChatGPT profiles were created based on the three personas and one control.

3.7 Conducting the Experiment

The three personas were firstly introduced to ChatGPT in the following way:

Hello ChatGPT, I am a < insert persona here >. I have the following skills < list of skills from Table 2 > and I want to pursue a career in Enterprise Architecture. I am enrolled in a course that has the following objectives < list objectives from Table 4 here >. I need to complete an assessment.

< Enter key >

This is assessment 1.

< Enter questions one by one >

This is assessment 2.

< Enter case study >

< Enter key >

< Request for essay >

< Enter key >

This is assessment 3.

< Enter case study >

< Enter key >

< Based on the case study above, answer the following question >

< Enter question one by one and record responses >

< Repeat for each persona >

For the control, there was no introduction. The assessments were pasted, and the responses were recorded.

4 Data Analysis and Interpretation

Each assessment was marked independently by both authors based on the marking rubric. Each author also recorded comments for each question. Once all the assessments were marked, the marks were compared, and the comments were consolidated. Average scores were calculated and then compared. The assessments were then grouped to form a matrix to compare the effects of using individual questions, essay type questions, no personas (the control) and personas.

4.1 Findings and Analysis

The three assessments were conducted as follows: (1) Control containing no persona information (2) Persona 1 (3) Persona 2 (4) Persona 3. Once all three assessments were conducted, the answers were downloaded into a text file and then independently marked by the authors. Marks for each answer along with comments for each answer were captured and discussed. This resulted in 120 datapoints (3 assessments x 10 questions x (1 Control + 3 Personas)). Once the authors discussed the comments relating to each answer, their comments were consolidated. The marks and comments for each assessment are accessible from supplementary material [29].

The marks and consolidated comments for assessment 1 are accessible from supplementary material [29]. The minimum mark scored by ChatGPT was 72% and the highest mark was 92%. ChatGPT seemed to generate appropriate answers to most of the questions but struggled to keep the responses concise. There seemed to have been confusion between the concept of an EAF and an EA evaluation framework. Archimate which is an EA design tool was included as an EAF presumably due to Archimate being mentioned in settings that relate to EA. Some of the answers were similar to each other which could suggest that the use of personas did not significantly influence the generation of the responses.

The marks and consolidated comments for assessment 2 are accessible from supplementary material [29]. The marks for assessment 2 show a drastic decline with the lowest mark at 0% and the highest mark at 50%. Overall, the answers were too short, contained little to no context related to the case study and were not relevant to the personas provided. In cases where answers were more substantiated, there was a lack of structure.

The marks and consolidated comments for assessment 3 are accessible from supplementary material [29]. The lowest mark for assessment 3 was 50% and the highest mark for assessment 3 was 84%. In this assessment, a lack of contextualization to the case study was noted. In some cases, the answers to the control were more detailed and scored higher than the 3 personas. Overall, however the individual personas did not seem to influence the generation of the responses.

5 Discussion of Findings

A summary of the marks scored across all three assessments is presented in Table 5.

Table 5. Summary of marks scored for each assessment.

	Average scores (% rounded to the next whole number)				
Assessment	Control	Persona 1	Persona 2	Persona 3	Overall
1	82	80	82	85	82
2	0	39	44	5	22
3	80	60	77	69	72

Assessment 1 was not contextualized to a particular scenario and contained questions which were not related to each other. Assessment 1's overall mark of 82% was the highest amongst the three assessments. Even though the responses were often too long, they contained sufficient and relevant detail to score marks. Assessment 2 which was based on a case study contained a high degree of contextualization. A single structured essay type response was required for this assessment. The responses received however were unstructured and lacked sufficient detail. ChatGPT attempted albeit poorly to piece together elements of EA with the healthcare case study but failed to relate these components. This resulted in the lowest overall mark of 22%. Assessment 3, an intersection of assessment 1 and 2 was contextualized to the case study and contained individual questions. The 72% mark recorded for assessment 3 was due to the detail and structure provided in the answers. Marks were however deducted due the answers lacking contextual relevance to the case study. ChatGPT therefore seemed to prefer structured questions (queries) as the generation of text could be more confined to a particular component. The introducing of personas into the queries seemed to make no difference to the responses. ChatGPT's lack of contextualization to the personas however could be due to the prompts. Future research could introduce the personas in further detail. The results of the three assessments have been repositioned in Fig. 2.

Can be provided by student

Determined by lecturer

	Persona provided	No persona provided
Individual answers required	76%	81%
Essay required	29%	0%

Fig. 2. Effect on marks based on question types and personas.

The marks obtained for assessment 1 and 3 were combined based on the individual structuring of the questions. The most notable variance in marks can be observed between the type of structuring.

5.1 Recommendations

Based on these findings we would recommend the following measures to be considered when setting essay assignments for large classes in low-resource environments:

- Introducing a word or character count on individual questions to ensure that students who use ChatGPT would have the opportunity to summarize or rewrite responses. This supports student engagement with the subject matter
- Contextualized structured essay type questions can be used in cases where educators want students to immerse themselves in the details of the case study. Should students require assistance from ChatGPT, they would need to create appropriate queries to generate appropriate responses. The individual responses would then need to be merged by the student, which supports engagement with the subject matter
- Educators could add a further dimension to their questions by introducing a persona to the scenario. ChatGPT did not adapt its responses to the personas which were provided. Students would then be encouraged to study the related subject matter to contextualize the responses to a particular persona. Alternatively, essay responses could be structured to require the students to engage with the subject matter in a manner that incorporates aspects related to their own personal contexts.

5.2 Implications

Considering Gen AI's ability to answer short questions, curriculum designers would need to consider limiting short questions and to introduce more case studies and essay-type questions with specific contexts. Concerns over academic integrity could be answered by detailed and clear policies that students and instructors could refer to. Students should be made aware of whether they may use Gen AI for an assessment and to what extent. Students should also be made aware of the possibilities that excessive use of Gen AI for the completion of assessments may inhibit their critical thinking skills. Generally speaking, it may be possible to introduce more invigilated assessments. In an OdeL environment however, additional invigilated assessments may not be feasible.

5.3 Limitations of This Study and Future Research

This study considered a single course in Enterprise Architecture from a narrative or essay perspective. Enterprise Architecture also involves feasibility studies through the use of weighted matrices. Future research could incorporate other forms of questions necessitating the construction of weighted feasibility matrices. Additionally, newer versions of Gen AI are capable of generating images. Since Enterprise Architecture also involves graphically modelling complex organizations, this could be incorporated into future research.

The authors used new OpenAI accounts to conduct the experiments which would limit the background knowledge that ChatGPT would know about the user. Considering the lack of background knowledge, ChatGPT could have generalized its responses to the questions and may have disregarded the personas. Future research could incorporate mature user profiles with more (user or persona) context.

For the moment, ChatGPT and other Gen AI tools have been described as disruptors of education and learning. Future research could assess Gen AI's abilities from the opposite perspective, as a teaching or tutoring aid for students.

6 Conclusions

Generative AI technologies such as ChatGPT have disrupted educational assessments especially those in the form of written essays or short questions. Those who use Generative AI in educational settings stand to benefit in ways that promote better language use in the case of non-native speakers and in the way of content creation for subjects which require text-based answers. The downside to using Generative AI is the undermining of academic integrity (plagiarism and repeatability) and the stifling of key skills (creativity and critical thinking). This study used three tailored assessments within the EA domain to determine whether contextualization to a case study and learner contexts (personas) influenced the answers generated by ChatGPT. The results showed that the greatest influence on the performance of ChatGPT was the structuring and contextualizing of questions. Educators should consider contextualizing questions by using case studies and should request detailed essays or reports. In the case of short questions, it is recommended that word or character limits should be enforced owing to ChatGPT's inability to summarize its answers whilst maintaining the appropriate context.

The assessments created for this research required textual answers. Future research could extend the assessments to include tables, images and graphs. Though these elements can be created by existing AI tools, the context and relevance to the essay text should be tested. This research experimented with ChatGPT as the generative AI tool, future research could incorporate other generative AI tools such as Microsoft Copilot.

Disclosure of Interests. The authors have no competing interests to declare that are relevant to the content of this article.

Appendix 1

Assessment 1: Open-ended questions (50 marks).

1. What is Enterprise Architecture (EA)? (2 marks).
2. When was EA first developed and by whom? (2 marks).
3. Why is EA needed? (5 marks).
4. What is the role of an Enterprise Architect? (4 marks).
5. What is the difference between an EA view and viewpoint? (4 marks).
6. What is a stakeholder concern? Provide an example of a concern. (3 marks).
7. Name and describe (in your own words) five commonly used Enterprise Architecture Frameworks (EAFs). (10 marks).
8. What is an EA evaluation framework and how is it used by organisations? (8 marks).
9. Select an evaluation framework and use it to compare the Zachman Framework with TOGAF. (8 marks).
10. Which framework would you select to use in the healthcare industry and why? (4 marks).

Appendix 2

Assessment 2: Case study (50 marks).

A large hospital chain runs an old patient management system that only integrates to other systems via file transfer. The CIO of the company wants to remove this system and implement a newer system that has advanced integration capabilities. The newer system can also link to the call centre service solution. The CIO sees this capability as an opportunity to merge the customer care call centre with the admissions and accounts department. This will result in changes to the staff profiles and teams. She has appointed a new manager for each of the three portfolios and a solutions architect to manage the new cloud infrastructure.

You have been appointed as the new Enterprise Architect. Your role is to assist the CIO in planning and implementing the move to the new solution. The hospital board members are uncertain about the need for EA and would rather use their existing project manager to manage the new implementation. You have the backing of the CIO, but you still need to justify your portfolio to the board.

Your first task is to create an EA project document that clearly defines EA and why it is vital to this project. You must also justify your chosen framework and create a textual model for the project. The CIO would like to use the TOGAF EAF but has asked you to make the final decision on which EAF to use by using an evaluation framework.

Ensure that you consider the stakeholders concerns, views and viewpoints. Take all the information provided into consideration so that the board can clearly understand the role of EA in the project and organization. This must be included in your document.

Your document must follow the layout of a standard essay and must contain the necessary references. The length should be between 1 500 and 2 000 words.

Appendix 3

Assessment 3: Deconstructed case study (50 marks).

Read the case study below and answer the following questions.

A large hospital chain runs an old patient management system that only integrates to other systems via file transfer. The CIO of the company wants to remove this system and implement a newer system that has advanced integration capabilities. The newer system can also link to the call centre service solution. The CIO sees this capability as an opportunity to merge the customer care call centre with the admissions and accounts department. This will result in changes to the staff profiles and teams. She has appointed a new manager for each of the three portfolios and a solutions architect to manage the new cloud infrastructure.

You have been appointed as the new Enterprise Architect. Your role is to assist the CIO in planning and implementing the move to the new solution. The hospital board members are uncertain about the need for EA and would rather use their existing project manager to manage the new implementation. You have the backing of the CIO, but you still need to justify your portfolio to the board.

1. Provide a background of EA to the board members by explaining what EA is and provide a brief history? (4 marks).
2. Why does the hospital group need EA? (5 marks).
3. Explain your role on the current project and going forward. (4 marks).
4. Explain what is meant by a stakeholder concern and provide a few examples. (3 marks).
5. Provide and describe a short list of views and viewpoints related to the project. (4 marks).
6. Name and describe five commonly used Enterprise Architecture Frameworks (EAFs). (10 marks).
7. Explain to the board how you used an appropriate evaluation framework to determine which EAF to use. (12 marks).
8. If you decided to use TOGAF, compare it with the Zachman framework using the evaluation framework otherwise, compare your chosen framework with TOGAF. (8 marks).

References

1. Chaka, C.: Generative AI chatbots—ChatGPT versus youchat versus chatsonic: use cases of selected areas of applied english language studies. Int. J. Learn. Teach. Educ. Res. **22**(6), 1–19 (2023). https://doi.org/10.26803/ijlter.22.6.1

2. Lund, B.D., Wang, T., Mannuru, N.R., Nie, B., Shimray, S., Wang, Z.: ChatGPT and a new academic reality: artificial Intelligence-written research papers and the ethics of the large language models in scholarly publishing. J. Assoc. Inf. Sci. Technol. **74**(5), 570–581 (2023). https://doi.org/10.1002/ASI.24750
3. Dwivedi, Y.K., Kshetri, N., Hughes, L., Slade, E.L., Jeyaraj, A., Kar, A.K., et al.: So what if ChatGPT wrote it? Multidisciplinary perspectives on opportunities, challenges and implications of generative conversational AI for research, practice and policy. Int. J. Inf. Manage. **71**, 102642 (2023). https://doi.org/10.1016/j.ijinfomgt.2023.102642
4. AlAfnan, M.A., Dishari, S., Jovic, M., Lomidze, K.: ChatGPT as an educational tool: opportunities, challenges, and recommendations for communication, business writing, and composition courses. J. Artif. Intell. Technol. (2023). https://doi.org/10.37965/jait.2023.0184
5. Gregorcic, B., Pendrill, A.: ChatGPT and the frustrated Socrates. Phys. Educ. **58**(3), 035021 (2023). https://doi.org/10.1088/1361-6552/acc299
6. Du Plessis, L., Smit, I.: Navigating source code plagiarism challenges: strategies to mitigate the impact of COVID-19 disruptions. Progressio (2024). https://doi.org/10.25159/2663-5895/13677
7. Eke, D.O.: ChatGPT and the rise of generative AI: threat to academic integrity? J. Responsible Technol. **13**, 100060 (2023). https://doi.org/10.1016/j.jrt.2023.100060
8. Dahl, B.M., Vasset, F., Frilund, M.: Students' approaches to scientific essay writing as an educational method in higher education: a mixed methods study. Soc. Sci. Humanit. Open **7**(1), 100389 (2023). https://doi.org/10.1016/j.ssaho.2022.100389
9. Geerling, W., Mateer, G.D., Wooten, J., Damodaran, N.: Is ChatGPT smarter than a student in principles of economics? SSRN Working Paper (2023). https://doi.org/10.2139/ssrn.4356034
10. Sweeney, S.: Who wrote this? essay mills and assessment—considerations regarding contract cheating and AI in higher education. Int. J. Manag. Educ. **21**(2), 100818 (2023). https://doi.org/10.1016/j.ijme.2023.100818
11. Malik, A.R., Pratiwi, Y., Andajani, K., Numertayasa, I.W., Suharti, S., Darwis, A.: Marzuki: exploring artificial intelligence in academic essay: higher education students' perspective. Int. J. Educ. Res. Open **5**, 100296 (2023). https://doi.org/10.1016/j.ijedro.2023.100296
12. Choi, J., et al.: ChatGPT goes to law school. J. Legal Educ. **387** (2022). https://doi.org/10.2139/ssrn.4335905
13. Lo, C.K.: What is the impact of ChatGPT on education? a rapid review of the literature. Educ. Sci. **13**(4), 410 (2023). https://doi.org/10.3390/educsci13040410
14. Cingillioglu, I.: Detecting AI-generated essays: the ChatGPT challenge. Int. J. Inf. Learn. Technol. **40**(3), 259–268 (2023). https://doi.org/10.1108/IJILT-03-2023-0043
15. Mohammadzadeh, Z., Ausloos, M., Saeidnia, H.R.: ChatGPT: high-tech plagiarism awaits academic publishing green light. Non-fungible token (NFT) can be a way out. Library Hi. Tech. News. **40**(7), 12–14 (2023). https://doi.org/10.1108/LHTN-04-2023-0067
16. Cotton, D.R.E., Cotton, P.A., Shipway, J.R.: Chatting and cheating: ensuring academic integrity in the era of ChatGPT. Innov. Educ. Teach. Int. **61**(2), 228–239 (2024). https://doi.org/10.1080/14703297.2023.2190148
17. Gilson, A., et al.: How does ChatGPT perform on the united states medical licensing examination? the implications of large language models for medical education and knowledge assessment. JMIR Med. Educ. **9**, e45312 (2023). https://doi.org/10.2196/45312
18. Anthony Jnr, B.: Managing digital transformation of smart cities through enterprise architecture—a review and research agenda. Enterp. Inf. Syst. **15**(3), 299–331 (2021). https://doi.org/10.1080/17517575.2020.1812006
19. Ylinen, M., Pekkola, S.: Looking for a five-legged sheep. In: Proceedings of the 19th Annual International Conference on Digital Government Research: Governance in the Data Age, pp. 1–8. ACM, New York (2018). https://doi.org/10.1145/3209281.3209353

20. Thönssen, B., von Dewitz, M.: A label is not enough—approach for an enterprise architecture role description framework. Proc. Comput. Sci. **138**, 409–416 (2018). https://doi.org/10.1016/j.procs.2018.10.058
21. Betterteam: Enterprise architect job description. https://www.betterteam.com/ (2023). Accessed 11 May 2023
22. RealIRM: EA Bootcamp. https://realirm.com/training/ea-frameworks/course/ea-bootcamp-training (2023). Accessed 11 May 2023
23. EA Learning: Applied business architecture. https://www.ealearning.com/our-courses/courses/applied-business-architecture-virtual-classroom.html (2023). Accessed 11 May 2023
24. Knowledge Academy: Enterprise architect training. https://www.theknowledgeacademy.com/za/courses/enterprise-architect-training/ (2023). Accessed 11 May 2023
25. Ma, M., Bui, G.: Implementing continuous assessment in an academic English writing course: an exploratory study. Assess. Writ. **53**(1), 100629 (2022). https://doi.org/10.1016/j.asw.2022.100629
26. DHET: TVET curriculum instruction (2023). https://www.dhet.gov.za/Technical%20and%20Vocational%20Education%20and%20Training%20Co/2023%20REPORT%20191%20ICASS%20Guidelines.pdf
27. Seyoum Beyene, Y., Seyoum Wolde-Mariam, G.: The implementation of continuous assessment in writing classes of Jimma College of Teachers Education. Ethiop. J. Educ. Sci. **10**(1), 109–135 (2014). https://www.ajol.info/index.php/ejesc
28. Halawi, L.A., McCarthy, R.V., Pires, S.: An evaluation of e-learning on the basis of Bloom's taxonomy: an exploratory study. J. Educ. Bus. **84**(6), 374–380 (2009). https://doi.org/10.3200/JOEB.84.6.374-380
29. Moonsamy, W., Lotriet, H.: Supplementary material. figshare (2025). https://doi.org/10.6084/m9.figshare.28005941.v1

Leveraging Abstract Syntax Trees To Generate Instructive Hints In Programming

Marc Levin[1], Herman Kandjimi[1,2](✉), and Aslam Safla[1]

[1] School of IT, Department of Computer Science, University of Cape Town, Woolsack Drive, Cape Town 7701, Rondebosch, South Africa
{lvnmar013,kndher001}@myuct.ac.za, hkandjimi@nust.na, aslam.safla@uct.ac.za

[2] Faculty of Computing and Informatics, Namibia University of Science and Technology, 13 Jackson Kaujeua Street, Windhoek, Namibia

Abstract. Introductory programming education is constantly challenged with how to provide effective, personalized guidance to struggling novices. AST-based hints generation emerges as a potential solution, marrying abstract syntax tree analysis with generative AI to offer tailored, instructive feedback for Python learners. Existing hint generation systems like ITAP and GPT4Hints-GPT3.5Val have approached hint generation through path construction and generative models, respectively. Both approaches to hint generation have shown promise in generating human-like hints, but each has its own limitations. These approaches either provide highly instructive hints that are often too explicit or more abstract but may lack the specificity necessary for effective guidance. Our study combines the strengths of both approaches to provide students with hints that are both instructive and abstract but do not give away the solution. We provide a detailed overview of the AST-based hints system, including requirements gathering, the system architecture and features. The system is evaluated through path construction testing and A/B testing with speculative analysis. The results from path construction and A/B testing demonstrate that AST-Hints is moderately effective at generating human-like hints, faster than human tutors, with its success strongly related to the quality of the goal solution and hint relevance.

Keywords: Programming · Abstract Syntax Tree · Generative AI · Instructive Hints · Python

1 Introduction

Students in introductory programming courses frequently encounter difficulties in solving programming exercises [6]. Identifying and correcting errors in code can be challenging, particularly without immediate access to educators or teaching assistants. This issue is amplified in large classes where such resources are

L. Nel et al. (Eds.): SACLA 2025, CCIS 2770, pp. 33–50, 2026.
https://doi.org/10.1007/978-3-032-12457-9_3

limited [33]. Instructive hints can be an effective tool in these scenarios, offering guidance to help students identify and correct errors in their code. However, generating effective hints presents its own challenges. These hints must balance being informative while remaining sufficiently abstract to promote critical thinking and problem-solving skills.

The use of abstract syntax trees (ASTs) in programming education tools shows promise in generating human-like hints [5,28]. ASTs are tree representations of a program's syntactic structure, capturing the relationships between different code elements. Comparing a student's AST to a goal AST allows for the identification of differences and suggestion of modifications to bring the student's code closer to the correct solution. This approach can generate instructive hints that guide students toward the correct solution while enhancing their understanding of the underlying concepts.

Python was selected for our case study due to its popularity in introductory programming courses because of its readability and simplicity [8,14]. Its clear syntax makes it suitable for teaching fundamental programming concepts such as control structures, data types, and functions.

Generative artificial intelligence (AI) models have demonstrated potential in various applications, including natural language processing. These models, trained on large datasets, can generate human-like responses to input prompts [23]. In programming education, generative AI models can potentially provide hints to students based on their code and the desired outcome. However, these models may struggle to generate hints that balance informativeness and abstraction, as they follow a fixed objective function and may prioritize correctness over pedagogical value [24,25].

Combining AST-based instructive hint generation with generative AI models could address this challenge, leveraging the strengths of both approaches to provide students with effective and adaptive guidance. This integration may enable the generation of hints that are both informative and conducive to learning.

This study presents a system that implements this combination, utilizing the differences between a student's AST and a goal AST to generate instructive hints using an AST comparison module, which is then refined by a generative AI module to provide more abstract natural language hints. The system consists of two main modules: the AST comparison module and the generative AI hint module, integrated within a command line interface (CLI). A CLI was chosen as the user interface for the implementation to facilitate interoperability, allowing the system to be integrated with existing educational platforms or tools.

The rest of the paper is structured as follows: the first section provides an overview of the literature on related work, followed by details on the experimental design and methodology, including the system design and implementation of the system, outlining its architecture, features, and testing methodology. We then conclude by discussing the evaluation results, the system's implications and potential areas for future research.

2 Related Work

Programming education encounters several challenges primarily due to high cognitive complexity, limited resources, and unrealistic expectations placed on students [2]. Multiple studies indicate that students often struggle with conceptual understanding, Huang et al. [16] points out that a lack of programming semantics and structure comprehension negatively affects self-efficacy, leading to the composition effectâĂŤwhere students find it challenging to integrate component skills, such as code tracing, which impedes their ability to develop cohesive programming competence. Additionally, several studies [1,7,13] highlight that students face difficulties with abstract concepts, such as arrays, loops, functions, and program design. Medeiros et al. [22] emphasize that inadequate problem-solving and mathematical skills lead to higher dropout and failure rates among students.

Furthermore, exercise-related barriers can arise in various contexts. For instance, De Souza et al. [9] link the misinterpretation of programming structures such as loops and conditionals to a lack of timely and consistent feedback in programming tasks, which they propose could be resolved through an automated evaluation and feedback of student programs. Similarly, Butler and Morgan [7] note that insufficient feedback on high-level design hinders the application of object-oriented principles.

Research on automated feedback in programming education often focuses on identifying mistakes rather than providing guidance on problem-solving or the following steps [19]. Implementation issues, such as limited concrete examples and practice opportunities, hinder adequate feedback provision [29]. While tools for automated feedback generation exist, they typically lack the adaptability for teachers to customize them to specific needs [18,19]. A feedback-oriented platform for deliberate programming practice must be developed to address these challenges, offering carefully selected tasks with increasing difficulty and immediate feedback [29]. However, the diversity of feedback types may increase over time, with new techniques being applied to generate more helpful student feedback [19].

Research has shown that instructive hints can significantly improve students' problem-solving skills across various subjects. For example, a study by Jacobse et al. [17] found that students who used metacognitive hints while solving word problems performed better than their peers who did not have access to such hints. The results indicated that these hints enhanced problem-solving performance and improved metacognitive skills, suggesting that instructional hints play a crucial role in developing critical thinking skills in programming contexts. Similarly, in physics, providing computer-delivered hints improved students' strategic knowledge and problem-solving abilities, with hints available during the problem-solving process being the most effective [26]. In mathematics, a student-controlled computer program that offered hints for various problem-solving scenarios resulted in increased problem-solving abilities compared to traditional instruction [15].

Instructive hints can empower students to take control of their learning process. Yi et al. [35] explored the feasibility of using automated program repair tools as a form of hint generation. Their results indicated that while students struggled to utilize the hints provided effectively, the potential for automated hints to facilitate self-directed learning was evident. By offering targeted feedback, these hints can help students identify and rectify errors independently, fostering a sense of ownership over their learning.

Furthermore, Emerson et al. [11] identified misconceptions among novice programmers using block-based programming environments. By tailoring hints to address these misconceptions, educators can provide targeted support that helps students overcome specific barriers to understanding. This targeted approach not only aids in correcting misunderstandings but also reinforces the learning of fundamental programming concepts. This type of hint can influence student behaviour, as observed in a logic proof tutor where next-step hints and abstract high-level hints affected hint usage, rule applications, and time spent in the tutor.

Recent studies have explored using Large Language Models (LLMs) to provide automated feedback in programming exercises. CodEv, an automated grading framework, leverages LLMs to offer consistent and constructive feedback comparable to human evaluators [32]. However, research on concurrent programming exercises found limitations in LLM's ability to assess specific concurrency errors accurately. Additionally [12], studies have outlined that LLMs suffer from knowledge about task constraints, providing randomness in responses and, in worse cases, fabricating information (hallucinations); hence, instructor oversight is needed as such responses may confuse students [3,20]. Furthermore, open-source LLMs have shown promising results in generating and judging programming feedback, performing nearly on par with proprietary models [21], a critical finding that could address concerns about privacy and ethics in proprietary models. These findings indicate that LLMs show potential for automated feedback in programming education.

2.1 Selected Approach

Intelligent Teaching Assistant for Programming. The AST comparison module in our system is based on the Intelligent Teaching Assistant for Programming (ITAP) system developed by Rivers and Koedinger [28]. ITAP builds upon the hint factory method introduced by Barnes and Stamper [5], which provides next-step hints by comparing current solutions to past student solutions and a goal solution. ITAP enhances this approach with a novel path construction algorithm that generates new intermediate solutions. This algorithm creates a sequence of transformations to convert a student's solution into the goal solution. By applying subsets of these transformations to the student's code, ITAP generates multiple iterations of the solution. These iterations are then evaluated using a desirability metric, with the highest-scoring iteration's transformation steps used to generate hints. To ensure semantic differences do not affect hint generation, ITAP employs a canonicalization process on both the student's code and the goal code. The effectiveness of ITAP in generating instructive hints for programming exercises, as demonstrated in a study by Price et al. [27], led to its selection as the foundation for our system's AST comparison module. Additionally, ITAP has an MIT license[1] allowing modification and use in an academic context provided we cite the project.

Hint Generation and Evaluation Using GPTs. Phung et al. [25] introduced GPT4Hints-GPT3.5Val, a hint generation approach that utilizes Generative Pre-Trained Transformer (GPT) models from OpenAI [6]. In their system, GPT-4 functions as a "Teacher" model, while GPT-3.5 acts as a "Student" model, to create hints for programming exercises. The teacher model attempts to correct the student's solution and then generates both a concise hint and a detailed explanation of the proposed fix. The system then employs ten(10) student models that receive the student's original solution along with the detailed hint provided by the teacher model. These student models try to fix the buggy code based on the teacher's long-form hint. The outputs of the student models are evaluated against a set of test cases, and if the majority of the models' corrected code passes these tests, the concise hint is delivered to the student. If the threshold is not met, the teacher model generates a new hint. After a set number of attempts, if the success criteria are still unmet, no hint is generated. GPT4Hints-GPT3.5Val's technique was adapted for the generative AI hint module in AST-Hints. The teacher-student model setup proved to be effective in generating hints that closely resemble those given by a human tutor [24,25]. The GPT4Hints-GPT3.5Val system also has an MIT license[2]

Combining ITAP and GPT Hints. Our system combines several algorithms from ITAP with the generative AI hint generation method from GPT4Hints-GPT3.5Val. The path construction algorithm, desirability and distance algorithms from ITAP were modified and adapted into the AST comparison module, which generates instructive hints based on the differences between a student's code and a goal solution. The hint refining methodology from GPT4Hints-GPT3.5Val was adapted into the generative AI hint module, which uses OpenAI's GPT-4o-mini and GPT-3.5 models to provide more abstract hints to students. These separate modules were integrated into a command-line interface (CLI) to provide a comprehensive interface for generating hints. The combination is illustrated by the system architecture in Fig. 1

3 Experiment Design and Methodology

The following sections detail the experiment design and methodology used to evaluate the AST-based hints system. The evaluation comprises two main components: path construction testing and A/B testing with speculative analysis.

[1] https://github.com/krivers/ITAP-django.

[2] https://github.com/machine-teaching-group/lak2024_GPT4Hints-GPT3.5Val.

These components aim to assess the system's effectiveness in generating instructive hints for programming exercises and compare the hints generated by the system with those provided by human tutors.

3.1 System Design and Implementation

The system's architecture consists of three main components: the AST Comparison Module, the Generative AI Hint Module, and the Command Line Interface (CLI). A detailed architecture of the three modules and the overall process flow of the system is illustrated in Fig. 1.

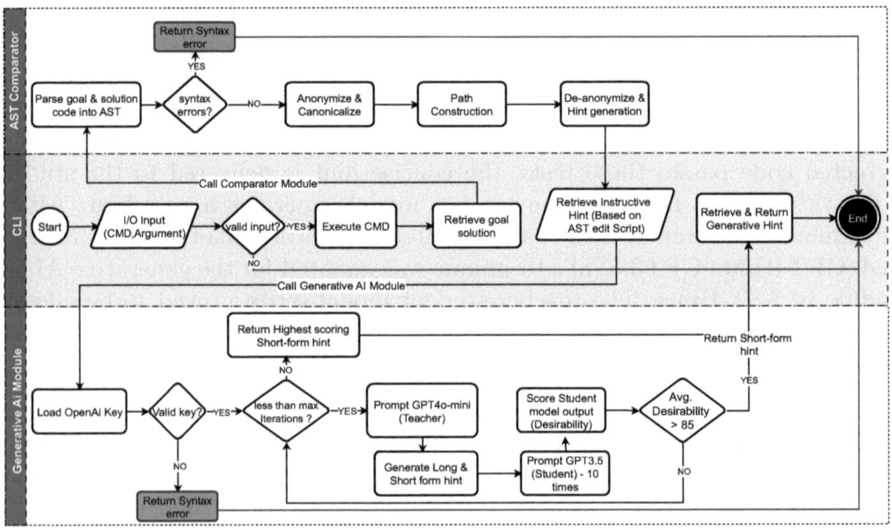

Fig. 1. Flow diagram depicting the architecture of AST-based hints system.

AST Comparison Module. The AST comparison module was built by refactoring ITAP's path construction algorithm to accommodate recent Python versions and fix existing bugs. The module takes in any two Python files, typically the student's code and the goal code, and generates a sequence of transformations to convert the student's code into the goal code. The module provides an entry point that first uses the autopep8 module to format the input files, ensuring consistent code style. This formatting is not necessary for the module to function, but improves the readability of the code during development, in a production environment this step would be omitted. The files are then parsed into ASTs using Python's built-in AST module, which rejects any code that is not evaluated, such as syntax errors. The ASTs are canonicalized and then passed to the path construction submodules, which produce the transformation steps. These steps are then passed to another submodule, which converts the transformation steps into human-readable hints. Finally, the hints are returned to the caller. In problem-solving, students may devise solutions that are semantically equivalent but syntactically diverse. Consequently, semantically equivalent ASTs may exhibit substantial syntactic variation. To mitigate syntactic variation, the module applies a set of normalization functions to standardize the AST structure, known as canonicalization.

Several transformations facilitate the canonicalization of student ASTs, which consist of nodes representing various code elements such as functions, variables, and expressions. Our canonicalization included *Constant folding*, *Dead code elimination*, *De Morgan's laws* and *Conditional redundancy* transformations.

The crucial step in the path construction algorithm is the evaluation of intermediate solutions. Each intermediate solution undergoes a validity assessment and those with syntax errors or compilation failures are discarded. Further viability validation employs a distance metric:

$$d\ (s,c) = \frac{change\_weight(s,c)}{max(\ weight(s), weight(c))} \tag{1}$$

d(s, c) denotes the distance between a given AST s and another AST c. Whereas $change\_weight(s,c)$ indicates the sum of the weights of changes between s and c, and *weight(s)* and *weight(c)* signify the weights of a given AST s and another AST c , respectively. The weight of an AST is the sum of the nodes' count, considering the node type and the number of children. The change weight sums the weights of the transformation operation's new and old values.

The distance between the goal AST and the intermediate solution is computed. Intermediate solutions with a longer distance from the goal AST than the student's AST are eliminated. The remaining intermediate solutions undergo a desirability metric application to select the most suitable solution:

$$D\ (c_n) = \frac{1}{6.0}(4 \cdot (1 - d(s,c_n)) + 2 \cdot (1 - d(g,c_n))) \tag{2}$$

$D(c_n)$ signifies the desirability of the code c_n, $d(s,c_n)$ represents the distance between the student's code s and the intermediate solution code c_n and $d(g,c_n)$ represents the distance between the goal code g and the intermediate solution code c_n. The desirability metric blends the distances between the student's code and the intermediate solution code and between the goal code and the intermediate solution code.

The desirability metric aims to identify the intermediate solution nearest to the goal code while remaining proximal to the student's code. This metric favours solutions closer to the student's code, as the primary goal is to provide hints that guide the student toward the correct solution. After selecting the most desirable intermediate solution, the transformation operations used to generate the solution from the student's AST are extracted, and the intermediate solution is now classified as the new goal code.

The hint generation process in the AST Comparison module yields instructive hints(transformation operations) that inform the student of the necessary changes to their code, guiding them toward the correct solution. However, these hints may not foster a profound understanding of underlying concepts. To address this limitation, the generative AI hint module provides more abstract and less explicit hints.

Generative AI Hint Module. The generative AI module was built from scratch, using a similar process as GPT4Hints-GPT3.5Val. The module takes in the student's code, the goal code, the exercise description, and the human-readable hint generated by the AST comparison module. The module utilizes OpenAI's API to access the GPT-4o-mini and GPT-3.5 models [23], these models are used as teacher and student models respectively.

The OpenAI's GPT-4o-mini (Teacher) model was fine-tuned with an aim to generate hints tailored to the specific student's code and the human-readable hint. This teacher model is configured to produce both a long-form hint, which is a paragraph that instructs on the application of the human-readable hint to the student's code, and a short-form hint, which succinctly summarizes the long-form hint. This methodology leverages the chain-of-thought technique to enhance response quality and reasoning capacity [34].

The OpenAI's GPT-3.5 (Student) models were fine-tuned to act as student agents focused on following instructions from the teacher model. These student models are tasked with applying the same long-form hint provided by the teacher model to generate revised code. The responses from the student models are then evaluated using the desirability metric, with a score above 85% being considered satisfactory. If the majority of responses from the student models meet this criterion, the short-form hint from the teacher model is selected. If not, the process is repeated with the teacher model generating a new set of long-form and short-form hints. This iterative process can occur up to three times, and ultimately, the short-form hint from the iteration with the highest score is presented to the student. This method is designed to ensure the generation of high-quality, meaningful guidance for the student.

CLI. The command line interface (CLI) serves as the user interface for the AST-based hints system. The CLI was created using a click, a Python library that simplifies the process of building command-line interfaces. The reason a CLI was chosen as the user interface is that it allows for interoperability with existing educational platforms or tools, and is installable via Python's package manager, pip. The click package was chosen for its automatic help page generation and built-in testing tools. The CLI was designed to be user-friendly, with clear and concise command descriptions and error messages.

3.2 Path Construction Testing

The AST comparison module was designed to generate a minimal number of transformation operations to convert a student's code into a target solution. To assess the efficacy of the path construction algorithm within the module, ten

Table 1. Summary of CLI commands in AST-based hints system

Command	Description
compare	Takes in two Python files and returns a human-readable hint generated by the AST comparison module.
generative-ai-hint	Takes in the student's code, the goal code, and the exercise description, and returns a hint generated by the generative AI hint module.
compare-using-strings	Wrapper for the compare command that takes input in the form of strings
generative-ai-hint-using-strings	Wrapper for the generative-ai-hint command that takes input in the form of strings.
help	Provides information on the available commands and their usage.

standard programming exercises were selected, each associated with a target solution. These target solutions were deliberately altered to introduce common novice errors, including control flow mistakes, out-of-bounds errors, and logical errors, resulting in "student" solutions with at least three errors each.

The student solutions were then compared to the original target solutions using the path construction algorithm. After generating the transformation steps and corresponding human-readable hints, these hints were manually applied to the student solutions. This process was repeated for each exercise, with the number of iterations required to transform the student solution into the target solution recorded. By recording the number of transformation operations generated and subsequently applied, the algorithm's efficiency and effectiveness in correcting student errors could be evaluated. The exercises were sourced from LeetCode, an online platform that is known for hosting a range of programming exercises suitable for novice programmers [8].

3.3 A/B Testing and Speculative Analysis

The study employed an A/B testing approach to evaluate the system's effectiveness in generating hints for programming exercises. This involved a comparative analysis of the hints generated by the AST-based hints system and those provided by human tutors for the same programming task. For our test case, students were given an assignment to create a Python script that prompts the user for five numbers, calculates their integer average, prints the average, and indicates whether the average is even or odd. We randomly divided a sample of 16 students into two cohorts: Group A received hints from the AST-based hints system, while Group B received hints from human tutors. The random assignment of students to each group aimed to minimize potential sources of bias and ensure a fair comparison between the two hint sources. The study was conducted during a routine practical session in an introductory programming course. Students were recruited on a voluntary basis and provided informed consent before participating in the study, they were further informed about the study's purpose and procedures. A web platform was designed using React, Django, SQLite3, Docker, and Nginx to deliver the hints. Students were presented with a programming exercise and could request a hint by visiting the website, pasting their code. For Group A, the requests were processed by the AST-based hints system, and the generated hints were displayed on the site. For Group B, the requests were forwarded to a human tutor who reviewed the code and provided a hint.

All hint requests and responses, whether automated or human-generated, were timestamped. Students were encouraged to apply the hints to their code and submit it to Automarker, an auto-grading software, before requesting additional hints. This process was managed by enforcing a three-minute cooldown period between hint requests. The enforcement of a cooldown was inspired by a study done by Baniassad et al. [4] which asserted that there are cases where students rely on the feedback in the form of generated hints in place of learning the desired knowledge base and that a period between requests being enforced can help mitigate this issue. To carry out the A/B testing a single-goal solution for the exercise was written before the study, as a basis for the system generating hints, which might have led to a reduced diversity of the generated hints and potentially affected the quality of the hints provided to students.

The submissions from Group A were used to evaluate the performance of the AST-based hints system in generating hints from a single-goal solution. The submissions from Group B were used to perform a speculative analysis. We manually modified the code submitted by Group B to generate a set of individualized goal solutions that were semantically equivalent to the original goal solution. The hints generated using the individualized goal solutions were then compared to the hints generated by the tutors for the same student submissions. This technique emulates the clustering system's functionality and allows for a more accurate comparison between the hints generated by AST-Hints and human tutors.

The measure of performance for submissions in group A was the average time taken to generate a hint as well as the hint's relevance. A hint was considered relevant if it referenced the student's code, both in structure and content. The measure of performance for the speculative analysis done on submissions from group B was the hint equivalency to the human-generated hints and the time taken to generate a hint, both from the tutor and from the AST-based hints system. A hint was considered equivalent if it conveyed the same information as the human-generated hint, even if the wording differed. Equivalency was scored on a scale of 1 to 5, with 1 indicating no similarity and 5 indicating complete similarity. The results of the A/B testing and speculative analysis will be discussed in the next section.

4 Results and Discussion

4.1 Path Construction Testing

The path construction algorithm was tested across ten exercises, with results indicating a moderate level of effectiveness in transforming erroneous student solutions into correct ones. As illustrated in Fig. 2, the algorithm consistently required an equal number of operations to correct the introduced errors for most of the exercises, demonstrating a one-to-one mapping between errors introduced and corrective operations. This reflects the algorithm's capability to methodically identify and rectify discrepancies in student code.

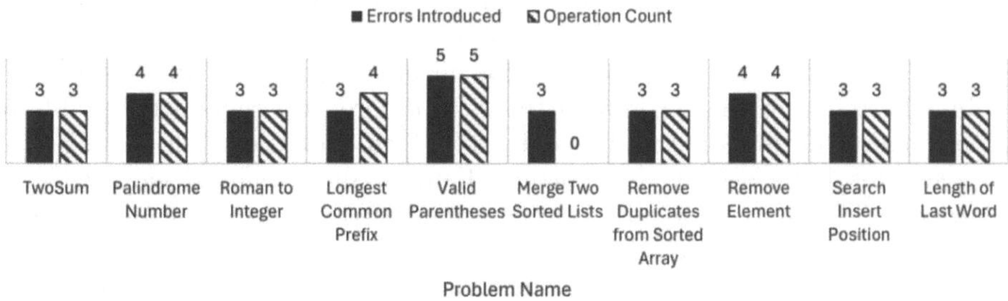

Fig. 2. Results of the path construction testing.

For eight out of the ten problems, the algorithm successfully achieved the necessary corrections within the same number of iterations as the errors introduced, affirming its robustness in handling common programming mistakes. However, the "Longest common prefix" exercise deviated from this trend, requiring four iterations to correct three errors. This anomaly was due to the algorithm's introduction of a variable that lacked a corresponding equivalent in the goal code. Although the algorithm generated a DeleteOperation to remove the variable, the disruption it caused to a logical operation necessitated an additional iteration for full correction. This case highlights a limitation in the current implementation of the algorithm, particularly in the handling of newly introduced variables that do not align with the logical structure of the goal code.

A significant outlier was observed in the "Merge Two Sorted Lists" exercise. Here, the student solution contained three errors, but the algorithm failed to parse the code post-canonicalization and anonymization. The underlying issue was traced to a limitation in the Python AST library, which struggled to revert the AST into a valid Python structure due to a missing attribute. This parsing failure appeared to be exacerbated by the presence of multiple class definitions within a single source file, suggesting a more general limitation in the library's ability to handle complex code structures.

The results demonstrate the path construction algorithm's general efficacy but also reveal areas for improvement. The consistent performance across most exercises suggests that the algorithm is well-suited for correcting typical student errors. However, the anomalies encountered indicate that the algorithm's reliance on the AST library introduces certain limitations, particularly when dealing with structural complexity in ASTs.

In summary, the path construction algorithm has demonstrated moderate potential in transforming erroneous code into correct solutions with minimal iterations, addressing the limitations exposed in this testing phase will be essential for further refinement and robustness of the system.

4.2 A/B Testing and Speculative Analysis

Group A submitted a total of 15 hint requests, with an average response time of 38.6 s from request to hint generation. In comparison, Group B also submitted 15 requests, but the average response time was significantly longer, at 186 s (or 3 min and 6 s). The average hint generation time for the system was notably shorter than that of human tutors, a difference largely attributable to the automated nature of AST-based hints, which processes code submissions and generates hints swiftly. In contrast, human tutors require more time to review code, identify errors, and formulate instructive hints, resulting in longer response times. Additionally, the practical session's context in which the evaluation took place may have influenced the time taken by tutors to generate hints, as they might have been more deliberate in their responses, considering the students' learning objectives and the educational context. The tutors noted that they took additional time to determine what the student was struggling with. This indicated that more information was needed to generate hints that were relevant to the student's specific issues. This discovery should be considered in future iterations of the system, as it suggests that the system may benefit from additional context to generate more relevant hints, without the need for human intervention.

Regarding the relevance of the hints, Group B received consistently relevant hints, as these were generated by human tutors. In contrast, Group A's hints were relevant in only 4 out of 15 cases. Two responses were entirely discarded because the AST-Hint CLI returned an error code, caused by a bug in the comparison algorithm that improperly parsed range expressions. The relevance issues in AST-Hints were likely influenced by the methodology used to convert transformation operations into human-readable hints. The goal solution for the evaluation contained boilerplate code absent from the student submissions, and the path construction algorithm tended to favour operations that minimized the distance between the student's code and the goal code. This resulted in hints focusing on adding irrelevant code rather than correcting existing code. This issue was further compounded by the generative AI hint module. When the teacher model received an instructive hint suggesting the addition of irrelevant code or the replacement of relevant code with irrelevant code, it generated hints that were similarly irrelevant. In five cases, the teacher model attempted to correct the erroneous instructive hint, resulting in hints that were irrelevant to the student's code. Ultimately, the use of a single-goal solution for the evaluation led to the generation of irrelevant hints.

To address the limitations of the A/B testing, a speculative analysis was conducted using submissions from Group B. The results of this analysis can be seen in Table 2 and Fig. 3. The findings indicate that, on average, the hints generated by the system using a diverse set of individualized goal solutions received an average equivalence rating of 3.3 out of 5. The equivalence ratings indicate a clear potential for the generated hints, with a success rate of more than 80% shown in the results. These results demonstrate that the LLM can effectively target the specific elements that require change in the student code, providing precise guidance without loss of time. This suggests that the hints produced by AST-Hints were moderately similar to those provided by human tutors in a speculative context. It is important to note that this analysis represents a best-case scenario, as each student submission was matched with a tailor-made goal solution, which may not be feasible in a real-world scenario. Additionally, the hints were generated in a controlled environment, which may not reflect the variability of student submissions in practice. These results suggest that AST-based hints system has the potential to generate hints comparable to those provided by human tutors when the system is tailored to individual student submissions. However, the system's performance is likely influenced by the quality of the goal solution and the diversity of student submissions.

On average, the system took 28.8 s to generate a hint using the individualized goal solutions, a time lower than the average during the A/B testing. This reduction in time can be attributed to the improved quality of the goal solutions, which enabled the system to generate hints more efficiently. The results indicate that the quality of the goal solution has a significant impact on the performance of AST-based hints in generating timely hints. When using individualized goal solutions, the system generated hints 7.5 times faster than human tutors on average. This demonstrates the potential of the system to provide rapid feedback to students, enhancing the learning experience and promoting self-directed learning, particularly in educational settings where students benefit from immediate feedback to progress in their studies.

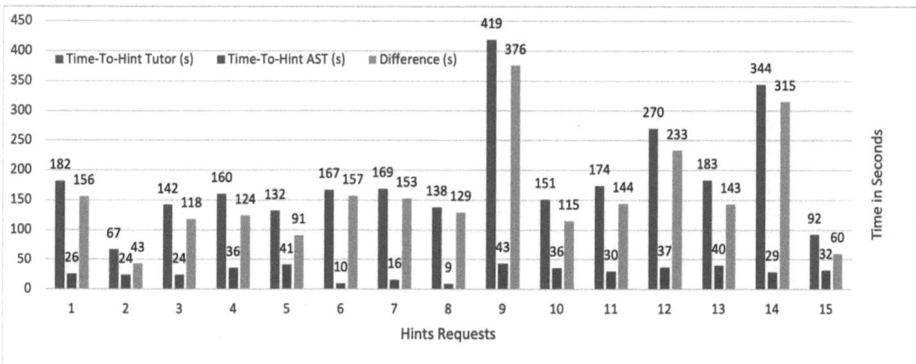

Fig. 3. Sample hints and time difference between human tutor and AST system hints

Table 2. AST-Hints with Equivalence Rating and Timing Differences in Seconds

Tutor Hint	AST-Hint	Equivalence Rating	Time-To-Hint Tutor	Time-To-Hint AST-Hints	Difference (Seconds)
Insure using double slash for integers values	Accumulate the total of the values first, then divide by 5 to find the average.	1	182	26	156
The ave variable should not be within the for loop. You only need to calculate the average once after you get the total of the input values.	Accumulate the total of the entered values before dividing by 5 to calculate the average correctly.	5	67	24	43
The value variable should sum the total of each input. Currently, the value variable is being reset to each input from the user. Use something like a += operator to actually sum the inputs.	Make sure to accumulate the input values in ave before calculating the average.	5	142	24	118
Try making the loop to ask input from the user then add all the values up then display.	Make sure to calculate the average using the total sum of all inputs, not just the last input value.	5	160	36	124
The second if statement can just be an else... and try using the loop to ask those numbers	Use else to print the odd message only when the average is not even.	4	132	41	91
Rather than int(average), use the round function to round the average to the nearest integer.	Use an f-string to correctly display the rounded average instead of the count of numbers.	1	167	10	157
You have first display the average then print whether it is odd or even	Print the rounded average before checking if it is even or odd to follow the correct output order.	5	169	16	153
The last line being outputted should be the first line being outputted.	Make sure to print the rounded average before checking if it is even or odd.	5	138	9	129
There would be no point in the while loop if you already have your values	Consolidate your print statements for even and odd cases into a single conditional block after calculating the average.	1	419	43	376
The if statement is incorrect and the ave/2 == 0; it would be the wrong condition.	Use (ave % 2 == 0) to check if the average is even.	5	151	36	115
The if statement is incorrect. It should check that the average is an even number which means it has no remainder (use % operator)	Use average % 2 == 0 to check if the average is even.	5	174	30	144
The elif statement is unnecessary. A simple else statement with no condition will do.	Calculate the average after the loop to ensure it uses the total sum of all entered numbers.	1	270	37	233
Try to divide with double slashes and not 1	Calculate the average after the loop to ensure it reflects all five numbers entered.	1	183	40	143
The average only needs to be calculated once, it does not need to be in the for loop.	Calculate the average after the loop to ensure it uses the total sum of all five numbers.	5	344	29	315
The average only needs to be calculated once, so it does not need to be in the for loop	Use int() to safely convert user input to an integer instead of eval().	1	92	32	60

5 Conclusion, Limitations and Future Work

The AST-based hints system demonstrates the potential to generate hints for novice Python programmers, that are semantically similar to human tutors, faster than human tutors by leveraging ASTs and generative AI. The system's path construction algorithm was successful in converting erroneous student code into correct solutions with minimal transformations, indicating the robustness of the AST-based approach. Moreover, the generative AI hint module showed promise, particularly when applied to individualized student submissions, in producing hints that moderately align with those generated by human tutors.

However, the evaluation also highlighted significant areas for improvement, particularly regarding the relevance and instructiveness of the generated hints. The current methodology for converting transformation operations into human-readable hints often resulted in outputs that were not directly applicable to the student's code. This issue was exacerbated by the generative AI hint module's dependence on a single-goal solution, which limited its adaptability across diverse student submissions.

To enhance the relevance and instructiveness of the hints, future work should focus on refining the hint-generation process. This could involve incorporating more context-awareness into the hint generation algorithm, enabling the system to provide hints that are more tailored to the student's specific code and errors. A student could provide the line number of the code they are struggling with or a description of the issue, which could be used to generate more relevant hints. Moreover, the system could be extended to consider the student's previous submissions and learning history, allowing for more personalized and adaptive hint generation.

The current system compares the entire structure of the student's code with the goal code, which can lead to less targeted hints. Future research could explore segmenting the code into smaller, semantically meaningful units, such as functions or loops, and generating hints that are contextually relevant to each unit. This approach could reduce the bias towards operations that add or remove code and instead focus on addressing specific issues within these units.

While Python was chosen as the implementation language due to its prevalence in introductory programming courses and its robust AST library, future work might consider exploring the implementations in other programming languages. Languages with a strong typed system and functional programming paradigm could offer potential advantages in the safety and implementation of the path construction algorithm, particularly with recursive structures and tree-based transformations [30].

Finally, while the use of OpenAI's API was relatively cost-effective (calculated to be \$0.0053 US\$s or around 1 South African cent per hint request), it introduces risks related to reproducibility and long-term reliability due to the reliance on an external service. To mitigate these risks, future work could investigate alternative generative AI frameworks, such as the open-source LLaMA models [31] or DeepSeek-Coder [10]. Self-hosting and fine-tuning models on domain-specific data could provide greater control over the hint generation process, improve reproducibility, and reduce dependency on third-party APIs. In summary, while AST-based hint system has shown promise in generating rapid and effective programming hints, particularly through its integration of ASTs and generative AI, several areas remain where the system can be refined and enhanced. Addressing these challenges will be crucial for realizing the full potential of automated hint generation in educational contexts, ultimately leading to a more tailored and effective learning experience for novice programmers.

Acknowledgments.. This work is financially supported by the Hasso Plattner Institute for Digital Engineering through the HPI Research School in Information and Communications Technology for Development (ICT4D) at the University of Cape Town.

References

1. Ali, M., Zamzuri, A.: Difficulties in learning programming: views of students. In: ICCIE2012: International Conference on Current Issues in Education (Jan 2012). https://doi.org/10.13140/2.1.1055.7441
2. Azaiz, I., Kiesler, N., Strickroth, S.: Feedback-Generation for programming exercises with GPT-4. ITiCSE 2024: Proceedings of the 2024 on Innovation and Technology in Computer Science Education **1**, 31–37 (7 2024https://doi.org/10.1145/3649217.3653594
3. Balse, R., Valaboju, B., Singhal, S., Warriem, J.M., Prasad, P.: Investigating the potential of GPT-3 in providing feedback for programming assessments. In: ITiCSE 2023: Proceedings of the 2023 Conference on Innovation and Technology in Computer Science Education **1**, 292–298 (June 2023). https://doi.org/10.1145/3587102.3588852
4. Baniassad, E., Zamprogno, L., Hall, B., Holmes, R.: STOP THE (AUTOGRADER) INSANITY: regression penalties to deter autograder overreliance. In: SIGCSE 2021: Proceedings of the 52nd ACM Technical Symposium on Computer Science Education, pp. 1062–1068 (3 2021). https://doi.org/10.1145/3408877.3432430
5. Barnes, T., Stamper, J.: Toward automatic hint generation for logic proof tutoring using historical student data. Springer-Verlag (2008). https://doi.org/10.1007/978-3-540-69132-7_41
6. Bennedsen, J., Caspersen, M.E.: Failure rates in introductory programming. ACM SIGCSE Bull. **39**(2), 32–36 (2007) https://doi.org/10.1145/1272848.1272879
7. Butler, M., Morgan, M.: Learning challenges faced by novice programming students studying high level and low feedback concepts. ascilite Singapore 2007, pp. 99–107 (Jan 2007). https://research.monash.edu/en/publications/learning-challenges-faced-by-novice-programming-students-studying
8. Coignion, T., Quinton, C., Rouvoy, R.: A performance study of LLM-Generated Code on LeetCode. In: EASE 2024: Proceedings of the 28th International Conference on Evaluation and Assessment in Software Engineering, vol. 14, 79–89 (June 2024). https://doi.org/10.1145/3661167.3661221
9. De Souza, L.M., Felix, I.M., Ferreira, B.M., Brandão, A.A.F., De Oliveira Brandão, L.: I know what you coded last summer. In: Anais do XXXII Simpósio Brasileiro de Informática na Educação (SBIE 2021), pp. 909–920 (Nov 2021). https://doi.org/10.5753/sbie.2021.218673

10. DeepSeek-Ai, Z.Q., et al.: DeepSeek-Coder-V2: breaking the barrier of Closed-Source Models in Code Intelligence. arXiv (Cornell University) (June 2024). https://doi.org/10.48550/arxiv.2406.11931
11. Emerson, A., et al.: Cluster-Based analysis of novice coding misconceptions in Block-Based programming. In: SIGCSE 2020: Proceedings of the 51st ACM Technical Symposium on Computer Science Education, pp. 825–831 (Feb 2020). https://doi.org/10.1145/3328778.3366924
12. Estevez-Ayres, I., Callejo, P., Hombrados-Herrera, M.A., Alario-Hoyos, C., Kloos, C.D.: Evaluation of LLM tools for feedback generation in a course on concurrent programming. Inter. J. Artifi. Intel. Educ. (May 2024). https://doi.org/10.1007/s40593-024-00406-0
13. Giannakoulas, A., Xinogalos, S.: A critical review of primary school students' difficulties in learning programming through educational games. J. Educ. Comput. Res. (2024). https://doi.org/10.1177/07356331241309074
14. Haldeman, G., et al.: Providing meaningful feedback for autograding of programming assignments. In: SIGCSE 2018: Proceedings of the 49th ACM Technical Symposium on Computer Science Education, pp. 278–283 (Feb 2018). https://doi.org/10.1145/3159450.3159502
15. Harskamp, E., Suhre, C.: Schoenfeld's problem solving theory in a student controlled learning environment. Comp. Educ. **49**(3), 822–839 (2006). https://doi.org/10.1016/j.compedu.2005.11.024
16. Huang, Y., Schunn, C.D., Guerra, J., Brusilovsky, P.: Why students cannot easily integrate component skills: An investigation of the composition effect in programming. ACM Trans. Comput. Educ. **24**(3), 1–37 (2024). https://doi.org/10.1145/3673239
17. Jacobse, A.E., Harskamp, E.G.: Student-controlled metacognitive training for solving word problems in primary school mathematics. Educ. Res. Evalua. **15**(5), 447–463 (2009). https://doi.org/10.1080/13803610903444519
18. Keuning, H., Jeuring, J., Heeren, B.: Towards a systematic review of automated feedback generation for programming exercises. In: ITiCSE 2016: Proceedings of the 2016 ACM Conference on Innovation and Technology in Computer Science Education, pp. 41–46 (July 2016). https://doi.org/10.1145/2899415.2899422
19. Keuning, H., Jeuring, J., Heeren, B.: A systematic literature review of automated feedback generation for programming exercises. ACM Trans. Comput. Educ. **19**(1), 1–43 (2018). https://doi.org/10.1145/3231711
20. Kiesler, N., Lohr, D., Keuning, H.: Exploring the potential of large language models to generate formative programming feedback. In: 2021 IEEE Frontiers in Education Conference (FIE) (Oct 2023). https://doi.org/10.1109/fie58773.2023.10343457
21. Koutcheme, C., Dainese, N., Sarsa, S., Hellas, A., Leinonen, J., Denny, P.: Open source language models can provide feedback: evaluating LLMs' ability to help students using GPT4AsAJudge. In: ITiCSE 2024: Proceedings of the 2024 on Innovation and Technology in Computer Science Education, vol. 1, pp. 52–58 (July 2024). https://doi.org/10.1145/3649217.3653612
22. Medeiros, R.P., Ramalho, G.L., Falcao, T.P.: A systematic literature review on teaching and learning introductory programming in higher education. IEEE Trans. Educ. **62**(2), 77–90 (2018). https://doi.org/10.1109/te.2018.2864133
23. OpenAI: GPT-4 Technical Report. arXiv (Cornell University) (Jan 2023). https://doi.org/10.48550/arxiv.2303.08774

24. Phung, T., et al.: Generative AI for programming education: benchmarking ChatGPT, GPT-4, and human tutors. In: ICER 2023: Proceedings of the 2023 ACM Conference on International Computing Education Research, vol. 2, pp. 41–42 (Aug 2023). https://doi.org/10.1145/3568812.3603476
25. Phung, T., et al.: Automating human tutor-style programming feedback: leveraging GPT-4 tutor model for hint generation and GPT-3.5 student model for hint validation. In: LAK 2024: The 14th Learning Analytics and Knowledge Conference, Kyoto, Japan, pp. 12–23 (Mar 2024). https://doi.org/10.1145/3636555.3636846
26. Pol, H.J., Harskamp, E.G., Suhre, C.J., Goedhart, M.J.: How indirect supportive digital help during and after solving physics problems can improve problem-solving abilities. Comput. Educ. **53**(1), 34–50 (2009). https://doi.org/10.1016/j.compedu.2008.12.015
27. Price, T.W., et al.: A comparison of the quality of Data-Driven Programming hint generation algorithms. IJAIED **29**(3), 368–395 (2019). https://doi.org/10.1007/s40593-019-00177-z
28. Rivers, K., Koedinger, K.R.: Data-driven hint generation in vast solution spaces: a self-improving python programming tutor. IJAIED **27**(1), 37–64 (2015). https://doi.org/10.1007/s40593-015-0070-z
29. Sánchez, M., Salazar, P.: A feedback-oriented platform for deliberate programming practice. In: ITiCSE 2020: Proceedings of the 2020 ACM Conference on Innovation and Technology in Computer Science Education (June 2020). https://doi.org/10.1145/3341525.3393996
30. Tamarit, S., Vigueras, G., Carro, M., Mariño, J.: A haskell implementation of a rule-based program transformation for C programs. In: Pontelli, E., Son, T.C. (eds.) PADL 2015. LNCS, vol. 9131, pp. 105–114. Springer, Cham (2015). https://doi.org/10.1007/978-3-319-19686-2_8
31. Touvron, H., et al.: LLAMA: Open and Efficient Foundation Language Models (Feb 2 2023). https://arxiv.org/abs/2302.13971
32. Tseng, E.Q., Huang, P.C., Hsu, C., Wu, P.Y., Ku, C.T., Kang, Y.: CODEV: an automated grading framework leveraging large language models for consistent and constructive feedback. In: 2021 IEEE International Conference on Big Data (Big Data), pp. 5442–5449 (Dec 2021). https://doi.org/10.1109/bigdata62323.2024.10825949
33. Watson, C., Li, F.W.: Failure rates in introductory programming revisited. In: ITiCSE 2014: Proceedings of the 2014 Conference on Innovation & Technology in Computer Science Education, pp. 39–44 (2014).https://doi.org/10.1145/2591708.2591749
34. Wei, J., Wang, X., Schuurmans, D., Bosma, M., Chi, E., Le, Q., Zhou, D.: Chain-of-Thought prompting elicits reasoning in large language models. arXiv (Cornell University) (Jan 2022). https://doi.org/10.48550/arxiv.2201.11903
35. Yi, J., Ahmed, U.Z., Karkare, A., Tan, S.H., Roychoudhury, A.: A feasibility study of using automated program repair for introductory programming assignments. In: ESEC/FSE 2017: Proceedings of the 2017 11th Joint Meeting on Foundations of Software Engineering, pp. 740–751 (Aug 2017). https://doi.org/10.1145/3106237.3106262

Beyond Language Barriers: Programme-Specific Effects of English Medium Instruction in South African Computer Science Education

Rouxan C. Fouché(✉)

Department of Computer Science and Informatics, University of the Free State, Bloemfontein, South Africa
foucherc@ufs.ac.za

Abstract. In South African higher education, English serves as the primary medium of instruction despite only 24 percent of undergraduate students citing English as their first language. This study investigates how language difficulties affect first-year Computer Science students' perceived module difficulty and engagement patterns across different technical disciplines at the University of the Free State. Analysis of survey data from 226 first-year IT students revealed distinct patterns across different module types: programming courses showed no significant difficulty differences between language groups, challenging assumptions about language barriers in technical education; business computing modules demonstrated the most pronounced challenges, while mathematical modules unexpectedly showed lower perceived difficulty among students with language difficulties. Student engagement analysis revealed higher classroom participation and increased informal peer learning engagement among students with language difficulties, suggesting compensatory learning strategies. Based on Cognitive Load Theory and Linguistic Relativity Theory, these findings show that the unique requirements of each subject area influence the cognitive load experienced during technical learning. Programming's universal syntax provides natural support that reduces unnecessary cognitive load, while business modules' contextual demands increase it. These insights advance theoretical frameworks for understanding multilingual technical education and provide evidence-based guidance for developing differentiated support strategies in post-colonial educational contexts.

Keywords: Computer science education · English medium instruction · Higher education · Language barriers · Multilingual learning · Student perception

1 Introduction

In South African higher education, English serves as the primary medium of instruction [1, 2], creating unique challenges in technical education [3]. English serves as both the medium of instruction and an entry requirement, despite being the first language of only 24% of South African undergraduate students [2]. At the University of the Free State (UFS), the Bachelor of Science in Information Technology (BSc IT) degree,

L. Nel et al. (Eds.): SACLA 2025, CCIS 2770, pp. 51–68, 2026.
https://doi.org/10.1007/978-3-032-12457-9_4

offered by the Department of Computer Science and Informatics (CSI), includes varied programmes blending core Computer Science with specialised disciplines such as Mathematics, Statistics, Physics, Chemistry, and Business Management [4].

While existing research has explored the general influence of language proficiency on academic performance in South African higher education [5–7], less attention has been given to how language difficulties impact student experiences across different technical and scientific disciplines. Specifically, while studies have documented the broader academic challenges faced by non-native English speakers [8, 9], few have investigated how students' perceptions of module difficulty vary across diverse combinations of Computer Science and other disciplines within the South African context.

This paper examines the impact of language barriers on academic experiences in first-year BSc IT education in a South African university, focusing on three key areas:

1. The perceived module difficulty in core Computer Science courses;
2. Language difficulties across different programme combinations; and
3. The impact of language challenges on student engagement and sense of belonging within the CSI department.

The significance of this study lies in its exploration of how various technical disciplines interact with language challenges in South African higher education. By examining core IT modules and disciplinary combinations, the study provides insights into which aspects of technical education are more resilient to language barriers and which require additional support. The results can inform language policies and support strategies in linguistically diverse higher education contexts locally and abroad.

The paper is structured as follows: Sect. 2 presents the literature review and theoretical frameworks; Sect. 3 describes the methodology; Sect. 4 presents the results; Sect. 5 discusses the results and implications; Sect. 6 provides the conclusion; and Sect. 7 outlines the limitations and future research directions.

2 Literature Review and Theoretical Frameworks

This review synthesises research on the impact of language proficiency on technical learning in higher education, with an emphasis on the UFS's BSc IT degree. Based on Cognitive Load Theory and Linguistic Relativity Theory, it investigates how language challenges affect student performance across several technical areas.

2.1 Theoretical Framework

This investigation of language challenges in technical education is guided by two key frameworks, namely Cognitive Load Theory (CLT) and Linguistic Relativity Theory (LRT). These frameworks help explain how language interacts with technical learning, particularly in IT higher education.

CLT theorises that learning tasks compete for limited cognitive resources, such as when a student decodes English error messages while learning to code. This can potentially overwhelm non-native speakers with additional language processing demands.

CLT, developed by Sweller [10], focuses on cognitive resource allocation during learning tasks. In IT higher education, students manage intrinsic load (understanding logic and algorithms), extraneous load (navigating syntax), and germane load (connecting concepts and problem-solving). Non-native English speakers face a higher cognitive load as a result of processing content in English. However, the formal syntax of programming languages could reduce cognitive load once foundational concepts are mastered [11].

In programming courses, the formal syntax helps non-native speakers by providing a consistent, language-independent structure. In contrast, business computing modules increase cognitive load due to the requirement of understanding both technical and business terminology in a non-native language [12].

LRT, proposed by Whorf [13], suggests that a student's native language shapes their understanding of technical concepts, for instance, by influencing how they interpret abstract programming logic differently from English-native peers. Therefore, LRT suggests that native language influences cognitive processes. This may affect students' understanding of technical concepts like programming logic and algorithms in IT higher education.

Together, CLT and LRT highlight the challenges in specific modules. For example, in math-based courses, universal symbolic notation lessens linguistic load, while courses combining technical and business concepts increase cognitive demands due to multiple linguistic and conceptual frameworks.

These theoretical perspectives are particularly relevant in South Africa's multilingual context, where eleven official languages create unique cognitive demands [14]. The absence of direct translations for technical terms in indigenous South African languages adds another layer of complexity to the cognitive load experienced by students [15, 16].

These perspectives emphasise the need to address cognitive load and linguistic influences on technical concept formation for IT education in multilingual contexts. Identifying these factors can facilitate the development of targeted teaching strategies to enhance student performance across various modules.

2.2 Language and Technical Education

Technical education involves language challenges beyond basic comprehension. It includes academic language, subject-specific terminology, and technical discourse patterns [10]. Existing research shows that English proficiency significantly impacts performance in technical subjects, with stronger English skills correlating with a better understanding of technical concepts [3]. In South African higher education, where English is the medium of instruction [1], these challenges place additional cognitive demands on non-native English speakers.

Guo's international study [17], involving 840 learners from 86 countries, found that while English is commonly used in programming, core programming concepts are more accessible, regardless of language background. However, business and contextual content presented greater challenges. Other studies, such as Foley [18], show that limited fluency in English restricts students' ability to grasp technical concepts thoroughly. Madadzhe [19] points out that this language barrier can prevent students from demonstrating their true understanding of content.

Technical education requires students to navigate several linguistic demands, including academic language, specialised terminology, and abstract concepts, often using symbolic notations. These challenges are particularly difficult for non-native English speakers, impacting their comprehension and communication of complex ideas. The interaction between language proficiency and technical learning is essential, as students must both understand and articulate content in assessments and practical applications [17].

In South African higher education, challenges are intensified by the linguistic diversity of the student population [14, 20]. While European institutions have developed strategies to maintain academic standards while supporting linguistic diversity in technical education [21], South African institutions must adapt these approaches to local conditions [6, 7]. This adaptation requires balancing international competitiveness with support for students from diverse linguistic backgrounds [8, 9].

The linguistic challenges observed in present-day computer science education reflect broader historical patterns in South African technical higher education. Post-apartheid language policies from the 1990s onward have identified the transition from mother-tongue primary education to English-medium higher education as a persistent barrier in science and mathematics learning [22]. Setati's [23] foundational work in the early 2000s documented similar patterns of differential performance across language groups in mathematics education, demonstrating how students learning in their second language faced significantly greater cognitive demands than their mother-tongue counterparts [24].

The challenges students face vary across different modules. In the BSc IT degree at UFS, students must balance core Computer Science modules with specialised content from related fields. Understanding how language challenges differ across these modules is crucial for developing targeted support strategies. The following section will delve into these module-specific challenges.

2.3 Module-Specific Language Challenges in Technical Education

Different modules in the UFS BSc IT programme present unique linguistic and cognitive challenges for non-native English speakers due to the unique demands of each programme.

Core Computer Science Foundation. All six BSc IT programmes share a foundation in Computer Science, where students may face challenges in programming modules. While programming syntax follows universal rules, understanding programming concepts requires abstract thinking in English. Guo [17] found that non-native speakers struggle with English error messages and debugging tasks despite handling syntax well.

Science-Based Programmes. In the Computer Science with Chemistry programme, students must navigate both technical computing and chemical terminology, including complex laboratory procedures and safety language [25]. In the Computer Science with Mathematical Statistics programme, while mathematical notation is largely language-independent, translating statistical concepts can be cognitively demanding [26]. The Computer Science with Mathematics programme involves abstract mathematical concepts alongside programming, with theoretical discussions increasing the cognitive load related to language processing [17]. Finally, the Computer Science with

Physics programme requires students to integrate complex physics terminology, mathematical notation, and programming concepts, which might be especially challenging during theoretical discussions and labs [27].

Business-Oriented Programme. In the Computer Science for Business and Management programme, students must master technical and business vocabulary, with additional cultural nuances that may be challenging for non-native speakers [28–30].

Data Science Programme. Combining Computer Science, Mathematics, and Statistical Terminology creates complex linguistic challenges as students integrate concepts from three distinct technical languages [4].

These module-specific challenges highlight the need for tailored support strategies to address technical demands and students' language development needs. The implementation of module-specific support strategies must consider South Africa's unique linguistic landscape [14, 20]. While international approaches offer valuable insights [21], practical support must address the specific challenges faced by students working in a language that often lacks technical vocabulary in their mother tongue [15, 16]. This understanding guides the development of pedagogical strategies that use linguistic diversity as a resource rather than just a challenge [6, 18].

3 Methodology

3.1 Research Design and Sampling

A quantitative approach was employed to examine first-year Computer Science students' linguistic challenges at the UFS. The research explored how language difficulties impact students' perceptions of module difficulty across various technical disciplines.

The study involved 226 first-year IT students from the CSI Department in 2023 and 2024. Of these, 67 students reported language difficulties, while 159 did not. The sample reflected South Africa's multilingual higher education context, with participants speaking various indigenous languages and English.

Participants were selected using purposive and convenience sampling methods. The purposive approach focused on students enrolled in the BSc IT program, while convenience sampling targeted accessible first-year students. Participation was voluntary, with no negative consequences for non-participants [31].

3.2 Data Collection and Questionnaire Design

This study investigated the effects of English medium instruction (EMI) on first-year BSc IT students at the University of the Free State, focusing on those with language difficulties. A non-experimental descriptive design used surveys to collect quantitative data via self-assessment questionnaires, ideal for capturing students' perceptions [29]. Participants completed a Computer Science Academic Experience questionnaire using a 5-point Likert scale. The questionnaire assessed perceived module difficulty (1 = Very easy to 5 = Very difficult), language challenges, and engagement patterns (1 = Strongly agree to 5 = Strongly disagree).

Though the questionnaire covered broad student experiences, this paper targets (1) language difficulties' impact on module difficulty across technical disciplines, (2) engagement patterns (e.g., classroom participation, collaboration), and (3) their link to departmental belonging. All participants gave informed consent. Adapted from prior student attrition studies [30–32], the questionnaire had two sections: Section A used Likert-scale and yes/no questions for nuanced insights, and Section B gathered demographics (e.g., gender, age, home language). This design explored language-related challenges in IT modules while retaining a broader view of student experiences.

3.3 Data Analysis

The data were prepared and checked for missing values, ensuring completeness for all respondents. All questionnaire responses were numerically coded and captured in Excel, then exported to SPSS Statistics for Windows, version 29.0. Descriptive statistics (means, standard deviations) were calculated for each measure. Independent samples t-tests were conducted to compare both module difficulty ratings and engagement patterns between students with and without language difficulties, with normality and equal variances assumed due to sample size robustness ($n = 226$ overall, $n \geq 30$ per group for key analyses). Statistical significance was set at $p < 0.05$, and Cohen's d was used to assess effect sizes. This methodical approach allowed for a comprehensive examination of how language difficulties impact both students' perceived module difficulty across different technical disciplines and their patterns of academic engagement.

3.4 Reliability and Validity

One way to ensure the reliability and validity of a questionnaire is to employ questions and concepts that have already been validated in previous studies [32, 33]. With this in mind, the questionnaire was developed by incorporating and adapting the previously validated questionnaires used in several studies. All respondents received the same questionnaire, which resulted in the data being better suited to compare responses since the same questions were answered, which increased reliability. The validity of the questionnaire was improved by mainly using closed-ended questions, thus simplifying the analysis of the responses [31]. All the participants were given the same information and tested under the same conditions as far as possible [33].

4 Results

Three key areas were examined while analysing the BSc IT students' experiences: participant demographics and linguistic backgrounds, perceived module difficulty across different subjects, and patterns of student engagement. Statistical comparisons focused on differences between students reporting language difficulties and those without, using t-tests and effect size calculations.

4.1 Participant Demographics

The demographic profile of the 226 first-year BSc IT student participants provides context for understanding the linguistic landscape of the study. Male students (67.7%, n = 153) significantly outnumbered female students (32.3%, n = 73), with a mean age of 20 years (range: 18–35). The majority (96.0%, n = 217) fell within the 18–25 age bracket.

Linguistic diversity emerged as a defining characteristic (See Table 1). Only 9.3% (n = 21) of the participants reported English as their home language despite it being the primary medium of instruction. The most prevalent home languages were Zulu (17.3%, n = 39), Southern Sotho (15.5%, n = 35), and Xhosa (13.7%, n = 31). All eleven of South Africa's official languages were represented among the participants, reflecting the linguistic diversity typical of South African higher education contexts. As noted in the methodology, 29.6% of participants reported experiencing language difficulties, while 70.4% did not. This distribution forms the basis for the comparative analyses.

Table 1. Home Language Distribution of Participants

Language	Participants	Percentage
Zulu	39	17.3%
Southern Sotho	35	15.5%
Xhosa	31	13.7%
Northern Sotho	29	12.8%
English	21	9.3%
Tswana	18	8.0%
Afrikaans	15	6.6%
Tsonga	13	5.8%
Venda	11	4.9%
Swati	7	3.1%
Ndebele	7	3.1%

4.2 Perceived Module Difficulty

The analysis of perceived module difficulty showed distinct patterns across different modules within the BSc IT curriculum. Due to varying enrollment patterns across programmes, statistical analysis focused on module types with large enough sample sizes to ensure robust interpretation. For clarity in reporting group comparisons, M_LD is used to denote the mean scores for students with language difficulties and M_NLD for students without. These notations are used consistently throughout the presentation of results. The pattern of effects shown in Fig. 1 reveals three distinct categories of language impact:

1. **Strong Positive Effects (Business modules)**: Business Calculations 1 showed the largest effect (d = 1.266, 95% CI [0.631, 1.891]), indicating substantially higher perceived difficulty for students with language difficulties.
2. **Strong Negative Effects (Mathematical/Physics modules)**: Physics (d = –0.786, 95% CI [–1.368, –0.197]) and Calculus (d = –0.448, 95% CI [–0.795, –0.100]) showed lower perceived difficulty among students with language difficulties.
3. **Negligible Effects (Programming modules)**: Core programming modules showed minimal effects (d = 0.017, 95% CI [–0.269, 0.304]), suggesting language-independent learning processes.

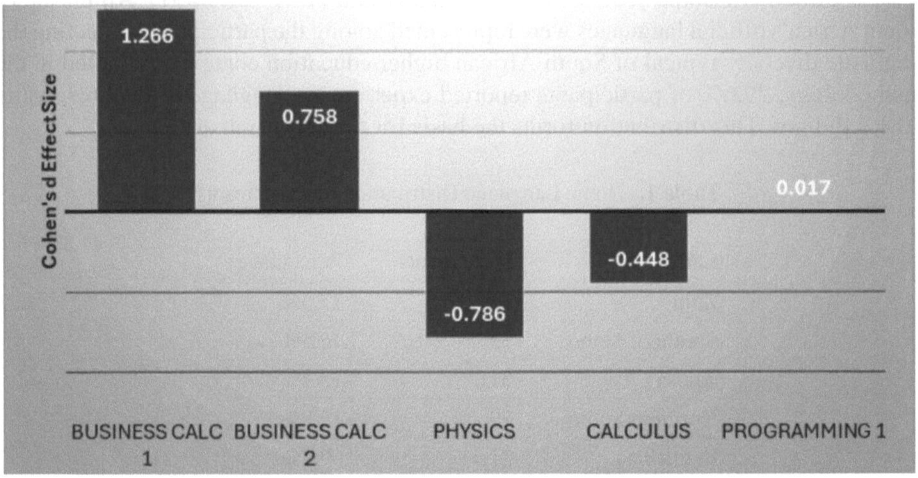

Fig. 1. Effect sizes (Cohen's d) for perceived module difficulty across modules.

The core Computer Science modules, which had the largest and most representative samples, revealed consistent patterns across both language groups. Computer Literacy modules (n = 163–187) showed minimal differences between students with and without language difficulties (Computer Literacy 1: Cohen's d = 0.249, p = .135; Computer Literacy 2: Cohen's d = 0.145, p = .362).

Programming modules with the largest sample sizes (n > 220) showed remarkably consistent perceptions between groups. Introductory Programming in C# Part 1 showed negligible differences (M_LD = 2.85, M_NLD = 2.83, t(221) = 0.119, p = .905, Cohen's d = 0.017), as did Part 2 (M_LD = 3.47, M_NLD = 3.43, t(223) = 0.277, p = .782, Cohen's d = 0.041). Additional core Computer Science modules also supported the pattern of negligible language effects, including Internet and Web page Development (M_LD = 2.70, M_NLD = 2.57, d = 0.145) and Introduction to Computer Hardware (M_LD = 3.26, M_NLD = 3.28, d = -0.021). These consistently small effect sizes across all core programming modules further strengthen the finding that fundamental computing subjects show resilience to language barriers.

Mathematics-related modules (n > 115) revealed an unexpected pattern, with significantly lower perceived difficulty among students with language difficulties. This trend was evident in both Calculus (n = 157, M_LD = 3.39, M_NLD = 3.86, p = .012, Cohen's d = −0.448) and Calculus and Algebra (n = 117, M_LD = 3.55, M_NLD = 4.13, p = .003, Cohen's d = −0.602). The Precalculus modules had insufficient enrollment numbers (n < 30 in the language difficulties group) for robust statistical analysis, particularly because fewer students in the BSc IT programme require these foundational mathematics modules.

Business-related modules demonstrated the most pronounced language-related effects. Business Calculations 1 showed the most significant effect size in the study (n = 59, M_LD = 4.00, M_NLD = 2.64, p < .001, Cohen's d = 1.266), with Business Calculations 2 showing a similar though slightly reduced effect (n = 65, M_LD = 3.88, M_NLD = 3.06, p = .011, Cohen's d = 0.758). Business Functions revealed a moderate effect size (n = 56, M_LD = 3.06, M_NLD = 2.65, p = .219, Cohen's d = 0.367), suggesting students with language difficulties found this module somewhat more challenging, though the difference did not reach statistical significance. This pattern aligns with, but is less pronounced than, the stronger effects observed in the Business Calculations modules. This potentially indicates that different business content types present varying degrees of language-related challenges.

Physics modules, while showing interesting patterns, had limited sample sizes that warrant cautious interpretation. Mechanics, Optics and Electricity (n = 54) demonstrated significantly lower perceived difficulty among students with language difficulties (M_LD = 3.33, M_NLD = 4.06, p = .009, Cohen's d = -0.786). However, other specialised physics variations had insufficient sample sizes (n = 15–34) for robust statistical analysis.

Statistical modules showed distinctive patterns from both pure mathematics and business modules. Introductory Statistics (n = 62, M_LD = 2.92, M_NLD = 2.66, p = .395, Cohen's d = 0.224) showed a small positive effect, while Introductory Probability Theory (n = 42, M_LD = 3.33, M_NLD = 3.33, p = 1.000, Cohen's d = 0.000) showed no effect at all. Neither difference reached statistical significance. This suggests that statistical content, combining mathematical notation with specialised concepts, may present different linguistic challenges than pure mathematics or business applications.

Several modules across the curriculum had sample sizes too small for meaningful statistical comparison (n < 30), including chemistry modules, business management modules, and industrial psychology modules. These sample size limitations reflect the diverse nature of the BSc IT programme streams, where students select different combinations of modules based on their chosen specialisation.

Table 2 summarises the effect sizes and statistical significance across all modules with sufficient sample sizes for analysis. These findings indicate that the relationship between language difficulties and perceived module difficulty varies substantially across subject areas.

Table 2. Effect Sizes and Statistical Significance for Perceived Module Difficulty by Language Group

Module Category	Module Name	n	Cohen's d	p-value	Interpretation
Core Computer Science	Computer Literacy 1	187	0.249	0.135	Small effect, non-significant

(*continued*)

Table 2. (*continued*)

Module Category	Module Name	n	Cohen's d	p-value	Interpretation
	Computer Literacy 2	163	0.145	0.362	Small effect, non-significant
	Intro Programming C# Part 1	223	0.017	0.905	Negligible effect
	Intro Programming C# Part 2	225	0.041	0.782	Negligible effect
	Web Development	221	0.145	0.321	Small effect, non-significant
	Computer Hardware	219	–0.021	0.887	Negligible effect
Mathematics	Calculus	157	–0.448	0.012	Medium effect, significant
	Calculus and Algebra	117	–0.602	0.003	Medium effect, significant
Physics	Physics (Mechanics, Optics, Electricity)	54	–0.786	0.009	Large effect, significant
Business	Business Calculations 1	59	1.266	<0.001	Large effect, significant
	Business Calculations 2	65	0.758	0.011	Large effect, significant
	Business Functions	56	0.367	0.219	Medium effect, non-significant
Statistics	Introductory Statistics	62	0.224	0.395	Small effect, non-significant
	Probability Theory	42	0.000	1.000	No effect

4.3 Student Engagement and Belonging

The analysis of student engagement patterns revealed differences between students with and without language difficulties across several academic dimensions. Participants responded to statements about their academic behaviours and social integration on a 5-point Likert scale (1 = Strongly agree, 5 = Strongly disagree).

Classroom Participation. Students with language difficulties reported higher participation in class discussions (responding to 'I ask questions in class or contribute to class discussion') (M_LD = 2.82, SD = 1.180) than those without (M_NLD = 3.09, SD = 1.240). Although this difference was not statistically significant ($t(224) = -1.501$, $p = .135$), the effect size (Cohen's d = 0.219) suggests a small, potentially meaningful impact on classroom dynamics. This finding challenges the assumption that language barriers hinder verbal engagement in technical courses.

Academic Behaviours. In terms of class attendance (responding to 'I skip classes'), students without language difficulties reported slightly better attendance (M_NLD = 3.23, SD = 1.317) than those with language difficulties (M_LD = 3.07, SD = 1.197), though this difference was not significant ($t(224) = -0.813$, $p = .417$). For preparation (responding to 'I come to class without completing readings'), students with language difficulties reported slightly better preparation (M_LD = 2.81, SD = 0.988) compared to those without (M_NLD = 2.77, SD = 1.202; $t(224) = 0.232$, $p = .817$). On punctuality (responding to "I have been late several times"), both groups reported similar behaviours, with students with language difficulties slightly more punctual (M_LD = 3.25, SD = 1.283) than those without (M_NLD = 3.21, SD = 1.378; $t(224) = 0.235$, $p = .815$).

Social Engagement and Belonging. In collaborative behaviours (responding to "I work with classmates outside of class"), students with language difficulties reported slightly lower formal collaboration (M_LD = 3.15, SD = 1.258) compared to those without (M_NLD = 3.12, SD = 1.380; $t(224) = 0.152$, $p = .879$). For informal peer learning (responding to "I study with other students"), students with language difficulties reported more peer study engagement (M_LD = 3.07, SD = 1.329) compared to their peers (M_NLD = 3.38, SD = 1.348; $t(223) = -1.559$, $p = .120$). Finally, in terms of belonging (responding to "I feel like I belong to the Computer Science Department"), students with language difficulties reported a lower sense of belonging (M_LD = 2.60, SD = 1.303) compared to those without difficulties (M_NLD = 2.40, SD = 1.296). However, this difference was not statistically significant ($t(223) = 1.047$, $p = .296$, Cohen's d = -0.153).

These findings highlight that while students with language difficulties show higher classroom participation and similar academic behaviours, they demonstrate mixed patterns in collaborative learning, with higher informal peer study but lower formal collaboration. They also report a somewhat lower sense of belonging within the academic community.

5 Discussion

This study highlights a challenging linguistic environment at the UFS. While 24% of South African university students speak English as their first language [2], only 9.3% of BSc IT students in this study are native English speakers. This suggests that our findings regarding language barriers are especially relevant in contexts with lower English proficiency in Computer Science education. Despite over 90% of students studying in a non-native language, our results indicate that certain aspects of Computer Science education appear to transcend language barriers.

5.1 Theoretical Interpretation Across Programme Structures

The differing patterns of perceived difficulty across different module types reveal important insights about the relationship between language barriers and technical education.

Core Computer Science Modules. This study found that core programming modules were highly resilient to language barriers, with minimal perceived difficulty differences between students with and without language challenges. Programming languages' structured, rule-based syntax reduces cognitive load once the basic concepts are mastered, making them largely independent of natural language. The consistent patterns (Cohen's d between 0.017 and 0.145) suggest that computer science education accommodates linguistic diversity through its universal syntax. This aligns with Guo's [17] findings and extends them to the South African multilingual context. This finding is particularly significant for computer science educators in linguistically diverse settings, as it suggests that programming education may offer a more accessible pathway to technical careers for non-native English speakers in South Africa and abroad.

Computer Science with Mathematics Programme. Students with language difficulties found mathematics modules easier, which supports both CLT and LRT theories. Mathematics uses universal symbols that work independently of any specific language. This gives students with language challenges access to learning systems that reduce the cognitive load needed for language processing. As Guo [17] observed, mathematical notation creates alternative routes to understanding that avoid language barriers entirely.

Computer Science with Mathematical Statistics Programme. Statistical modules showed only small differences between student groups, which supports CLT's ideas about how the brain manages cognitive resources. Statistics combines visual elements like graphs and charts with mathematical symbols, creating several different ways for students to understand concepts. This variety helps balance the mental workload even when students face language challenges. When statistical concepts are taught alongside programming, students gain even more ways to access the same content, which may help overcome language-related difficulties.

Computer Science with Physics Programme. Students with language challenges found physics modules easier, which supports both theoretical frameworks. Physics uses mathematical symbols, visual aids like diagrams, and hands-on experiments to teach concepts. These different approaches give students multiple ways to understand the material without relying heavily on language skills. This approach aligns with CLT's principle of using various representation methods to spread the mental workload across different cognitive systems.

Computer Science with Chemistry Programme. Chemistry modules had too few students to allow for reliable statistical analysis. However, the theoretical frameworks suggest that chemistry's lab-based learning could provide cognitive support similar to the visual aids used in physics. When students combine hands-on lab work with programming concepts, they may gain multiple ways to understand the content. This possibility needs further research with larger groups of students to confirm.

Computer Science for Business and Management Programme. Students with language difficulties found business modules harder, which supports CLT's prediction about cognitive overload. These students must simultaneously process technical content and specialised business language, which may overwhelm them. Business Calculations showed the strongest negative effects, while Business Functions had a more moderate impact. This suggests that different types of business content create varying levels of language challenge. These findings align with Guo's research [17], which showed that business-context programming was particularly difficult for non-native English speakers. This highlights a global challenge when combining business and technical content in education.

Data Science Programme. Students in this programme, which combines mathematics, statistics, and programming, appear to have developed effective strategies to manage cognitive load across multiple technical domains, as evidenced by their performance across core modules.

5.2 Student Engagement Patterns

The engagement results challenge common beliefs about how language barriers affect students in higher education. Students with language difficulties demonstrated higher classroom participation than their peers without such difficulties, likely representing a compensatory strategy to overcome comprehension gaps. This active approach matches Guo's [17] findings that non-native English speakers develop adaptive learning methods when dealing with technical content.

The academic behaviour data shows a complex picture. Students without language difficulties had slightly better class attendance, while those with language difficulties showed slightly better class preparation and similar punctuality. These mixed patterns suggest that students use different approaches to manage their academic responsibilities when studying in a non-native language.

The difference between formal and informal engagement is especially interesting. While structured group activities showed minimal differences between student groups, those with language difficulties reported more informal peer study sessions despite feeling less connected to their department overall. This creates an "active learning with weaker belonging" pattern. These students actively seek peer learning opportunities to overcome language challenges while feeling less integrated into the broader departmental community.

The preference for informal peer study over formal collaboration among students with language difficulties likely stems from the comfort and support offered in self-selected, linguistically familiar groups, contrasted with the challenges of structured, mixed-language group work [17].

This engagement profile helps contextualise the module-specific findings. The combination of higher verbal participation and informal peer study with lower reported difficulty in mathematics and programming modules suggests that students with language difficulties employ multiple active strategies to navigate technical content successfully. By asking questions in class and studying with peers, they may clarify concepts through formal and informal discussion rather than relying solely on written materials.

5.3 Implications for Educational Practice

The finding that core computer science modules naturally work well for students with different language backgrounds has important implications for computer science education in multilingual settings. Programming education may provide both a pathway to technical careers and a model for making education more language-inclusive. Computer science departments could build on this natural advantage by:

- Highlighting how programming syntax works the same way across all languages in introductory courses
- Using programming examples to scaffold learning in more language-dependent content areas
- Developing teaching approaches that transfer the language-independent aspects of programming to other subject areas

For the Business and Management programme, where language challenges are most pronounced, support should focus on integrating business terminology with technical concepts. Practical interventions might include discipline-specific vocabulary development and explicit connections between business contexts and programming applications.

Educators should build on the natural advantages of universal symbols and visual elements in programs that combine Computer Science with Mathematics or Physics. Teaching methods that use multiple ways to represent concepts, such as symbols, diagrams, and hands-on applications, may help students overcome language barriers.

Several South African universities have implemented initiatives that could inform these approaches. Madadzhe's [19] multilingual glossaries could be particularly valuable in the Business and Management programme, while Mathematics and Physics programmes might benefit from greater emphasis on visual and symbolic learning materials.

To address engagement challenges, departments could build on the informal peer study that students with language difficulties already use naturally. This could help strengthen their sense of belonging in the department. Creating structured learning groups based on these existing peer study habits might help students apply their active learning strategies to other areas while feeling more connected to their department. Additionally, department-wide efforts to create more inclusive community environments could help all students feel they belong.

5.4 Integration with International Perspectives

These program-specific findings contribute to international research by showing how language barriers change depending on the combined technical subjects. This suggests that support strategies should be designed specifically for each program's structure rather than using a one-size-fits-all approach. While programming education shows strength against language barriers, as Guo [17] noted, our study goes further by identifying which subject combinations help reduce language challenges and which make them worse. Computer science educators worldwide can benefit from knowing that core programming courses create equal opportunities for students from different language backgrounds, while combined programs may need more focused support. These insights could inform technical education in multilingual contexts, especially in post-colonial settings where instruction is often in non-native languages.

6 Conclusion

This study reveals an important finding for computer science education in South Africa's multilingual higher education system: core computer science modules, especially programming courses, naturally overcome language barriers. In a context where only 9.3% of BSc IT students at the UFS are native English speakers, the discovery that programming modules show negligible differences in perceived difficulty between students with and without language difficulties (Cohen's d ranging from 0.017 to 0.041) suggests that computer science education offers a uniquely equitable learning environment in South Africa's complex linguistic landscape.

Core computer science education appears to overcome language barriers for several reasons. Programming languages use the same syntax worldwide, provide visual and hands-on feedback when code runs, and involve problem-solving that allows different valid approaches. This finding contrasts sharply with business-technical modules, which showed significant language-related challenges (Cohen's $d = 1.266$), while mathematics modules demonstrated unexpected advantages for students with language difficulties (Cohen's $d = -0.448$).

Students with language difficulties demonstrated higher verbal participation rates and comparable academic behaviours despite studying in a non-native language. However, they reported slightly lower feelings of departmental belonging, suggesting that while computer science content may naturally accommodate linguistic diversity, social integration remains an area for targeted support. The results indicate that while language barriers remain a significant challenge in South African higher education, computer science education might offer a unique solution that emerged naturally from the discipline's inherent characteristics.

7 Limitations and Future Research

Several limitations should be considered when interpreting these findings. Sample sizes varied across modules, with core Computer Science modules having larger cohorts ($n > 220$) and some specialised modules having smaller representations ($n < 30$). The cross-sectional design captures student experiences at a specific point rather than tracking how language-related challenges evolve over time. Additionally, while perceived module difficulty patterns were identified, academic performance measures were not included.

Future research should:

- Investigate exactly how programming education becomes more accessible despite language barriers;
- Conduct longitudinal studies to understand how this advantage develops throughout degree programs;
- Include direct academic performance data alongside perception measures;

- Include high school English performance data and university English proficiency scores in addition to self-reported language difficulties;
- Examine whether similar benefits exist in other technical disciplines; and
- Explore how computer science education's natural advantage might support multilingual education more broadly.

Despite these limitations, the study's central finding offers hope for equitable technical education in multilingual contexts. Computer science education serves as a pathway to technical careers and a model for language-inclusive education in South Africa's diverse higher education landscape.

Disclosure of Interests. The author has no competing interests to declare relevant to this article's content.

Statement on Ethics. Ethical clearance for this study was granted by the General/Human Research Ethics Committee of the UFS (Ethical clearance number: UFS-HSD2024/0178). Informed consent was secured from all participants, ensuring they understood the research objectives and their right to withdraw at any time.

References

1. Department of Higher Education and Training: The Language Policy Framework for Public Higher Education Institutions. Pretoria (2020)
2. Department of Higher Education and Training: South African Survey of Student Engagement Report. Pretoria (2021)
3. Childs, P.E., O'Farrell, F.J.: Learning science through English: an investigation of the vocabulary skills of native and non-native English speakers in international schools. Chem. Educ. Res. Pract. **4**, 233–247 (2003)
4. UFS Department of Computer Science and Informatics: Undergraduate Programmes Yearbook 2025 (2025)
5. Van Rooy, B., Coetzee-Van Rooy, S.: The language issue and academic performance at a South African university. South. Afr. Linguist. Appl. Lang. Stud. **33**, 31–46 (2015). https://doi.org/10.2989/16073614.2015.1012691
6. Coetzee-Van Rooy, S.: Complex systems, multilingualism and academic success in South African higher education. South. Afr. Linguist. Appl. Lang. Stud. **28**, 309–321 (2010). https://doi.org/10.2989/16073614.2010.548021
7. Coetzee-Van Rooy, S., Botha, W.: English-medium instruction in higher education in South Africa. In: Bolton, K., Botha, W., Lin, B. (eds.) The Routledge Handbook of English-Medium Instruction in Higher Education, pp. 311–323. Routledge, London (2024). https://doi.org/10.4324/9781003011644
8. Ngidi, S.A., Mncwango, E.M.: University students' perspectives on an English-only language policy in higher education. J. Transdiscipl. Res. South. Afr. **18** (2022). https://doi.org/10.4102/td.v18i1.1189
9. Webb, V.: English as a second language in South Africa's tertiary institutions: a case study at the University of Pretoria. World Engl. **21**, 49–61 (2002). https://doi.org/10.1111/1467-971X.00231
10. Sweller, J.: Cognitive load during problem-solving: effects on learning. Cogn. Sci. **12**, 257–285 (1988). https://doi.org/10.1207/s15516709cog1202_4

11. Sweller, J.: Cognitive load theory and educational technology. Educ. Technol. Res. Dev. **68**, 1–16 (2020). https://doi.org/10.1007/s11423-019-09701-3
12. Jewels, T., Albon, R.: "We don't teach English, we teach in English": teaching non-native English speaking university students. Learn. Teach. High. Educ. Gulf Perspect. **9**, 3–31 (2012)
13. Whorf, B.L.: Language, Thought, and Reality: Selected Writings of Benjamin Lee Whorf. MIT Press, Cambridge (2012)
14. Department of Higher Education and Training: Language Policy for Higher Education (2020)
15. Emsley, M.R., Modiba, M.A.: Multilingualism in South African universities is a fallacy: a critical realist perspective. Afr. Perspect. Res. Teach. Learn. **8**, 150–167 (2024). https://doi.org/10.70875/v8i3article12
16. Khumalo, L.: Intellectualization through terminology development. Lexikos **27**, 252–264 (2017)
17. Guo, P.J.: Non-native English speakers learning computer programming: barriers, desires, and design opportunities. In: Proceedings of the Conference on Human Factors in Computing Systems. ACM (2018). https://doi.org/10.1145/3173574.3173970
18. Foley, A.: Language policy in higher education in South Africa: implications and complications. South Afr. J. High. Educ. **18**, 57–71 (2004)
19. Madadzhe, R.N.: Using African languages at universities in South Africa: the struggle continues. Stellenbosch Pap. Linguist. Plus **58**, 205–218 (2019). https://doi.org/10.5842/58-0-843
20. UFS: Language Policy of the University of the Free State (2023)
21. Wilkinson, R., Gabriëls, R. (eds.): The Englishization of Higher Education in Europe. Amsterdam University Press, Amsterdam (2021)
22. Heugh, K.: Multilingual education policy in South Africa constrained by theoretical and historical disconnections. Annu. Rev. Appl. Linguist. **33**, 215–237 (2013). https://doi.org/10.1017/S0267190513000135
23. Setati, M.: Access to mathematics versus access to the language of power: the struggle in multilingual mathematics classrooms. S. Afr. J. Educ. **28**, 103–116 (2008)
24. Setati, M.: Teaching mathematics in a primary multilingual classroom. J. Res. Math. Educ. **36**, 447–466 (2005)
25. Rees, S., Kind, V., Newton, D.: Meeting the challenge of chemical language barriers in university-level chemistry education. Isr. J. Chem. **59**, 470–477 (2019). https://doi.org/10.1002/ijch.201800079
26. Dunn, P.K., Carey, M.D., Richardson, A.M., McDonald, C.: Learning the language of statistics: challenges and teaching approaches. Stat. Educ. Res. J. **15**, 8–27 (2016). https://doi.org/10.52041/serj.v15i1.255
27. Taibu, R., Ferrari-Bridgers, F.: Physics language anxiety among students in introductory physics course. Eurasia J. Math. Sci. Technol. Educ. **16** (2020). https://doi.org/10.29333/ejmste/111993
28. Aina, J.K., Ogundele, A.G., Olanipekun, S.S.: Students' proficiency in English language relationship with academic performance in science and technical education. Am. J. Educ. Res. **1**, 355–358 (2013). https://doi.org/10.12691/education-1-9-2
29. Ouanhlee, T.: Effect on non-native English speakers of utilising English for business. Int. Bus. Res. **16**, 16–35 (2023). https://doi.org/10.5539/ibr.v16n9p16
30. Vishwakarma, V.K.: Translating cultural nuances: challenges and strategies. ELT Voices **13**, 80–90 (2023)
31. Trochim, W.M., Donnelly, J.P., Arora, K.: Research Methods: The Essential Knowledge Base. Cengage, Boston (2016)

32. Stausberg, M.: Surveys and questionnaires. In: Stausberg, M., Engler, S. (eds.), The Routledge Handbook of Research Methods in the Study of Religion, pp. 461–482. Routledge, New York (2022)
33. Silverman, R.M., Patterson, K.L.: Qualitative Research Methods for Community Development. Routledge, New York (2021). https://doi.org/10.4324/9781003172925

A Framework for Integrated Project and Context-Based ICT Education

Jacqui Muller[1] and Japie Greeff[1,2,3](✉)

[1] Belgium Campus iTversity, Pretoria, South Africa
{muller.j,greeff.j}@belgiumcampus.ac.za
[2] Optentia Research Unit, North-West University, Vanderbijlpark, South Africa
[3] National Institute for Theoretical and Computational Sciences (NITheCS), Vanderbijlpark, South Africa
https://www.belgiumcampus.ac.za/ ,
https://optentia.co.za/,https://nithecs.ac.za/

Abstract. The evolving landscape of Information and Communication Technology (ICT) education necessitates innovative teaching methodologies that bridge the gap between academic theory and industry practice. This study proposes the Integrated Project & Context-Based Learning (IPCBL) framework, which integrates project-based learning (PBL), context-based learning (CBL), and Integrated Learning (IL) interdisciplinary approaches to enhance student engagement, competency development, and real-world application of skills. Using Design Science Research (DSR) methodology, the study iteratively develops and evaluates the IPCBL framework to ensure its effectiveness in fostering deep learning and problem-solving skills.

The framework is tested within an ICT module focusing on the Internet of Things (IoT), where students engage in capstone projects that progressively build technical and analytical skills while aligning with industry requirements. Through an industry-aligned curriculum incorporating external certifications, the IPCBL framework successfully enhances student motivation, critical thinking, and professional readiness. The study further explores technical considerations, assessment methodologies, and scalability of the framework within higher education.

Results indicate that IPCBL fosters a structured learning approach that aligns academic outcomes with workforce expectations. Future research will focus on refining the framework, incorporating structured curriculum rubrics, and optimizing external training integration. Ultimately, the IPCBL framework contributes to ICT education by promoting an integrated, skill-based, and industry-relevant learning experience.

Keywords: Computer Science Education · Teaching and Learning · Assessment · Integrated Project & Context-Based Learning

1 Introduction

The rapid evolution of Information and Communication Technology (ICT) education has created a pressing need for innovative teaching and learning method-

L. Nel et al. (Eds.): SACLA 2025, CCIS 2770, pp. 69–83, 2026.
https://doi.org/10.1007/978-3-032-12457-9_5

ologies that better equip students with practical, industry-relevant skills [12]. Traditional assessment methods often lack the integration of real-world applications, leading to a disconnect between academic theory and industry practice [10]. The challenge lies in designing a framework that not only enhances student engagement but also promotes competency-based learning through project-driven and context-aware education, as expressed by Pratisto and Danoetirta [21] and Molina-García et al. [18].

This study addresses this challenge by proposing an Integrated Project & Context-Based Learning (IPCBL) framework, which merges project-based learning (PBL), context-based learning (CBL), and integrated learning (IL) methodologies into a cohesive approach. The primary research objective is to develop and evaluate a framework that fosters deep learning, problem-solving, and skill acquisition within an ICT education context. The study aims to propose a framework that can be used to bridge the gap between the undergraduate ICT studies and the ICT industry.

The decision to adopt PBL, CBL, and IL approaches in this initial framework was intentional, serving as a foundational step in exploring pedagogies that bridge academic theory and industry application. These three were selected due to their proven alignment with real-world ICT practices and their complementary strengths in promoting critical thinking, practical skill development, and interdisciplinary learning. However, this selection is not exhaustive; it provides a starting point for iterative research. Future iterations of the study will explore additional approaches such as game-based learning to further enhance and adapt the framework for diverse learning contexts and technological advancements.

2 Research Method

Design Science Research (DSR) can be used as a research methodology that promotes the creation of innovative and practical solutions to real-world problems. According to Gregor and Hevner [7], DSR involves the systematic development and evaluation of artefacts (including frameworks, systems, theories or applications) that are designed to address specific problems. Gregor et al. [6] suggest that DSR enables design, implementation, and evaluation of new information systems and technologies. Vaishnavi [24] notes that DSR is an iterative process that involves the application of design principles and techniques to create new knowledge and solutions.

Vaishnavi [24] notes that the use of iterative DSR cycles allow researchers to refine and improve solutions through the process of continuous evaluation, testing, feedback and refinement. Cennamo and Kalk [5] and Zydney et al. [28] similarly argue that iterative cycles are an essential aspect of DSR, as they enable researchers to develop and refine their solutions based on feedback from end-users and stakeholders.

Figure 1 illustrates how the existing knowledge contribution of other researchers will be used as the foundation for gaining awareness of the problem before iteratively developing a framework (through various steps) that contribute back to the knowledge base in various ways.

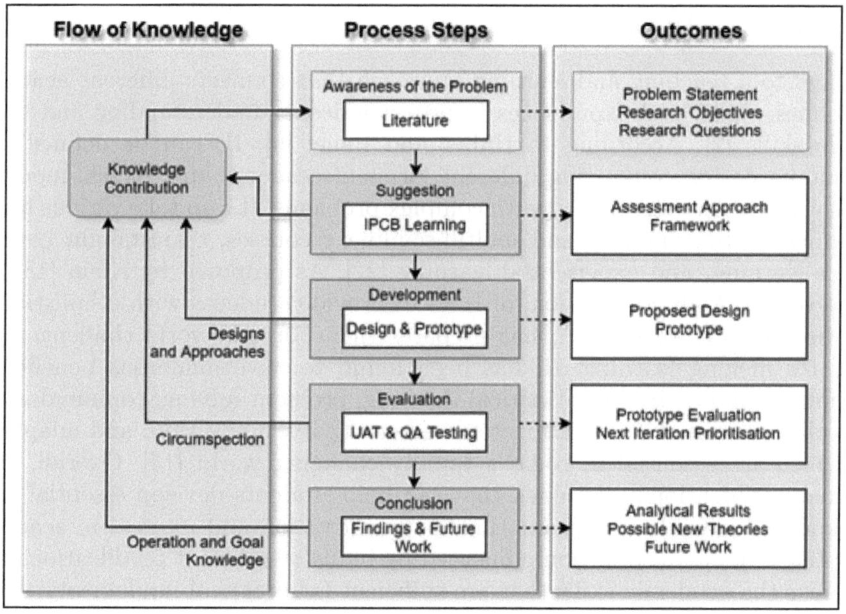

Fig. 1. Research Method

By incorporating multiple evaluation and/or feedback loops and cycles of testing and refinement, DSR researchers can improve the quality as well as effectiveness of their artifacts to ensure that they are well-suited to the function and non-functional requirements. This iterative approach allows for the creation of *practical and innovative solutions that are well-grounded in the realities of the problem domain.* In this study, the framework was developed iteratively, leveraging insights from existing research while refining the implementation through multiple evaluation loops. The problem being addressed is the need for an effective and scalable approach to integrating PBL and CBL within ICT education.

3 Combining Learning Approaches

The field of ICT education has undergone significant changes in recent years, driven by the need to prepare students for the rapidly evolving digital world [25]. Wang [26] positions the integration of different concepts with learning which motivates the choice of combining of PBL, CBL, and IL approaches. The aim is to engage students in real-world projects that are situated within relevant contexts and require the integration of different disciplines and skills. By combining learning approaches, ICT educators aim to provide students with a comprehensive and immersive learning experience that prepares them for the demands of the digital workforce [23].

3.1 Integrated Learning

IL refers to a teaching and learning approach that connects different academic disciplines, skills, and experiences to promote deeper understanding and transferable skills [2]. According to Huber and Panel [9], IL can be defined as a curriculum design connecting different forms of academic disciplines, modes of inquiry and knowledge to deal with complex problems. IL can take various forms, including interdisciplinary and multidisciplinary courses, team-taught courses, service learning, and experiential learning [22]. As proposed by Klein [13] and supported by Alali [1], the goal of IL is to provide students with a holistic and interdisciplinary perspective that prepares them for real-world challenges and promotes lifelong learning. IL has been found to have numerous benefits for students, including improved critical thinking, problem-solving, communication, and collaboration skills. It also promotes creativity, innovation, and adaptability, which are essential in today's rapidly changing world [14]. Overall, IL is a valuable educational approach that can help students develop essential skills and knowledge while also promoting their motivation and interest in academic disciplines. IL can also be complimented by industry-relevant certifications that recognise the academic skills that are sufficient for practical implementation.

3.2 Project-Based Learning

PBL is an educational approach that introduces students to real-world projects that enable their development of essential knowledge and skills [8]. As put forward by Widiyati and Pangesti [27] - in PBL, students work collaboratively to investigate and respond to complex questions, problems, or challenges, using critical thinking, problem-solving, and decision-making skills. They typically engage in a process of inquiry, design, and reflection, with the goal of developing deep understanding and transferable skills [3].

According to Guo et al. [8] and supported by Boss and Krauss [4], PBL has been found to have numerous benefits for students which included improved motivation, engagement and achievement. It also promotes the development of essential skills (like communication, collaboration, creativity and innovation) which are highly valued in professional workspaces, as seen in the Slovakian study [17]. PBL is a valuable educational approach that helps students develop the essential skills and knowledge needed to be productive participants of the workforce, while promoting motivation and interest in academic disciplines [10].

3.3 Context-Based Learning

CBL is referred to as an educational approach that incorporates real-world problems and challenges, allowing students to learn through practical application and inquiry-based learning [11]. This approach allows students to work collaboratively to develop and implement solutions addressing issues within specific communities or societies, applying academic knowledge to real-world contexts to enhance the students skillset [20]. According to Krajcik et al. [15], CBL is an effective way to engage students while creating learning environments that are industry-relevant. This approach allows students to see the practical applications of technology and the effect it has on day-to-day activities. CBL encourages students to develop the relevant problem-solving skills (like critical thinking and communication skills). Additionally, CBL also increases student motivation and interest in their domains, as well as improve their professional literacy [16].

3.4 Integrated Project and Context-Based Learning

The goal of IPCBL is to combine the individual approaches of CBL, PBL and IL with the aim of realising the benefits of each separate approach when they are all brought together.

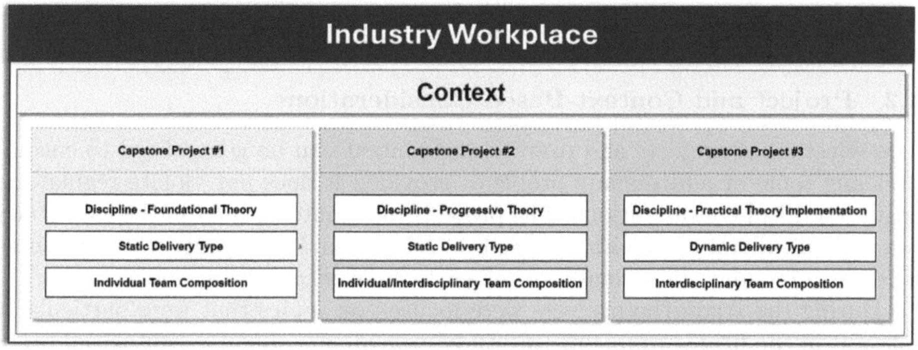

Fig. 2. Integrated Project & Context-Based Learning

As illustrated in Fig. 2, all projects within a specific module are given within a specific context or problem. Each project, referred to as a capstone project, is subject to its own nature and discipline that students need to acquire to complete the project. In each project students need to develop the fundamental subject matter expertise. In retrospect, the composition of each project will contribute to the IL aspect of the module as the composition of each project should replicate a real-world scenario, ideally resulting in differing compositions for each project.

4 Technical Considerations

4.1 Technology Considerations

In [19] it was suggested that the benefits of automated marking were dependent on the architecture and technology stack, but this has been revised to reflect a technology-agnostic perspective. IPCBL can be achieved through initiatives spanning across various technological solutions, with different automation tools, data visualisation platforms, and cloud-based services offering viable alternatives, in ICT based projects. For automation, UiPath or Automation Anywhere could be used instead of Power Automate. Similarly, while Power BI was selected for data visualisation, equivalent functionality could be achieved using Qlik or Tableau. For cloud-based services, Microsoft Azure was used, but other platforms such as AWS Lambda or Google Cloud Functions could provide similar functionality. The selection of the specific technology stack in the use cases used as part pf this study were based on several factors. The balance between module outcomes and skills requirements from industry partners had to be mitigated through the projects. Integration with the existing university infrastructure, which includes a Microsoft-based LMS and Active Directory authentication, played a significant role in technical considerations as well. Ease of deployment and maintenance was also prioritised, alongside cost considerations relevant to the university setting. Additionally, personal expertise in the selected technologies enabled efficient development and implementation. These choices do not imply exclusivity but rather illustrate one possible approach to achieving an effective automated marking assistant.

4.2 Project and Context-Based Considerations

The selection of projects and overarching context can be generalized to encompass any topic or address any problem, provided it does not violate regulatory, legal, or ethical considerations. The projects and contexts used in the case study were specifically aligned with the needs of relevant industry partners at the time. These can be adapted annually to reflect technological advancements.

During the study the projects were focused on topics that were particularly relevant in the field throughout the study, providing a valuable contextual problem statement that could be broken down into smaller projects, each incorporating various concepts and technologies. The proposed approach was tested across three iterations, each representing a distinct use case with a different contextual premise, yet consistently producing the same deductions from the results.

Each project had its own context and business context briefing associated. At a high-level, the summary of the three iterations rendered interesting results, illustrated in Fig. 3. All three iterations had specific contexts associated with the project, while following the same semester structure. The third iteration included a smaller set of students. The study has seen over 600 students accumulate over 7300 badges and certifications.

4.3 Validation Considerations

As part of the initiative to integrate student skills development with industry requirements, it is essential to ensure that the skills being developed align with both academic and industry expectations. From an academic perspective, the goal is to meet the outcomes of each module in a degree, but can be passed by achieving all of the sub-minimums and a passing grade. From an industry perspective, the skills acquired are assessed against industry certification standards. To evaluate the success of this initiative, students should be able to translate their academic knowledge into an industry-recognised certification. As

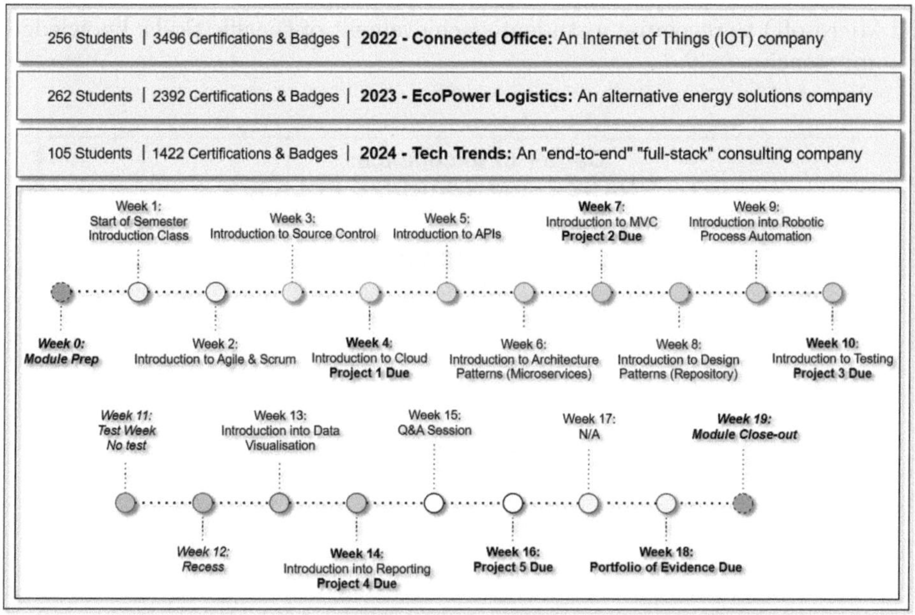

Fig. 3. Iteration Results

part of the use case, the concept of industry training and certification was also incorporated.

5 Connected Office Use Case: Analysis of Results

As part of an experiment trialled for six months within an ICT development module, specifically focused on assisting students with the adaptation of new technologies and polishing their integration skills, students were given a high-level technical architecture with an overarching context for all content delivered throughout the semester. The overarching theme was "Connected Office" relating to the concept of the Internet of Things (IoT). All concepts were introduced to students within the Connected Office context, even from a theoretical perspective. Figure 4 illustrates the high-level technical architecture presented to students to explain the layers of the architecture that they would be working with throughout the semester, in different capstone projects, all tying back into the main IoT theme.

A continuous learning approach was used in the module to assess students, with a portfolio of evidence (POE) submitted by the students at the end of the semester to show the work they had managed to complete throughout the semester, along with community contribution and external training (badges and certifications). This was done through the incorporation of external badges and certifications provided by industry reputable providers (like UiPath, LinkedIn and Microsoft) to recognise a student's achievement of specific skills, knowledge, or competencies.

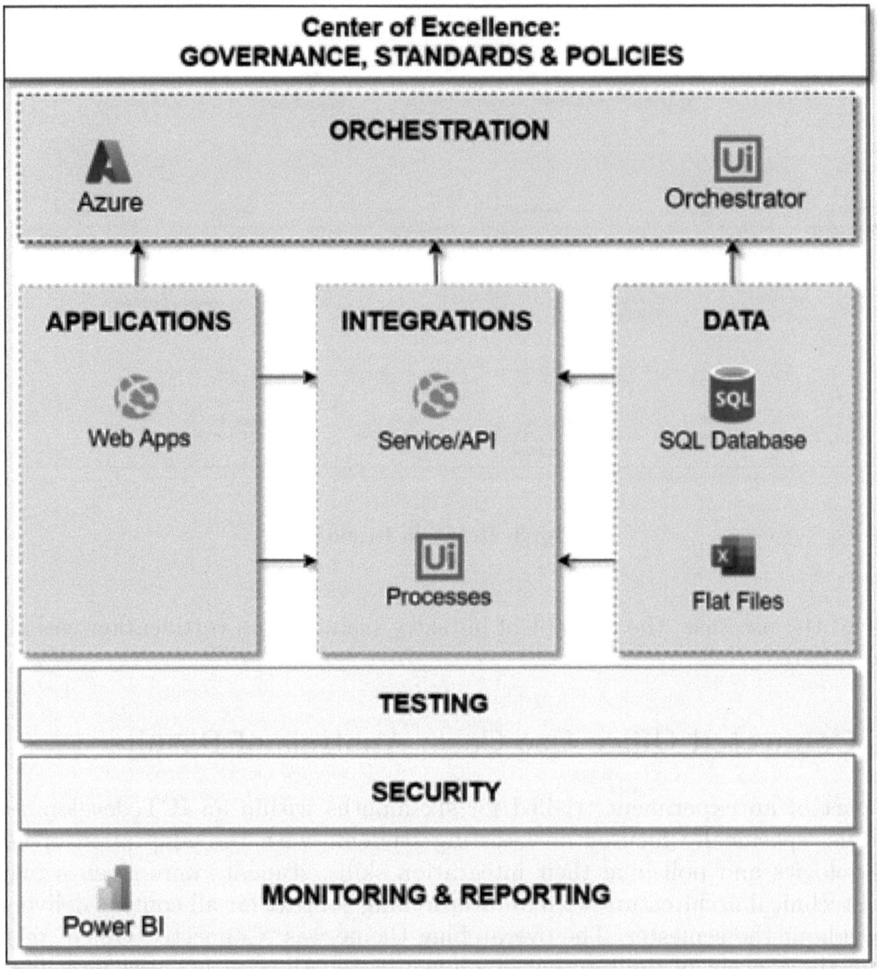

Fig. 4. Module Context

As illustrated by Fig. 5, each project was issued as a capstone project with all white blocks outlined in black demonstrating where new components had to be created as part of the designated project. All grey blocks refer to pre-developed components (from previous projects) that had to be reused to complete the objectives, changing the composition of each project while remaining separate capstone projects, all relating to the overarching IoT theme within the module context.

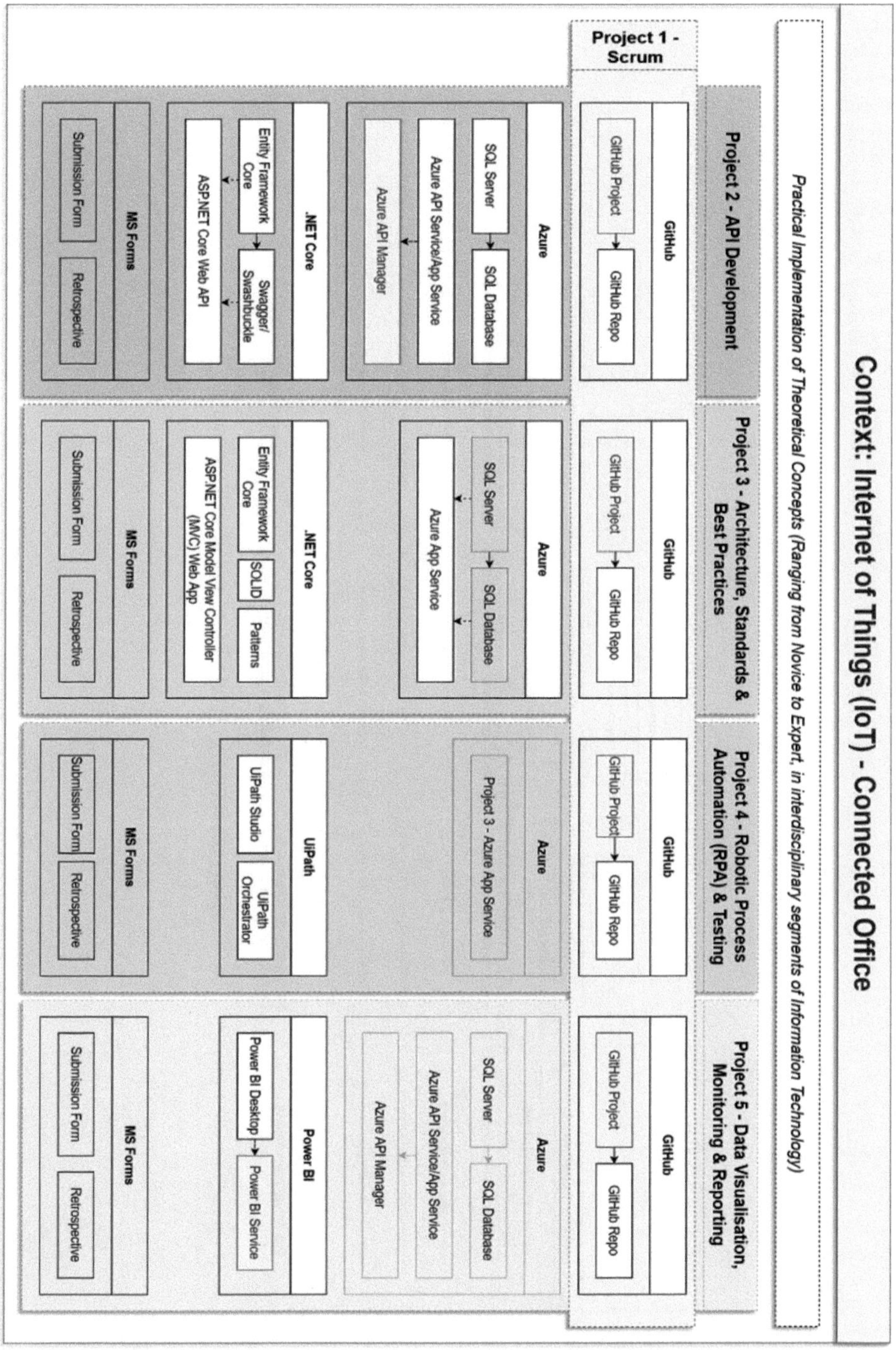

Fig. 5. Implemented Integrated Project Context-Based Learning

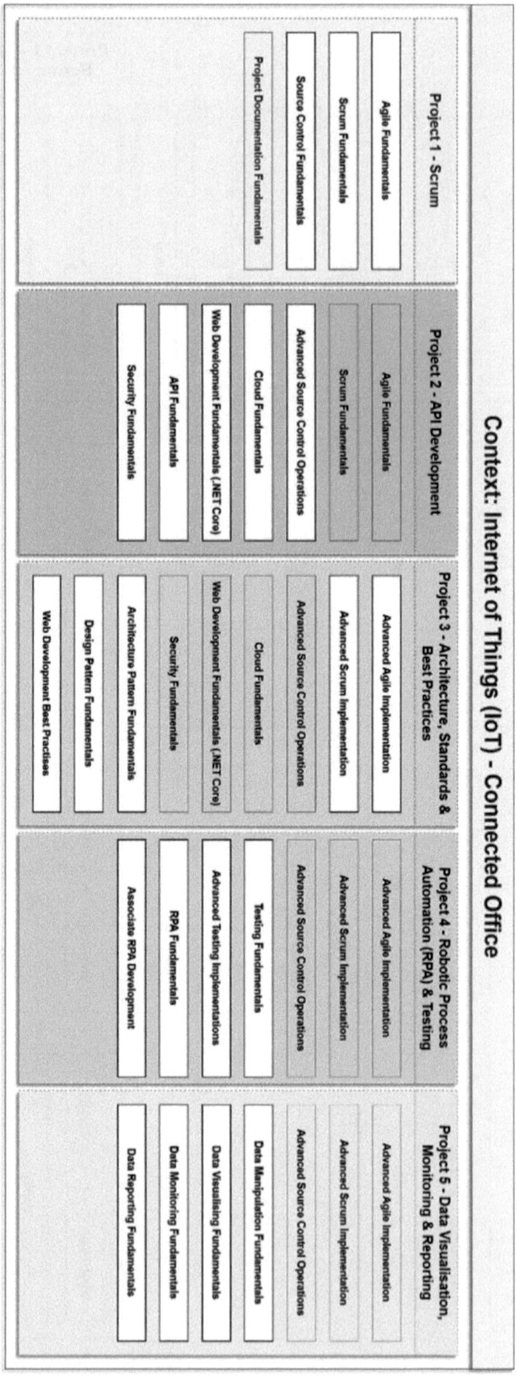

Fig. 6. Implemented Integrated Project Context-Based Learning with Certification Paths

The context provided by Fig. 5, enabled the introduction of external training and certification by well-respected issuers, like Microsoft and UiPath, related to the content and context of the module. Figure 6 demonstrates how each project encapsulated recommended external training, resulting in external certifications, relating to the context of each capstone project as well as the context of the module as a whole. The white blocks, outlined with black borders depicts new categories of skills that need to be acquired whereas the transparent blocks assume the skills mastered through the completion of previous projects, adding to the integrated disciplinary nature of all of the capstone projects. The white blocks illustrate additional knowledge to be acquired through the module which will be coupled with external badges and certifications.

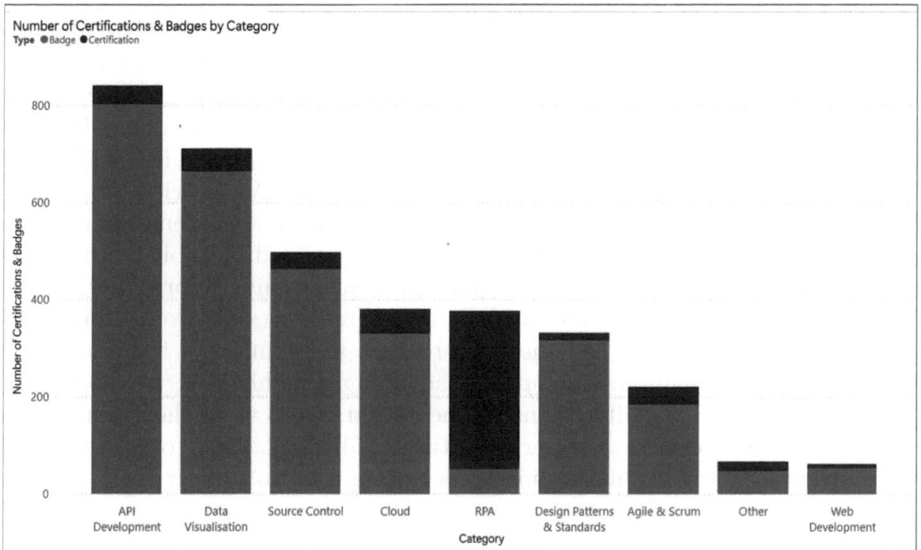

Fig. 7. Badges and Certifications Obtained

As a result of this approach, across approximately 256 students, 3 495 certifications were achieved, of which 2 914 were badges. Majority of the students obtained 11 badges and 2 certifications, on average. Figure 7 illustrates the division of certifications and badges across major categories, in alignment with the capstone projects. The highest number of certifications was obtained for API development, followed by data visualisation. The lowest number of certifications were obtained for the web development category which can be explained by the order of the capstone projects. Project 2 focused on API development using the same technical framework as web development which featured in Project 3, showing a growth in skills with a reduced need for upskilling as projects continued to build on top of one another. The projects built on one another in context and knowledge but were still separate projects. If a student did not complete a project, the next project would not be impacted. Students were given the resources needed for each project to still succeed, regardless of the results of their previous project.

Apart from the iterative review of student feedback and continuous monitoring of student progress, the implementation of the proposed framework was evaluated using Quality Assurance (QA) and User Acceptance Testing (UAT) to identify any potential enhancements.

The criteria presented in Table 1 were selected based on established educational theory and best practices in ICT curriculum design. Sources such as [3,11,13], and [15] highlight the significance of motivation, knowledge transfer, and real-world application as indicators of effective pedagogy. Additionally, the inclusion of external certification reflects current trends in aligning academic learning with industry benchmarks [19].

Due to the nature of the module, all external training was to be planned and completed based on the students' need thereof. As such, no strict deadlines were enforced and, in some cases, it did result in students completing the training long after the submission of the designated project was due. That was the biggest takeaway from the testing and evaluation process. This was changed to be connected to project deadlines in later iterations. Along with the evaluation process, multiple advantages were realised from the concatenation of three learning approaches into one single approach, summarised in Table 1. The information represented in Table 1 shows that different learning approaches can be followed to realise benefit, however there are gaps that occur from using these approaches individually. When these approaches are combined, the benefits of all approaches are realised. The specific advantages highlighted were based on critical reflection between iterations by the authors as to what they would hope to achieve. In future work a larger literature study is planned to explore what other advantages and evaluation methods can be used to further maximise the benefit to students.

Table 1. Advantages of Different Learning Approaches

Advantage	CBL	PBL	IL	IPCBL
Improved motivation & engagement	X	X	–	X
Improved retrospective understanding of critical concepts	X	X	X	X
Development of essential skills	X	X	–	X
Transferability of knowledge	X	X	X	X
Real-world application	X	X	X	X
Encourages critical thinking	X	X	X	X
Encourages creative thinking	–	–	X	X
Encourages problem solving	X	X	X	X
Encourages external training & certification	–	X	–	X

6 Future Work

The learnings from this iteration of the study will enable the future iterations to encapsulate the evaluation feedback into the improvement of the approach as a framework. The future work items include:

- Encapsulate the approach proposed in [19] to develop a curriculum shaped specifically to incorporate pre-defined skills that can be aligned to a module-outcome-level binary rubric.
- Enhance the template of the content required in the portfolio of evidence that illustrates the progression of student skills and application of knowledge through the IPCBL learning approach.
- Introduce external training milestones into the approach to ensure certificates are obtained timeously and within integrated capstone project context, contributing to the overarching module context.

7 Conclusion

This study introduced the IPCBL framework as a solution to bridging the gap between academic learning and industry needs in ICT education. By integrating PBL and CBL, the framework promotes deep learning, problem-solving, and competency development. The study demonstrated that a structured, technology-agnostic approach to integrating students into the working environment by exposing them to industry relevant badges and certifications while maintaining academic integrity was possible. Future iterations of this research will refine the IPCBL framework through further empirical validation, ensuring that it remains adaptable to evolving educational and technological landscapes. Ultimately, the framework contributes to advancing ICT education by fostering a more integrated, skill-based, and industry-aligned learning environment.

Acknowledgments. Gratitude is extended to North-West University for providing the opportunity and necessary support to implement this research. The university's commitment to academic excellence and innovation has played a crucial role in facilitating this study. Sincere appreciation is also conveyed to the mentors whose invaluable guidance, insightful feedback, and continuous encouragement have been instrumental in shaping this research. Thanks are also due to all those who contributed, directly or indirectly, to the success of this work. Their support is greatly appreciated.

Disclosure of Interests. The authors have no competing interests to declare that are relevant to the content of this article.

References

1. Alali, R.: Enhancing 21st century skills through integrated stem education using project-oriented problem-based learning. Geo J. Tourism Geosites **53**, 421–430 (2024)
2. Ali, W.: Online and remote learning in higher education institutes: a necessity in light of covid-19 pandemic. High. Educ. Stud. **10**, 16–25 (2020)
3. Bell, T., Urhahne, D., Schanze, S., Ploetzner, R.: Collaborative inquiry learning: models, tools, and challenges. Int. J. Sci. Educ. **32**, 349–377 (2010)
4. Boss, S., Krauss, J.: Reinventing project-based learning: Your field guide to real-world projects in the digital age. Int. Soc. Technol. Educ. (2022)
5. Cennamo, K., Kalk, D.: Real World Instructional Design: An Iterative Approach to Designing Learning Experiences. Routledge (2019)
6. Gregor, S., Chandra Kruse, L., Seidel, S.: Research perspectives: the anatomy of a design principle. Assoc. Inf. Syst. (2020)
7. Gregor, S., Hevner, A.R.: Positioning and presenting design science research for maximum impact. MIS Quart. 337–355 (2013)
8. Guo, P., Saab, N., Post, L.S., Admiraal, W.: A review of project-based learning in higher education: student outcomes and measures. Int. J. Educ. Res. **102**, 101586 (2020)
9. Huber, M., Panel, C.P.: Integrative learning as an intellectual art. In: Association of American Colleges and Universities Network Conference on Integrative Learning, pp. 1–7 (2005)
10. Janse Van Rensburg, J.: Project-based learning guidelines for it higher education. In: ICT Education: 50th Annual Conference of the Southern African Computer Lecturers' Association, SACLA 2021, pp. 67–81. Springer (2022)
11. Javed, U., Shaukat, K., Hameed, I.A., Iqbal, F., Alam, T.M., Luo, S.: A review of content-based and context-based recommendation systems. Int. J. Emerg. Technol. Learn. (iJET) **16**, 274–306 (2021)
12. Khasawneh, M.A.S.: Closing the industry-academia gap in translation education; exploring collaborative strategies as tools for effective curriculum alignment. Kurdish Stud. **12** (2024)
13. Klein, J.T.: Integrative learning and interdisciplinary studies. Peer Rev. **7**, 8–10 (2005)
14. Klein, J.T.: Creating Interdisciplinary Campus Cultures: a Model for Strength and Sustainability. Wiley (2009)
15. Krajcik, J., Mcneill, K.L., Reiser, B.J.: Learning-goals-driven design model: developing curriculum materials that align with national standards and incorporate project-based pedagogy. Sci. Educ. **92**, 1–32 (2008)
16. Liu, X., Xu, J., Xu, X., Wang, Y., Cao, Y.: Context-based learning: a review of recent research and implications for science education. Res. Sci. Educ. **50**(1), 155–178 (2020)
17. Maros, M., Korenkova, M., Fila, M., Levicky, M., Schoberova, M.: Project-based learning and its effectiveness: evidence from slovakia. Interact. Learn. Environ. **31**, 4147–4155 (2023)
18. Molina-García, N., González-Serrano, M.H., Ordiñana-Bellver, D., Baena-Morales, S.: Redefining education in sports sciences: a theoretical study for integrating competency-based learning for sustainable employment in spain. Soc. Sci. **13**, 242 (2024)

19. Muller, J., Greeff, J.J.: The use of binary scales in rubrics to evaluate computer science assessments. In: ICT Education: 51st Annual Conference of the Southern African Computer Lecturers' Association, SACLA 2022, pp. 58–72. Springer (2022)
20. Nittayathammakul, V., Chatwattana, P., Piriyasurawong, P.: Conceptual framework of crowd context-based learning via iot wearable technology to promote digital health literacy. In: 5th International Conference on E-Society, E-Education and E-Technology, pp. 113–119 (2021)
21. Pratisto, E.H., Danoetirta, D.R.: Design and user analysis of a learning management system: student competency-based learning. IOTA J. **5**, 136–147 (2025)
22. Sabbir, M.M., Taufique, K.M.R.: ustainable employee green behavior in the workplace: integrating cognitive and non-cognitive factors in corporate environmental policy. Bus. Strateg. Environ. **31**, 110–128 (2022)
23. Truong, H.M.: Integrating learning styles and adaptive e-learning system: current developments, problems and opportunities. Comput. Hum. Behav. **55**, 1185–1193 (2016)
24. Vaishnavi, V.K.: Design Science Research Methods and Patterns: Innovating Information and Communication Technology. Auerbach Publications (2007)
25. Vassilakopoulou, P., Hustad, E.: Bridging digital divides: a literature review and research agenda for information systems research. Inf. Syst. Front. 1–15 (2021)
26. Wang, C., Shen, J., Chao, J.: Integrating computational thinking in stem education: a literature review. Int. J. Sci. Math. Educ. **20**, 1949–1972 (2022)
27. Widiyati, E., Pangesti, W.: Project-based learning in teaching speaking to young learners: is it effective? EduLite: J. English Educ. Literat. Cult. **7**, 71–81 (2022)
28. Zydney, J.M., Warner, Z., Angelone, L.: Learning through experience: Using design based research to redesign protocols for blended synchronous learning environments. Comput. Educ. **143**, 103678 (2020)

Development of the GE-ARCS-E Model to Evaluate the Impact of Gamification on Programming Students' Motivation and Engagement

Marisa Venter[1,2(✉)] and Lizette de Wet[1]

[1] Department of Computer Science and Informatics, University of the Free State, Bloemfontein, South Africa
marisa@cut.ac.za

[2] Department of Information Technology, Central University of Technology, Free State, Bloemfontein, South Africa

Abstract. Programming modules in higher education often face challenges such as low student motivation and engagement, exacerbated by traditional, teacher-centred methods that limit active participation. Gamification offers a transformative solution, enabling educators to redefine programming education through innovative, gamified learning activities and software applications. This approach fosters engagement, addresses existing challenges, and creates a dynamic learning environment, empowering students to succeed in their programming endeavours. This study aimed to develop and empirically evaluate a theoretical model to assess the influence of gamification elements on the motivation and engagement of first-year higher education internet programming students. Using the Stimulus-Organism-Response (S-O-R) framework, the GE-ARCS-E theoretical model was developed. Findings revealed that students' interaction with achievement-related and social-related game elements significantly predicted the attention and satisfaction dimensions of motivation. Additionally, the interaction of students with social-related game elements and the relevance dimension of motivation significantly predicted the confidence dimension of motivation. Lastly, confidence and satisfaction dimensions of motivation significantly predicted the academic engagement of first-year programming students. The study's scientific contribution lies in presenting a statistically validated theoretical model that measures the interaction of students with game elements and its predictive impact on ARCS motivation, while also quantifying the influence of motivation on academic engagement. A key recommendation is that institutions should invest in the development of customisable gamification tools and platforms tailored to programming education, enabling educators to design and adapt gamified learning experiences that align with specific course objectives and student needs.

Keywords: SEM · ARCS · higher education · computer programming

L. Nel et al. (Eds.): SACLA 2025, CCIS 2770, pp. 84–101, 2026.
https://doi.org/10.1007/978-3-032-12457-9_6

1 Introduction

Programming is easy … until it's not [1]. Undergraduate computer science students have consistently encountered difficulties in programming courses, a subject that has been thoroughly examined and discussed over several decades [2]. These challenges were further highlighted in a recent systematic literature review of 44 studies [3], which identified the two most significant obstacles in programming education: low motivation, mentioned in eight studies, and low engagement, reported in six studies. Traditional, teacher-centric teaching methods contribute to disengagement, demotivation, and boredom among programming students by limiting active engagement [4]. These methods fail to meet the expectations of modern students, who are accustomed to immediate gratification from digital experiences [5]. The failure of traditional teaching methods to meet the diverse needs of programming students incentivises educators to explore contemporary teaching strategies. Among these, gamification stands out, not merely as a trend, but as a promising foundation for transforming programming modules [6]. Gamification enhances interactivity, engagement, motivation and learning outcomes of programming students – outcomes that align with the preferences of digital natives [3, 6–8]. Gamification, generally understood as the integration of game design elements into non-game contexts, provides a flexible framework applicable across multiple disciplines [9]. In higher education, programming instructors can utilise gamified learning activities and software applications to develop innovative pedagogical approaches that support students in achieving success in their programming studies [2].

Although gamification is seen as a promising tool for enhancing motivation and engagement, unresolved gaps remain, as evidenced by Venter and de Wet [10], which will be discussed in Sect. 2.

2 Research Problem and Objectives

Multiple systematic reviews over several years highlight that much of the applied research on gamification lacks theoretical grounding [11–13]. Additionally, there has been limited academic focus on developing a theoretical framework for educational gamification to explain its impact on motivation and engagement in gamified learning environments [14].

Another identified gap concerns the way studies measure gamification elements and test their influence on dependent variables. When gamification elements are not measured as variables, and when the impact of these gamification elements on dependent variables are not statistically assessed, it is difficult to discern the true impact of gamification. Most research studies on the impact of gamification on user interaction, participation and engagement, failed to accurately capture users' authentic responses to their engagement with gamification features [15]. These studies, for example Berger et al. [16] and Hsu and Chen [17], do not treat gamification elements as variables, and do not measure the perceived importance that users attribute to gamification features or the frequency of user interaction with gamification features [12, 13]. Instead, these studies treat gamification as a research context and assume that, if a gamification element has been incorporated into a gamified environment, it automatically means that users have interacted with it

[15]. Subsequently, studies that do not incorporate gamification elements as predictors in their gamification models per se, do not allow conclusions to be drawn about how gamification elements have influenced the engagement of users [15].

To address the aforementioned gaps in the literature, this study aimed to develop a theoretical model and use it to empirically evaluate the influence of gamification elements on the motivation and engagement of first-year higher education internet programming students. This study is among the first in the gamification of higher education programming modules to operationalise game elements and to measure their impact on variables such as motivation and engagement of students. The following research question was used to guide this study: *Which theoretical model can be developed to evaluate the influence of gamification elements on the motivation and engagement of first year higher education internet programming students?*

3 Gamified Internet Programming Learning Environment

To assess the influence of gamification elements on the motivation and engagement of first-year Internet Programming students, a gamified learning environment was designed for the Internet Programming 1 module. The procedure that was used to design this gamified learning environment is addressed comprehensively in our previous research [18, pp. 4–6].

Various scholars in the gamification research domain have attempted to create categories to group game elements in order to facilitate the design and evaluation of gamified systems. Xi and Hamari [19] as well as Cui and Yang [20] credit Yee [21] for the three categories they used to categorise game elements, namely achievement, social and immersion. A summary of these three game element categories are provided in Table 1.

Using the conceptualisation of Xi and Hamari [19] and Cui and Yang [20], the gamified learning environment developed for the study incorporated three achievement-related elements, namely points, badges, and virtual currency. Furthermore, three social-related game elements—competition, cooperation, and leaderboards—were included. The achievement-related game elements were implemented using the following three gamified learning platforms: Khan Academy [22, 23], where students earned points for watching learning videos and completing programming activities; Codecademy [24, 25], where students earned badges for completing programming activities; and Gimkit, where students earned virtual currency for completing activities in the Fishtopia environment by successfully completing various quizzes [26].

Social game elements was implemented as follows: Competition was implemented using the Kahoot! platform [27], where students competed against each other during theory classes. Cooperation was implemented through a gamified group project where students worked in groups to design a website for a novel business idea. Student groups competed for the top five positions, with each receiving a prize of R1000. Leaderboards were created by ranking students based on three criteria: (1) the weekly points accumulated on Khan Academy, (2) the weekly badges earned on Codecademy, and (3) the weekly points obtained in the Kahoot! quizzes.

Table 1. Three game element categories [15, 16]

	Achievement-related game elements	Social-related game elements	Immersion-related game elements
Definition	Designed to provide rewards to users after they accomplish specified mileposts or activities, to address users' innate yearning for acknowledgement and achievement. Also serve as a mechanism to deliver feedback	Components that emphasise the significance of cooperation, social bonding and community development, nurturing a feeling of inclusivity and cohesion among users	Components crafted to construct compelling narratives or immersive experiences, enabling users to become thoroughly engrossed and fully immersed in the material
Game elements	Points, badges, trophies, medals, rankings, virtual currency, physical rewards, levels, progress bars	Competition, cooperation, leaderboards, social pressure	Story, theme, virtual characters, content unlocking, avatars

4 Development of Theoretical Model

The Stimulus-Organism-Response (S-O-R) framework was adopted as the overarching theoretical foundation for developing a theoretical model to assess the gamified learning environment in this study. This framework was originally introduced by Mehradian and Russell [28] and provides a theoretical foundation for understanding the relationships among three key components of person–environment interaction: stimulus, organism, and response. The stimulus refers to elements in a person's environment that activate or trigger certain internal processes. These internal processes are experienced by the individual as cognitive (thoughts) and affective (emotional) reactions, which together form the organism component. In essence, the organism represents the psychological and emotional state of the individual as they process and interpret environmental stimuli. This internal state, then influences the individual's behavioural responses or tendencies, referred to as the response [29].

The S-O-R framework has been widely applied in tourism, marketing and retail domains [30] and its utilisation within the gamification domain has been gaining traction over the past few years. It is viewed as one of the best explanations for the mechanism underlying gamification in educational settings [31]. The S-O-R framework has been used in various educational settings like mobile learning [32, 33], massive open online courses [34, 35] and virtual learning [30].

In the gamified programming learning environment of this study, the implemented game elements were regarded as the stimuli [36]. These game elements will, in turn, trigger or arouse the motivation of students (including various emotional and cognitive states) referred to as the organism. Enhanced motivation levels of students will positively influence the behavioural engagement responses of students. The high-level theoretical model of the study is shown in Fig. 1. The components of this model will be discussed next.

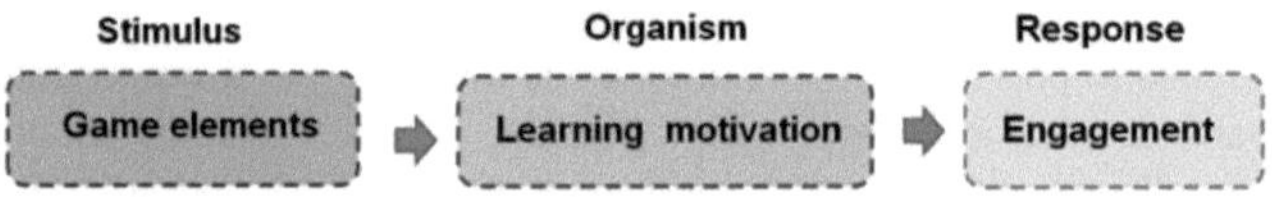

Fig. 1. High-level theoretical model of the study

4.1 Stimulus – Game Elements

The stimulus component of the theoretical model of the study comprised of the following two higher order variables:

- Achievement-related game elements comprised of the points, badges and virtual currency lower order variables.
- Social-related game elements comprised of the competition, collaboration and leaderboards lower order variables.

4.2 Organism – Learning Motivation

The ARCS model of motivation was developed with the aim of comprehensively understanding the key factors that influence motivation for learning [37]. When the four dimensions of the ARCS model namely attention, relevance, confidence and satisfaction are examined, it can be seen that the cognitive and affective dimensions of the organism category of the S-O-R framework are incorporated. The ARCS model's attention dimension evaluates whether learning materials capture students' attention, stimulate curiosity, and facilitate concentration, reflecting cognitive states influenced by game elements in a gamified environment. Similarly, the relevance dimension assesses how well learning content supports comprehension and aligns with students' goals, interests, and needs. Affective states triggered by game elements are represented by the confidence and satisfaction dimensions. The confidence dimension measures students' perceptions of competence and mastery, while the satisfaction dimension assesses enjoyment and overall contentment with the learning experience [38]. The different dimensions of ARCS motivation consequently impact student engagement.

Following a comprehensive review of the existing literature, four studies that used the ARCS model to evaluate the motivation of students in gamified programming environments were located. The context of these studies included game-based learning [39, 40], e-learning [41] and blended learning [42]. All four studies measured the success of the gamification endeavours by comparing the measurements of the ARCS dimensions for the experiential groups against the control groups, without measuring the level of interaction students had with game elements.

4.3 Response – Engagement

The cultivation of student engagement, specifically, is instrumental for achieving valued educational results such as academic progress and attainment [31]. Some studies have highlighted the enhancement of user engagement as the principal objective of gamification interventions [43, 44], especially in educational settings [31]. According to the S-O-R framework, the response category refers to the behavioural responses or behavioural tendencies that are a response to the cognitive and affective states of a person. In order to measure the engagement category of the study, the Higher Education Student Engagement Scale (HESES) was used [45]. The HESES scale refers to behavioural engagement of students as academic engagement and, therefore, this term was adopted by the current study. The measurement scale of academic engagement of the HESES includes two constructs, namely academic learning and online learning, which was incorporated in the current study to measure academic engagement.

4.4 Hypotheses of the Theoretical Model

Variables Influencing the Attention Dimension of Motivation. Empirical studies report that incorporating game design elements, such as badges and points, can effectively guide students' attention towards designated learning activities [46]. Furthermore, the competitive nature of the gamified tasks lead to heightened levels of student interest in learning activities [47]. Similarly, research findings indicate that leaderboards have the capability to focus students' attention on specific learning tasks [46]. Based on the preceding discussion, the following hypotheses are offered:

H_1a: Student interaction with achievement-related game elements is positively associated with the attention dimension of motivation.

H_1b: Student interaction with social-related game elements is positively associated with the attention dimension of motivation.

Variables Influencing the Relevance Dimension of Motivation. Various studies in educational contexts report statistically significant and positive relationships between the attention and relevance dimensions of the ARCS model [49, 50]. Based on the positive associations reported in these studies, it can be reasoned that, when instructional materials capture students' attention effectively, students are more likely to perceive the material as relevant. Consequently, the following hypothesis is proposed:

H_2: The attention dimension of the motivation is positively associated with the relevance dimension of motivation.

Variables Influencing the Confidence Dimension of Motivation. Rewarding the achievements of students is crucial for establishing a sense of accomplishment. In line with this perspective, gamification badges, points and virtual currency can serve as incentives to acknowledge success and enhance students' self-confidence for subsequent tasks [51]. The implementation of leaderboards in gamified learning environments indicates to students their ranking in relation to other students. These rankings, furthermore, encourage competition between students and lead to social comparison among peers [52]. Social comparison, in turn, can motivate students to attain higher levels of achievement, by positively influencing their confidence levels. Various studies reported statistically significant positive relationships between the relevance and confidence dimensions of motivation in educational settings [49, 50]. It can be argued that, when instructional materials are perceived as relevant, learners are more likely to see the value of engaging with the content. This increased perception of relevance can enhance students' confidence in their ability to understand and apply the material. The following hypotheses are consequently put forward:

H3a: Student interaction with social-related game elements is positively associated with the confidence dimension of motivation.

H3b: Student interaction with achievement-related game elements is positively associated with the confidence dimension of motivation.

H3c: The relevance dimension of motivation is positively associated with the confidence dimension of the motivation.

Variables Influencing the Satisfaction Dimension of Motivation. Gamification features such as group functionalities and chat options facilitate frequent communication, idea exchange and reciprocal interactions among students. These student interactions foster a stronger sense of connection and belonging among students [19]. When individuals experience camaraderie and establish close bonds with others, they often report heightened feelings of satisfaction [53]. Furthermore, an empirical study found that there was a statistically significant positive relationship between social interaction and overall satisfaction of users with mobile technology [54]. Additionally, Hamzah et al. [55] proposes that game elements such as badges and virtual currency can be used to reward learners and recognise their achievement and accomplishment to increase their satisfaction levels in gamified learning environments. Moreover, studies that empirically tested the relationship between the relevance dimension and the satisfaction dimension of the ARCS model found statistical significant relationships [49, 50]. The findings reported above led to the following hypotheses:

H4a: Student interaction with social-related game elements is positively associated with the satisfaction dimension of motivation.

H4b: Student interaction with achievement-related game elements is positively associated with the satisfaction dimension of motivation.

H4c: The relevance dimension of motivation is positively associated with the satisfaction dimension of the motivation.

Variables Influencing Academic Engagement. When students perceive themselves as capable of completing a task, they are inclined to participate in it actively [56]. The confidence dimension of motivation aligns with self-efficacy, which is an individual's trust in their capability to accomplish specific tasks successfully [57]. Students possessing higher levels of self-efficacy demonstrate increased behavioural engagement in the classroom, which leads to higher learning engagement levels [58]. An empirical study researching a first-year module at a university in Mauritius found that there was a significant and positive correlation between satisfaction with the module and engagement in the module [59]. Based on the preceding discussion, the following hypotheses are presented:

H5a: The confidence dimension of motivation is positively associated with academic engagement.

H5b: The satisfaction dimension of motivation is positively associated with academic engagement.

The theoretical model of the study, inclusive of hypotheses, are shown in Fig. 2. The researcher named this extended ARCS model the GE-ARCS-E model, where "GE" represents the independent game element variables, and "E" denotes the dependent academic engagement variable.

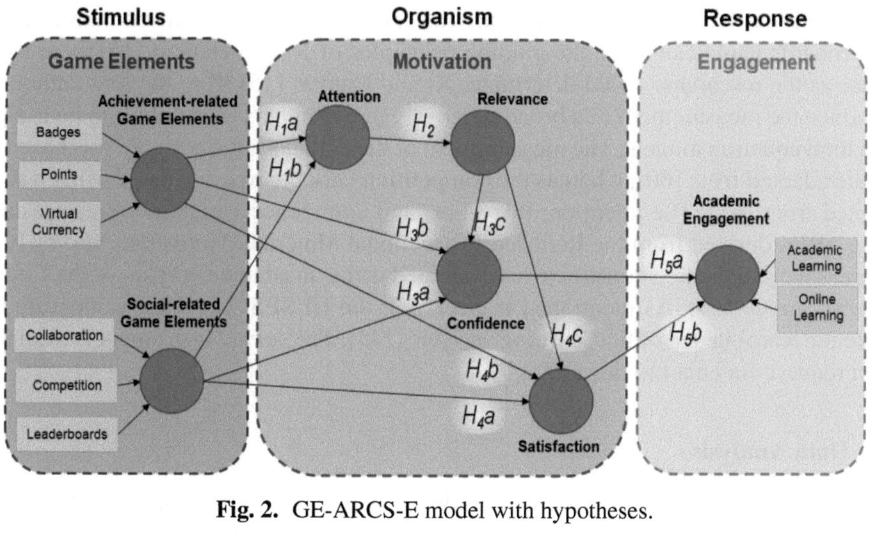

Fig. 2. GE-ARCS-E model with hypotheses.

5 Methodology

5.1 Research Design

A concurrent mixed methods approach was used, incorporating both quantitative and qualitative data collection. Quantitative data was gathered through a survey, while qualitative data was obtained via group interviews conducted at the end of the semester. This paper focuses solely on the quantitative data collected. The study population comprised 276 students enrolled in an Internet Programming 1 module at a South African university, of whom 179 formed the final sample by completing the questionnaire. This module is designed to develop students' proficiency in web programming, with a focus on HTML, CSS, and JavaScript. Participation in the survey was voluntary, and the survey link was distributed through the learning management system of the university. The study received ethical approval from the university where the research was conducted.

5.2 Survey Instrument

The survey instrument comprised four sections. Section 1 gathered demographic information, while Sect. 2 focused on data related to the game elements incorporated in the study. Section 3 examined students' motivation, and Sect. 4 assessed their engagement. The instrument employed multi-item summated rating scales, utilising a 7-point Likert scale with endpoints ranging from (1) Strongly Disagree to (7) Strongly Agree. In order to measure the interaction students had with the points, badges, virtual currency and leaderboards game elements, the guiding principles of Xi and Hamari [15] were used. As far as the researcher could determine, Xi and Hamari [15] were the first authors to introduce the measurement of a broad range of game elements as variables to be used in structural equation models. The measurement of the collaboration variable was based on a scale adapted from [60], whereas the competition variable was evaluated using a scale adapted from [61]. The attention, relevance, and confidence variables were measured using scales derived from the Reduced Instructional Materials Motivation Survey [62], whereas the satisfaction construct was evaluated using an adapted version of the Course Interest Survey [63]. As mentioned in Sect. 4.3, the HESES was used to measure the academic learning and online learning variables [45]. The survey instrument is available upon request via email to the author.

5.3 Data Analysis

The quantitative data for the study were analysed using SmartPLS4. SmartPLS4 provides a graphical user interface designed for variance-based partial least squares structural equation modelling (PLS-SEM).

6 Results

6.1 Biographical Data

Male students constituted the majority of survey respondents (58.66%), followed by female students (40.78%), with 0.56% identifying as belonging to the 'other' gender category. The age distribution of the sample was as follows: 18–19 years (35.75%), 20–21 years (41.34%), 22–23 years (12.29%), 24–25 years (3.91%) and 6.71% of students were older than 25 years.

6.2 PLS-SEM Analysis Results

The analysis of the PLS-SEM results was conducted in two stages. The first stage of evaluating these results comprised scrutinising the measurement models to establish the reliability and validity of the variables. Generally, if the measurement models conformed to the applicable threshold value, researchers can proceed with the second phase, which is the assessment of the structural model to determine the significance of the hypothesised relationships and the explanatory power of the structural model [64].

6.3 Stage 1: Assessment of Measurement Models

In the current study, the SEM model contained eight lower-order variables, four first-order variables, and three higher-order variables. The eight lower-order variables (badges, points, virtual currency, collaboration, competition, leaderboards, academic learning and online learning) were used to measure three higher-order variables. Badges, points, and virtual currency were used to measure the achievement-related game elements higher-order variable. Also, the three lower-order variables, namely collaboration, competition and leaderboards, were used to measure the social-related game elements higher-order variable. Furthermore, the academic learning and online learning lower-order variables were used to measure the academic engagement higher-order variable. The first-order variables were attention, relevance, confidence and satisfaction. All the first-order and lower-order variables were measured reflectively, while all the higher-order variables were measured formatively. The assessment of the measurement models was done in two steps. The reflective measurement model was assessed first followed by the assessment of the formative measurement model.

Assessment of the Reflective Measurement Model. The assessment measures of the reflectively measured first-order and lower-order variables are shown in Table 2. Internal consistency reliability were assessed by investigating the Cronbach's alpha (α) and composite reliability ($CRrho_A$). As indicated in Table 2, these values were higher than 0.7 threshold, confirming internal consistency of all variables [54].

Convergent validity were assessed by scrutinising the average variance extracted (AVE) which was above the 0.5 threshold, thereby indicating convergent validity of all variables [64]. To assess the indicator reliability, the factor loadings of the items that were used to measure each variable were investigated. In Table 2 the lowest and highest factor loading for items measuring each variable were indicated. Factor loadings were

Table 2. Lower-order and first-order variables assessment measures.

Variable	No. of items	Indicator factor loading range	α	CR rho_A	AVE
Academic learning	5	0.543 - 0.825	0.766	0.794	0.523
Attention	5	0.749 - 0.852	0.857	0.858	0.638
Badges	3	0.799 - 0.936	0.844	0.913	0.762
Collaboration	5	0.724 - 0.849	0.863	0.882	0.645
Competition	4	0.598 - 0.801	0.701	0.710	0.532
Confidence	5	0.711 - 0.890	0.884	0.899	0.686
Leaderboards	3	0.704 - 0.895	0.763	0.805	0.680
Online learning	5	0.600 - 0.817	0.772	0.777	0.526
Points	3	0.767 - 0.829	0.716	0.722	0.637
Relevance	4	0.810 - 0.904	0.899	0.903	0.768
Satisfaction	6	0.788 - 0.897	0.915	0.919	0.704
Virtual currency	5	0.753 - 0.806	0.837	0.850	0.597

evaluated using the following threshold ranges: 0.32 (poor), 0.45 (fair), 0.55 (good), 0.63 (very good), and 0.71 (excellent) [65]. As shown in Table 2, all factor loadings fell within acceptable ranges.

Assessment of Formative Measurement Model. In Table 3, the measures used to assess the validity of the higher order variable are indicated.

Table 3. Higher-order construct validity

Higher-order variables	Lower-order variables	VIF	Outer weights	p-values
Achievement-related game elements	Badges	1.682	0.374	0.006
	Points	1.827	0.499	0.002
	Virtual currency	1.130	0.416	0.006
Social-related game elements	Collaboration	1.361	0.445	<0.001
	Competition	1.369	0.497	<0.001
	Leaderboards	1.119	0.372	0.002
Academic engagement	Academic learning	1.340	0.506	<0.001
	Online learning	1.340	0.644	<0.001

First multicollinearity was assessed using the variance inflation factor (VIF). Ideally, VIF values less than or equal to 3 indicate no multicollinearity issues [64]. Collinearity did not pose any threat, as all VIF values were less than 3, as shown in Table 3.Next, the significance and relevance of outer weights were assessed. Outer weights are used in formative measurement models, where indicators contribute to and define the variable. They show how much each indicator contributes to the overall variable, with higher weights indicating a stronger contribution [64]. All outer weights were found statistically significant with p-values lower than 0.05, establishing the validity of the higher-order variables.

6.4 Results and Discussion of the Assessment of the Structural Model

The results of the assessment of the structural model are summarised in Table 4. All hypotheses of the study were supported except H3b. The explanatory power of the structural model is expressed in terms of the coefficient of determination (R^2), which indicates the proportion of the total variance of a dependent variable, explained by its associated independent variables. One of the most widely cited guidelines for assessing the strength of R^2 was used, where R^2 values above 0.67, 0.33, and 0.19 are considered substantial, moderate, and weak, respectively [66].

When the influence of various independent variables was investigated in the prediction of the four motivation dimensions of the ARCS model, the confidence dependent dimension had the highest R^2 value (0.609 in Table 4). The relevance ($\beta = 0.562$, $p < 0.001$) and the social-related game elements variable ($\beta = 0.205$, $p = 0.005$) collectively predicted 60.90% of the variability of the confidence variable. This represented a predictive power very close to the substantial level. The implication of this finding is that relevance of the learning material, as well as student's interaction with social- related game elements, all played a role to improve student confidence levels.

In contrast, the achievement-related game elements did not have a statistically significant influence on the confidence variable ($\beta = 0.148$, $p = 0.052$). The strong predictive role of relevance ($\beta = 0.562$, $p < 0.001$) in fostering confidence is also supported by Huang and Hew [46] who found that relevance in gamified learning environments enhances students' intrinsic motivation and self-efficacy, thereby boosting their confidence. The significant influence of social-related game elements ($\beta = 0.205$, $p < 0.005$) on confidence is consistent with a study on gamified systems which found positive and statistically significant relationships between social interaction game elements (coopetition, competition, comparison) and the attention, confidence and satisfaction constructs of the ARCS model [67].

The R^2 value of the relevance dependent variable (0.456) in Table 4 was the second highest in the structural model. The attention variable ($\beta = 0.675$, $p < 0.001$) predicted 45.6.7% of the variability of the relevance dependent variable. The implication of this finding is that, when students' attention levels are sustained, they will be more prone to understanding the learning material and to find it useful and relevant. This finding is consistent with other research that recognises heightened attention facilitates enhanced cognitive processing, thereby improving students' ability to comprehend and relate with the material [68].

When the R^2 value of the satisfaction dependant variable (0.444) is investigated, it can be seen that the social-related game elements variable ($\beta = 0.310$, $p < 0.001$),

Table 4. Explanatory power of the structural model

Hypothesis	Independent variable	β value	p-value	Dependent variable	R^2	Explanatory power
H_1a ✓	Achievement-related game elements	0.352	< 0.001	Attention	0.286	Weak
H_1b ✓	Social-related game elements	0.245	0.026			
H_2 ✓	Attention	0.675	< 0.001	Relevance	0.456	Moderate
H_3c ✓	Relevance	0.562	< 0.001	Confidence	0.609	Moderate
H_3a ✓	Social-related game elements	0.205	0.005			
H_3b X	Achievement-related game elements	0.148	0.052			
H_4a ✓	Social-related game elements	0.310	<0.001	Satisfaction	0.444	Moderate
H_4c ✓	Relevance	0.303	<0.001			
H_4b ✓	Achievement-related game elements	0.192	0.012			
H_5a ✓	Confidence	0.367	< 0.001	Academic engagement	0.389	Moderate
H_5b ✓	Satisfaction	0.335	< 0.001			

the relevance variable ($\beta = 0.303$, $p < 0.001$), and the achievement-related game elements variable ($\beta = 0.192$, $p = 0.012$) together predicted 44.4% of the variability of the satisfaction dependent variable. This represents a moderate predictive power. This finding suggests that the interaction of students with the social game elements, namely collaborating with each other on the group project, competing with each other on the Kahoot! platform, the relevance of the learning material and the interaction of students with points, badges and virtual currency, all played a role to enhance the satisfaction of students participating in the gamified programming learning environment. This finding aligns with a study which demonstrated that social game elements positively influence students' overall satisfaction with the learning process [54]. Additionally, research indicate that achievement-related game elements, such as points, badges, and virtual rewards serve as extrinsic motivators that reinforce positive behaviors and provide a sense of accomplishment and increase satisfaction [55].

The attention dependent variable had the lowest R^2 level (0.286) of all the ARCS dimensions. The achievement-related game elements variable ($\beta = 0.352$, $p < 0.001$) and the social-related game elements variable ($\beta = 0.245$, $p = 0.026$) collectively predicted 28.6% of the variability of the attention dependent variable, which is representative of a predictive power very close to a moderate level. This finding implies that the interaction of students with points, badges and virtual currency, as well as their collaboration on the group project, their competition in theory lessons on the Kahoot! platform and their interaction with the leaderboards, all contributed to attracting the attention of students to the learning activities they performed in the gamified programming learning environment.

Investigating the R^2 value of 0.389 of the last dependent variable in Table 4, it can be seen that the confidence ($\beta = 0.367$, $p < 0.001$) and satisfaction ($\beta = 0.335$, $p < 0.001$) variables collectively explain 38.9% of the variability of academic engagement, indicating moderate predictive power. This results is supported by prior research demonstrating that the satisfaction of students with gamified learning environments positively influences engagement in learning activities [59]. The significant role of confidence in predicting academic engagement aligns with existing literature, which posits that confidence in one's abilities is a key determinant of engagement, as it influences students' willingness to tackle challenges and persist in academic tasks [57].

7 Conclusion

The aim of this study was to address a gap in the literature by developing and empirically evaluating a theoretical model to assess the influence of gamification elements on the motivation and engagement of first-year higher education internet programming students. Using the Stimulus-Organism-Response (S-O-R) framework, the GE-ARCS-E theoretical model was developed. To the best of the researcher's knowledge, this study is among the first to measure the interaction students had with achievement-related and social-related game elements and to determine their impact on the ARCS dimensions of motivation in a first-year programming module. Additionally, it is one of the first studies to quantify the predictive potential of motivation on the academic engagement of first-year programming students. The GE-ARCS-E model provides higher education instructors with a formal, structured tool to evaluate the effectiveness of their gamification efforts, offering valuable insights for designing more engaging and motivating learning experiences.

However, this study has certain limitations. Firstly, it was conducted within a single internet programming module at one university in South Africa, which may limit the generalisability of the findings to the broader gamified programming learning domain. Secondly, as the study was conducted in a specific cultural context, the results may not be directly comparable to international student populations due to potential cultural differences. These limitations highlight the need for further research in diverse educational and cultural settings to validate and extend the findings.

A key recommendation is that institutions should invest in the development of customisable gamification tools and platforms tailored to programming education. Such tools would enable educators to design and adapt gamified learning experiences that align with specific course objectives and student needs, thereby enhancing motivation and engagement. Future research could also explore the applicability of gamification across different disciplines and cultural contexts. By addressing these areas, the potential of gamification as a transformative educational strategy can be further realised, contributing to more effective and inclusive programming education.

8 Disclosure of Interests.

The authors have no competing interests to declare that are relevant to the content of this article.

Acknowledgements. We would like to acknowledge the financial support provided by the Centre for Innovation in Learning and Teaching, through the Scholarship of Teaching and Learning office, funded by the Department of Higher Education and Training's (DHET) University Capacity Development Grant in South Africa. This support enabled the research and publication of this work. The views expressed are those of the authors and do not necessarily reflect those of the funding bodies.

References

1. Usman, M.: Programming is easy … until it's not: The truth about the programming mindset. https://dev.to/web_dev-usman/programming-is-easy-until-its-not-the-truth-about-the-programming-mindset-3d5j. Accessed 03 Mar 2025
2. Costa, J.M.: Using game concepts to improve programming learning: a multi-level meta-analysis. Comput. Appl. Eng. Educ. **31**, 1098–1110 (2023). https://doi.org/10.1002/cae.22630
3. Maryono, D., Budiyono, S., Akhyar, M.: Implementation of gamification in programming learning: literature review. Int. J. Inf. Educ. Technol. **12**, 1448–1457 (2022). https://doi.org/10.18178/ijiet.2022.12.12.1771
4. Kumar, B., Sharma, K.: A gamified approach to achieve excellence in programming. In: Proceedings of the - 4th International Conference Computer Science ICCS 2018, pp. 107–114 (2019). https://doi.org/10.1109/ICCS.2018.00026
5. Murillo-Zamorano, L.R., López Sánchez, J.Á., Godoy-Caballero, A.L., Bueno Muñoz, C.: Gamification and active learning in higher education: is it possible to match digital society, academia and students' interests? Int. J. Educ. Technol. High. Educ. **18** (2021). https://doi.org/10.1186/s41239-021-00249-y
6. Calles-Esteban, F., Hellín, C.J., Tayebi, A., Liu, H., López-Benítez, M., Gómez, J.: Influence of gamification on the commitment of the students of a programming course: a case study. Appl. Sci. **14** (2024). https://doi.org/10.3390/app14083475
7. De Pontes, R.G., Guerrero, D.D.S., De Figueiredo, J.C.A.: Analyzing gamification impact on a mastery learning introductory programming course. In: SIGCSE 2019 - Proceedings of the 50th ACM Technical Symposium on Computer Science Education, pp. 400–406 (2019). https://doi.org/10.1145/3287324.3287367
8. Mubin, S.A., Wee, M., Poh, A., Jantan, A.H.: Gamification in programming language learning: a review and pathway. Int. J. Adv. Res. Eng. Technol. **11**, 1148–1155 (2020). https://doi.org/10.34218/IJARET.11.12.2020.111
9. Dichev, C., Dicheva, D.: Gamifying education: what is known, what is believed and what remains uncertain: a critical review. Int. J. Educ. Technol. High. Educ. **14**, 1–36 (2017). https://doi.org/10.1186/s41239-017-0042-5
10. Venter, M., de Wet, L.: Systematic literature review of gamification design in higher education programming courses: methodological rigor exposed. In: Plácido da Silva, H., Cipresso, P. (eds.) Computer-Human Interaction Research and Applications. CHIRA 2024. CCIS, vol. 2370, pp. 1–8. Springer, Cham (2025). https://doi.org/10.1007/978-3-031-82633-7_16
11. Khaldi, A., Bouzidi, R., Nader, F.: Gamification of e-learning in higher education: a systematic literature review. Smart Learn. Environ. **10**, 1–31 (2023). https://doi.org/10.1186/s40561-023-00227-z

12. Seaborn, K., Fels, D.I.: Gamification in theory and action: a survey. Int. J. Hum. Comput. Stud. **74**, 14–31 (2015). https://doi.org/10.1016/j.ijhcs.2014.09.006
13. Van Gaalen, A.E.J., Brouwer, J., Schönrock-Adema, J., Bouwkamp-Timmer, T., Jaarsma, A.D.C., Georgiadis, J.R.: Gamification of health professions education: a systematic review. Adv. Heal. Sci. Educ. **26**, 683–711 (2021). https://doi.org/10.1007/s10459-020-10000-3
14. Treiblmaier, H., Putz, L., Lowry, P.B.: Research commentary: setting a definition, context, and theory-based research agenda for the gamification of non-gaming applications. AIS Trans. Hum.-Comput. Interact. **10**, 129–163 (2018). https://doi.org/10.17705/1thci.00107
15. Xi, N., Hamari, J.: Does gamification affect brand engagement and equity? A study in online brand communities. J. Bus. Res. **109**, 449–460 (2020). https://doi.org/10.1016/j.jbusres.2019.11.058
16. Berger, A., Schlager, T., Sprott, D.E., Herrmann, A.: Gamified interactions: whether, when, and how games facilitate self–brand connections. J. Acad. Mark. Sci. **46**, 652–673 (2018). https://doi.org/10.1007/s11747-017-0530-0
17. Hsu, C.L., Chen, M.C.: How gamification marketing activities motivate desirable consumer behaviors: focusing on the role of brand love. Comput. Human Behav. **88**, 121–133 (2018). https://doi.org/10.1016/j.chb.2018.06.037
18. Venter, M., De Wet, L.: The influence of player type on the motivation of students in a gamified programming learning environment. In: Gundu, T., Gcaza, N., Calitz, A. (eds.) ICT Education. SACLA 2024. CCIS, vol. 2397, pp. 1–16. Springer, Cham (2025). https://doi.org/10.1007/978-3-031-82478-4_1
19. Xi, N., Hamari, J.: Does gamification satisfy needs? A study on the relationship between gamification features and intrinsic need satisfaction. Int. J. Inf. Manag. **46**, 210–221 (2019). https://doi.org/10.1016/j.ijinfomgt.2018.12.002
20. Cui, Z., Yang, H.: From game elements to active learning intentions: exploring the driving factors in digital learning platforms. SAGE Open **13**, 1–16 (2023). https://doi.org/10.1177/21582440231208932
21. Yee, N.: Motivations of play in online games. J. Cyber. Psychol. Behav. **9**, 772–775 (2007)
22. Khan Academy: Khan Academy. https://www.khanacademy.org. Accessed 24 Jan 2024
23. Morrison, B.B., DiSalvo, B.: Khan academy gamifies computer science. In: Proceedings of the 45th ACM Technical Symposium on Computer Science Education – SIGCSE'14, pp. 39–44. Atlanta, Georgia, USA (2014). https://doi.org/10.1145/2538862.2538946
24. Codecademy: Codecademy. www.codecademy.com. Accessed 01 Jan 2024
25. Van Roy, R., Deterding, S., Zaman, B.: Uses and gratifcations of initiating use of gamifed learning platforms. In: 2018 ACM CHI Conference on Human Factors in Computing Systems (2018). https://doi.org/10.1145/3170427.3188458
26. Gupta, J.: What is Fishtopia in Gimkit? https://stealthygaming.com/what-is-fishtopia-gimkit/%0AWhat. Accessed 29 Apr 2024
27. Wang, A.I., Tahir, R.: The effect of using Kahoot! for learning – a literature review. Comput. Educ. **149**, 103818 (2020). https://doi.org/10.1016/j.compedu.2020.103818
28. Mehrabian, A., Russell, J.A.: An Approach to Environmental Psychology. The MIT Press, Cambridge (1974)
29. Islam, J., Rahman, Z.: The impact of online brand community characteristics on customer engagement: an application of stimulus-organism-response paradigm. Telemat. Inform. **34**, 96–109 (2017). https://doi.org/10.1016/j.tele.2017.01.004
30. Safdar, S., Ren, M., Chudhery, M.A.Z.: Cloud computing-based virtual learning environments: factors that build trust and satisfaction leading to acceptance. IEEE Trans. Eng. Manag. **71**, 4517–4529 (2024). https://doi.org/10.1109/TEM.2022.3218707
31. Thomas, N.J., Baral, R.: Mechanism of gamification: role of flow in the behavioral and emotional pathways of engagement in management education. Int. J. Manag. Educ. **21**, 100718 (2023). https://doi.org/10.1016/j.ijme.2022.100718

32. Peng, M.Y., Xu, Y., Xu, C.: Enhancing students' English language learning via M-learning: integrating technology acceptance model and S-O-R model. Heliyon. **9**, e13302 (2023). https://doi.org/10.1016/j.heliyon.2023.e13302
33. Yang, X.: Mobile learning application characteristics and learners' continuance intentions: the role of flow experience. Educ. Inf. Technol. **29**, 2259–2275 (2024). https://doi.org/10.1007/s10639-023-11910-6
34. Cheng, Y.M.: What makes learners enhance learning outcomes in MOOCs? Exploring the roles of gamification and personalization. Interact. Technol. Smart Educ. **21**, 308–330 (2024). https://doi.org/10.1108/ITSE-05-2023-0097
35. Shanshan, S., Wenfei, L.: Continuance intention to use MOOCS: the effects of psychological stimuli and emotions. Asia-Pac. Educ. Res. **33**, 27–45 (2024). https://doi.org/10.1007/s40299-022-00705-x
36. Ourdas, C., Ponis, S.: Evaluating the effects of gamification in behavioural change: a proposed SEM-based approach. Sustain. **15** (2023). https://doi.org/10.3390/su15065442
37. Keller, J.M.: Development and use of the ARCS model of instructional design. J. Instr. Dev. **10**, 2–10 (1987). https://doi.org/10.1007/BF02905780
38. Keller, J.M.: First principles of motivation to learn and e-learning. Distance Educ. **29**, 175–185 (2008). https://doi.org/10.1080/01587910802154970
39. Abbott, D.: Game-based learning for postgraduates: an empirical study of an educational game to teach research skills. High. Educ. Pedagog. **4**, 80–104 (2019). https://doi.org/10.1080/23752696.2019.1629825
40. Hao, K.C., Lee, L.C.: The development and evaluation of an educational game integrating augmented reality, ARCS model, and types of games for English experiment learning: an analysis of learning. Interact. Learn. Environ. **29**, 1101–1114 (2021). https://doi.org/10.1080/10494820.2019.1619590
41. Hamzah, W.M.A.F.W., Ali, N.H., Saman, M.Y.M., Yusoff, M.H., Yacob, A.: Influence of gamification on students' motivation in using e-learning applications based on the motivational design model. Int. J. Emerg. Technol. Learn. **10**, 30–34 (2015). https://doi.org/10.3991/IJET.V10I2.4355
42. Baah, C., Govender, I., Subramaniam, P.R.: Exploring the role of gamification in motivating students to learn. Cogent Educ. **10** (2023). https://doi.org/10.1080/2331186X.2023.2210045
43. Koivisto, J., Hamari, J.: The rise of motivational information systems: a review of gamification research. Int. J. Inf. Manag. **45**, 191–210 (2019). https://doi.org/10.1016/j.ijinfomgt.2018.10.013
44. Liu, D., Santhanam, R., Webster, J.: Toward meaningful engagement: a framework for design and research of gamified information systems. MIS Q. **41**, 1011–1034 (2017). https://doi.org/10.1007/s13398-014-0173-7.2
45. Zhoc, K.C.H., Webster, B.J., King, R.B., Li, J.C.H., Chung, T.S.H.: Higher education student engagement scale (HESES): development and psychometric evidence. Res. High. Educ. **60**, 219–244 (2019). https://doi.org/10.1007/s11162-018-9510-6
46. Huang, B., Hew, K.F.: Implementing a theory-driven gamification model in higher education flipped courses: effects on out-of-class activity completion and quality of artifacts. Comput. Educ. **125**, 254–272 (2018). https://doi.org/10.1016/j.compedu.2018.06.018
47. Gil-Doménech, D., Berbegal-Mirabent, J.: Stimulating students' engagement in mathematics courses in non-STEM academic programmes: a game-based learning. Innov. Educ. Teach. Int. **56**, 57–65 (2019). https://doi.org/10.1080/14703297.2017.1330159
48. Lin, Y., Wang, H.: Applying augmented reality in a university English class: learners' perceptions of creativity and learning motivation. Innov. Lang. Learn. Teach. **17**, 291–305 (2023). https://doi.org/10.1080/17501229.2022.2040513
49. Nel, G., Nel, L.: Motivational value of code.org's code studio tutorials in an undergraduate programming course. Commun. Comput. Inf. Sci. **963**, 173–188 (2019)

50. Velaora, C., Dimos, I., Tsagiopoulou, S., Kakarountas, A.: A game-based learning approach in digital design course to enhance students' competency. Inf. **13**, 1–25 (2022). https://doi.org/10.3390/info13040177
51. Ozdamli, F.: ARCS motivation model adapted to gamification applications on a programming language course. Int. J. Learn. Technol. **13**, 327–351 (2018). https://doi.org/10.1504/IJLT.2018.098502
52. Ho, J.C.S., Hung, Y.S., Kwan, L.Y.Y.: The impact of peer competition and collaboration on gamified learning performance in educational settings: a meta-analytical study. Educ. Inf. Technol. **27**, 3833–3866 (2022). https://doi.org/10.1007/s10639-021-10770-2
53. Deci, E.L., Ryan, R.M.: The "what" and "why" of goal pursuits: human needs and the self-determination of behavior. Psychol. Inq. **11**, 227–268 (2000)
54. Kim, Y.H., Kim, D.J., Wachter, K.: Smartphones: user engagement motivations effect on their value, satisfaction, and future engagement intention. In: 18th Americas Conference on Information Systems 2012, AMCIS 2012, vol. 6, pp. 4386–4395 (2012)
55. Hamzah, W.M.A.F.W., Ali, N., Saman, M.Y.M., Yusoff, M.H.: Enhancement of the ARCS model for gamification of learning. In: 2014 3rd International Conference on User Science and Engineering (i-USEr), pp. 287–291 (2014). https://doi.org/10.1109/IUSER.2014.7002718
56. Chen, J., Liang, M.: Play hard, study hard? The influence of gamification on students' study engagement. Front. Psychol. **13** (2022). https://doi.org/10.3389/fpsyg.2022.994700
57. Lopez-Garrido, G.: Bandura's self-efficacy theory of motivation in psychology. https://www.simplypsychology.org/self-efficacy.html. Accessed 09 Apr 2024
58. Linnenbrink, E.A., Pintrich, P.R.: The role of self-efficacy beliefs in student engagement and learning in the classroom. Read. Writ. Q. **19**, 119–137 (2003). https://doi.org/10.1080/10573560308223
59. Rajabalee, Y.B., Santally, M.I.: Learner satisfaction, engagement and performances in an online module: implications for institutional e-learning policy. Educ. Inf. Technol. **26**, 2623–2656 (2021). https://doi.org/10.1007/s10639-020-10375-1
60. Fu, F., Su, R., Yu, S.: EGameFlow: a scale to measure learners' enjoyment of e-learning games. Comput. Educ. **52**, 101–112 (2009). https://doi.org/10.1016/j.compedu.2008.07.004
61. Wirani, Y., Nabarian, T., Romadhon, M.S.: Evaluation of continued use on Kahoot! As a gamification-based learning platform from the perspective of Indonesia students. Procedia Comput. Sci. **197**, 545–556 (2021). https://doi.org/10.1016/j.procs.2021.12.172
62. Loorbach, N., Peters, O., Karreman, J., Steehouder, M.: Validation of the Instructional Materials Motivation Survey (IMMS) in a self-directed instructional setting aimed at working with technology. Br. J. Educ. Technol. **46**, 204–218 (2015). https://doi.org/10.1111/bjet.12138
63. Keller, J.M.: Tools to support motivational design. In: Motivational Design for Learning and Performance, pp. 267–295. Springer, Boston, MA (2010). https://doi.org/10.1007/978-1-4419-1250-3
64. Hair, J.F., Hult, G.T.M., Ringle, C., Sarstedt, M., Danks, N., Ray, S.: Partial Least Squares Structural Equation Modeling (PLS-SEM) Using R: A Workbook. Springer, Cham (2021). https://doi.org/10.1007/978-3-030-80519-7
65. Tabachnick, B.G., Fidell, L.S.: Using Multivariate Statistics. Pearson, New York (2019). https://doi.org/10.4324/9781315181158-21
66. Chin, W.W.: The partial least squares approach to structural equation modelling. In: Marcoulides, G.A. (ed.) Modern Methods for Business Research, pp. 295–336. Lawrence Erlbaum Associates, Mahwah, NJ (1998)
67. Orji, R., Reilly, D., Oyibo, K., Orji, F.A.: Deconstructing persuasiveness of strategies in behaviour change systems using the ARCS model of motivation. Behav. Inf. Technol. **38**, 319–335 (2019). https://doi.org/10.1080/0144929X.2018.1520302
68. Sailer, M., Homner, L.: The gamification of learning: a meta-analysis. Educ. Psychol. Rev. **32**, 77–112 (2020). https://doi.org/10.1007/s10648-019-09498-w

Quintuple Helix, the Informal Economy and Sustainable-Smart Innovations: Lessons to Be Learned from a Transdisciplinary Student Project

Carolien van den Berg[1(✉)] and Belinda Verster[2]

[1] Information Systems Department, University of the Western Cape, Cape Town, South Africa
cvandenberg@uwc.ac.za

[2] Department of Town and Regional Planning, Cape Peninsula University of Technology, Cape Town, South Africa
versterb@cput.ac.za

Abstract. This paper explores how the informal economy can act as a catalyst for sustainability and digital innovation through student-led interventions in marginalised communities. Drawing on a transdisciplinary project situated in the informal settlement of Dunoon, Cape Town, we apply the Quintuple Helix (QH) framework to examine how collaborative innovation unfolds across academia, government, industry, civil society, and the natural environment. The study investigates how student teams co-designed context-specific digital solutions in partnership with community and institutional actors. Our research is guided by the question: What insights does the QH framework offer for guiding transdisciplinary student projects focused on the informal economy? Using thematic analysis of student artefacts, reflections, stakeholder feedback, and researcher observations, we evaluate how knowledge co-creation contributes to sustainable-smart innovation. Findings highlight the importance of community engagement, inter-institutional collaboration, and sustainability-oriented design, while also identifying challenges such as limited industry involvement and scalability.

Keywords: Information Systems Education · Informal Economy · Digital Innovation · Quintuple Helix · Design Thinking · Innovation-Based Learning

1 Introduction

This paper presents findings from a transdisciplinary student project that investigated how digital interventions can address sustainability challenges within the informal economy of Dunoon, a marginalised settlement in Cape Town, South Africa. The informal economy has often been regarded as a challenge to urban planning and economic regulation, yet it plays a critical role in mitigating poverty and unemployment, especially in contexts marked by high youth unemployment and inadequate service delivery [1–3]. Rather than viewing informality as a deficit to be formalised, this paper adopts a

L. Nel et al. (Eds.): SACLA 2025, CCIS 2770, pp. 102–118, 2026.
https://doi.org/10.1007/978-3-032-12457-9_7

more inclusive perspective, recognising it as an adaptive and innovative system. In this context, student teams from three universities worked with community members to co-design sustainable-smart innovations. These digital solutions aimed to address locally relevant issues such as waste management, informal trade logistics, and skills development. The project was explicitly aligned with several Sustainable Development Goals (SDGs), notably SDG 1 (No Poverty), SDG 8 (Decent Work and Economic Growth), SDG 10 (Reduced Inequalities), and SDG 11 (Sustainable Cities and Communities).

To analyse the dynamics of collaboration within this complex environment, we apply the Quintuple Helix (QH) framework [4]. As an evolution of the Triple and Quadruple Helix models [5, 6], QH integrates five stakeholder systems: academia, industry, government, civil society, and the natural environment. It is particularly well-suited for sustainability-focused innovation because it explicitly includes environmental and social dimensions as drivers of knowledge creation and transformation.

The study is guided by the question: What insights does the QH framework offer for guiding transdisciplinary student projects focused on the informal economy? Through thematic analysis of student artefacts, reflective journals, partner feedback, and researcher observations, we examine how QH-informed collaboration contributes to context-sensitive, inclusive innovation. By embedding sustainability principles and digital co-creation into an educational setting, this work offers a practical model for engaging higher education in addressing real-world challenges in marginalised communities.

The paper is organised as follows: a theoretical overview of the literature to position the QH framework, followed by a discussion on the importance and challenges of the informal economy and the concepts embedded in the learning environment. The next section provides background on the student project, followed by the research methodology and the discussion and findings from the analysis of the QH framework.

2 Quintuple Helix Framework

The Quintuple Helix (QH) framework [4] represents an evolution of the innovation system frameworks that preceded it, namely the Triple Helix [5] and the Quadruple Helix [6]. This development was necessitated by the increasing complexity of innovation processes in the 21st century, where traditional models proved insufficient to capture the multifaceted dynamics of knowledge production and societal needs [7].

The original Triple Helix model identified three key actors, Academia (Universities), Industry, and Government, whose interplay fosters innovation. While effective, this model did not account for the growing role of broader societal participation in knowledge creation. The introduction of a fourth helix, Civil Society, recognised that end-users and communities influence technological development through their demand and participation [4]. This inclusion emphasised that knowledge generation and innovation are not exclusive to institutional actors but are co-produced with societal stakeholders. Building on this foundation, the QH further incorporated the Environment as a fifth dimension [4] to present an analytical framework where knowledge and innovation are connected with the environment.

As argued by Carayannis and Campbell [8] "The Quintuple Helix innovation system optimises societies and economies by fostering smart, sustainable, inclusive, and resilient development through cyber-physical ecosystems aligned with Industry 5.0 and Society 5.0".

Sustainability concerns have become critical in innovation discourse, requiring an integrated model that considers ecological impacts alongside economic and technological advancements [9, 10]. This addition ensures that innovation systems are aligned with long-term sustainable development goals by balancing technological progress with environmental responsibility. By adding these two helices of civil society and the natural environment, a comprehensive lens for analysing complex socioeconomic systems is provided [7]. This is of particular value when working in informal settlements, which are one of the most complex urban phenomena of our time.

The application of the QH framework as an analytical framework for reviewing the outcome of student projects during the fourth iteration in 2024 has the benefit of including a transdisciplinary focus to integrate different perspectives. It can be applied as a framework for understanding the complex relationships and interactions between various partners involved in innovation processes. It furthermore supports the concepts that we incorporate in our learning environment, such as Society 5.0, as it relates to the digital social innovations generated by student teams, as well as the inclusion of local lived knowledge within collaborative partnerships. It can also help to identify gaps or areas where collaboration or intervention may be needed to achieve the desired outcomes.

3 The Informal Economy: Its Importance and Challenges in South Africa

The informal economy plays a significant role in South Africa's broader economic landscape by generating employment opportunities and contributing to economic growth [11]. According to Musara and Nieuwenhuizen [12], South Africa's informal sector employs over 3.2 million individuals, accounting for approximately 19% of the country's total workforce. Despite these substantial contributions, the informal economy remains largely untapped in terms of policy support and investment, which limits its potential to address socio-economic challenges such as poverty and unemployment. To enhance its impact, greater efforts are required to integrate alternative resources, such as digital technologies, to foster growth and sustainability within the informal sector [13].

Despite its importance, the informal economy in South Africa faces numerous challenges that hinder its growth and integration into the broader economy. Key barriers include inadequate social protection, poor infrastructure, ineffective government policies, and restricted access to credit [11]. Additional challenges include low capitalisation, limited technology adoption, and insufficient support structures for informal enterprises. Daramola and Etim [14] further emphasise the barriers of inadequate digital skills, unreliable government support, high electricity costs, expensive internet access, and various health and safety concerns.

As mentioned above, integrating information and communication technologies (ICTs) also presents challenges for the informal economy, such as low adoption rates, lack of customised ICT solutions, and unequal access to digital resources [15]. These findings suggest that addressing digital and ICT adoption challenges is crucial for enhancing the productivity and sustainability of the informal sector. Overcoming these barriers requires targeted policies that recognise the informal economy as a legitimate sector, investment in digital literacy, and the provision of affordable technological solutions tailored to the needs of the informal sector.

Digital technologies have emerged as transformative tools for economic growth, particularly within the informal sector, such as e-commerce, financial services, supply chain management and efficiency [16–18]. Despite these opportunities, it also raises new risks in the form of digital exclusion or adverse incorporation [19]. Furthermore, the adoption of digital technologies within the informal economy remains limited, necessitating further research to explore the impact and implications of technology on informal enterprises [20].

4 Inclusive Design Through Sustainable-Smart Innovation

Our learning environment is informed by several key concepts that are critical for addressing contemporary challenges and fostering sustainable development. These concepts serve as guiding principles in the student projects to infuse inter- and transdisciplinary collaboration, societal engagement, and ethical considerations in higher education and beyond. The key focus is on sustainable-smart innovations, particularly in marginalised settings, where digital sustainability intertwines with inclusive innovation. Figure 1 provides an overview of the concepts that we apply.

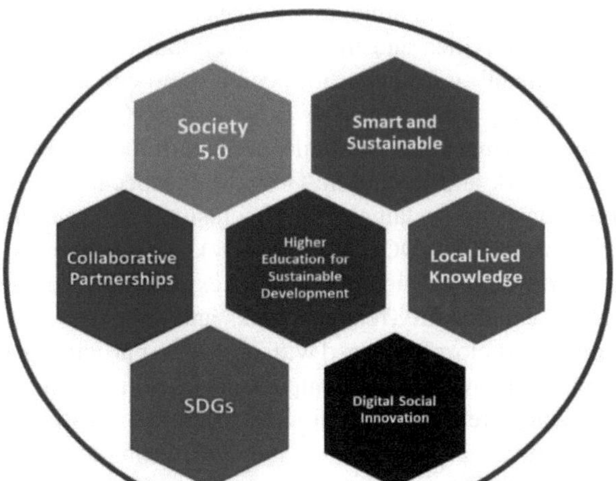

Fig. 1. Key Concepts for Inclusive Design Through Sustainable-Smart Innovation

Sustainable-smart innovations in this project are co-created through the collaboration of academia, industry, government, and communities to develop technology-enabled solutions that respond to real-world challenges. Our use of the term sustainable-smart innovation aligns with broader digital transformation goals, yet it is grounded explicitly in the socio-material realities of informal economies. This framing deliberately departs from more technologically deterministic models by centring community co-creation, the value of local knowledge, and ecological responsibility as foundational design principles. This approach resonates with the concept of Digital Social Innovation (DSI) as articulated by Serpa and Ferreira [21], which highlights the convergence of technological advancement, social needs, and inclusive innovation ecosystems. Rather than positioning technology as the sole driver of change, the emphasis is placed on collaborative processes that involve diverse stakeholders in shaping equitable and context-sensitive solutions. In doing so, sustainable-smart innovation becomes not only a means of technological progress but a pathway toward building more just, resilient, and inclusive societies.

Society 5.0 envisions an inclusive, technology-driven society that enhances social well-being and quality of life. It moves beyond economic competitiveness to emphasise co-created knowledge within public-private partnerships [7, 22]. Though relatively new in Africa, its principles of leveraging technology for social good, inclusivity, and sustainable development align with local challenges. This framework helps students critically engage with sustainability, resilience, and the agility needed for rapid socio-technological changes [23, 24].

Sustainable Development Goals (SDGs) provide a framework to consider sustainability both as an objective to be achieved and a method to get there [25]. Sustainability encompasses social development, economic development and environmental protection and within this framing, digital sustainability refers to "the development, deployment, and utilisation of digital resources and artefacts toward improving the environment, society, and economic welfare" [26]. What this highlights is the need to continuously think and act with sustainability in mind, thus not only as an end-of-project achievement but also as a driver of activities and thought. This dual role underscores the importance of tailoring sustainability strategies to specific socio-economic and environmental contexts, thus being highly context-sensitive. Several SDGs provide guidance in our engagement with the informal economy in the context of the specific informal community. SDG 8 (Decent Work and Economic Growth) is especially relevant, with targets 8.1, 8.2, and 8.4 emphasising sustainable and inclusive economic growth, innovation, and the circular economy [27]. SDG 1 (No Poverty), through targets 1.1, 1.4, and 1.5, underscores the importance of eradicating poverty, expanding access to technology, and building resilience to sustainability-related shocks and disasters. SDG 11 (Sustainable Cities and Communities) is closely aligned with our work, particularly target 11.6, which addresses the reduction of environmental impact, an urgent issue in informal economies where waste management remains a significant challenge. Lastly, SDG 10 (Reduced Inequalities), and in particular targets 10.2 and 10.3, promotes the social, economic, and political inclusion of all, and calls for the reduction of inequality through equal opportunity and equitable outcomes [27].

Partnerships: The growing urgency to address the future of our societies and planet requires collaborative partnerships that co-create sustainable solutions whilst enabling the equilibrium between ecological, economic and social concerns. This complex endeavour calls for an inter/transdisciplinary focus to circumvent the narrow lenses of disciplinary boundaries [28]. The application of a QH approach can integrate different perspectives to set the stage for sustainability priorities and considerations.

Local knowledge or local knowing refers to the know-how derived from the day-to-day lived realities of community members and students as members of their community. We recognise the value of local lived knowledge by valuing the intimate understanding that local communities often have of their environment and the challenges they face and that this knowledge should be used to inform and guide sustainable development efforts. We adhere to the following principles for engagement:

- Community knowledge is central to the projects and their associated technological solutions, resulting in unique perspectives and experiences.
- Complex social issues and context-specific environmental and economic challenges often cannot be well understood or resolved by "expert" research.
- Interventions from outside the community often have disappointing results with little uptake. This point is specifically relevant in the South African context with its resource shortages.
- Communities should have equal inclusion and collaboration in the identification, research, and resolution of community issues [29].

Collaborative technology development, reflection, and joint deliberation with respect for local agency and innovation can open new avenues toward responsible and societally oriented knowledge production and ethical technology development. We require solutions that are 'fit for purpose' to ensure alignment within the context of the user, thus striving for more equality and less coloniality in the (digital) society [30].

This study does not treat the informal economy, the student learning environment, and the QH framework as competing lenses, but rather as interdependent components. The informal economy provides a context where sustainability challenges are acute; the student project offers an interventionist platform and the QH framework enables a multi-stakeholder analysis of how innovation is co-produced across sectors. Together, these layers serve to interrogate the potential and limitations of transdisciplinary, sustainability-driven digital innovation.

5 The Student Project

This interdisciplinary student project was launched in 2021 and we are reporting on the fourth iteration that took place in 2024. Each of the previous iterations saw significant changes in the project, such as shifting the focus from numerous communities to a single community and including an international academic partner. Another substantive shift was changing the project theme from generalised community sustainability challenges to focusing solely on the informal economy as a significant contributor to sustainability and a driver for digital innovations.

The iteration in 2024 was rolled out as a Collaborative Online International Learning (COIL) project with student groups from Urban Planning (CPUT), Information Systems (UWC) and a multidisciplinary group of students from the Innovative Studio at Avans University of Applied Sciences (Netherlands).

The one constant throughout the four years was the application of Design Thinking as a method to structure the project in phases, as illustrated in Fig. 2.

The main objective of the student project is to develop community-specific digital innovations for local sustainability challenges.

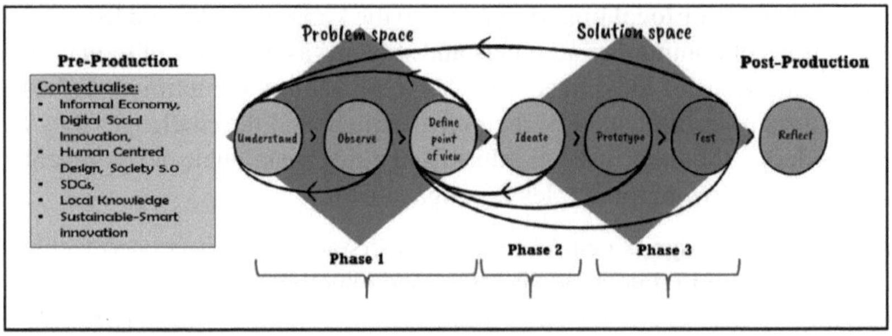

Fig. 2. Project Design Phases and Learning Activities (Adapted from Design Thinking Toolbook)

6 Methodology

The paper presents an analysis of findings from the fourth iteration of a longitudinal Design-Based Research (DBR) study. DBR is a methodological approach where researchers first develop an in-depth understanding of a problem before testing and refining solutions over multiple iterations [31]. This approach is particularly effective in developing both theoretical insights and practical solutions in collaboration with stakeholders within authentic settings.

To explore our research question, the QH framework was applied as an analytical lens, integrating Mode 3 knowledge application, which emphasises innovation networks and knowledge clusters within student projects [8]. For this iteration, we adopted a thematic analysis approach to examine artefacts generated by student teams, including design documentation, reflective journals, group presentations, and fieldwork notes, as well as observational notes from researchers and structured feedback from community and industry partners. Data collection occurred over four months, aligned with the project cycle.

A hybrid coding approach was used, combining inductive and deductive methods. Initially, a set of sensitising concepts drawn from the QH framework and literature was used to guide deductive coding (e.g., community engagement, sustainability, digital innovation). This was complemented by inductive coding to allow emergent themes to surface from student reflections and community feedback. Coding was conducted using ATLAS.ti and intercoder reliability was strengthened through independent coding by two researchers, followed by consensus meetings to resolve discrepancies. To ensure rigour, we triangulated across data types and participant groups, used member checking where feasible, and maintained a clear audit trail. The aim was to explore the contributions of each helix within the collaborative learning process, while identifying patterns of inclusive innovation and sustainability impact. This analysis has helped to identify gaps and develop interventions for future iterations while also contributing theoretical and practical insights.

Participants in the study included 35 BCom IS Honours students, 20 students from the Advanced Diploma in Urban and Regional Planning and 20 students from Avans University. The group project was integral to the overall learning outcomes and was assessed in the academic modules. Ethical approval for the study was obtained from both universities, and permission was granted by students for the inclusion of their reflections and findings in the analysis.

By employing DBR in a longitudinal framework, this study systematically refines design principles and explores sustainable-smart innovations through a transdisciplinary learning approach. The fourth iteration contributes to this ongoing process by incorporating broader stakeholder engagement and leveraging insights to enhance future interventions.

7 Findings and Discussion

Table 1 was used to analyse the data and identify gaps that can be addressed in subsequent iterations of the project.

7.1 Civil Society Helix

The Civil Society Helix in the QH framework emphasises the critical role of active community involvement in shaping project outcomes, assessing social impact, and fostering knowledge exchange among project stakeholders. Meaningful engagement with residents in Dunoon is an essential component to ensure that the proposed solutions address real challenges and promote sustainable-smart innovations aligned with social inclusion and equity.

Active Community Engagement. The effectiveness of the Civil Society Helix hinges on sustained and active community participation. Understanding local lived experiences is central to this initiative, and students conduct interviews and engage with community members to gain firsthand insights into the problems they face. This participatory approach ensures that potential solutions are co-developed rather than externally imposed. The reflections from students illustrate the significance of this engagement:

> *"One of the most valuable aspects of this assignment was the opportunity to conduct interviews and visit the Dunoon township. This interaction with the Dunoon residents allowed us to gather valuable insights and understand the challenges and needs of the community". (SJ)*

This interaction reinforced the importance of co-creation, where the voices and needs of the community guided project development. The project's success underscores the power of community-led initiatives:

> *"The success of this project serves as a testament to the power of community-led initiatives and the importance of engaging with local stakeholders in the development process. By putting the needs and voices of the community at the forefront, we were able to create solutions that are not only effective but also sustainable and empowering". (G2)*

Figure 3 depicts some examples of the student engagement in the community of Dunoon.

Fig. 3. Community Engagement

Prototyping and Knowledge Exchange. Another key measurement of the Civil Society Helix is the impact of potential solutions on addressing real community challenges. As part of the project, student groups developed prototype specifications, ensuring the feasibility of implementing solutions in the community. These prototypes included functional and non-functional requirements, user interface (UI) and user experience (UX) design, system architecture, database structures, security measures, and material selection for hardware components.

To enhance sustainability, the 2025 student cohort will refine these prototypes through further community testing, allowing for iterative improvements. The next phase, scheduled for 2026, will focus on piloting selected solutions within Dunoon. This phased approach ensures that solutions evolve in direct response to community feedback, reinforcing long-term engagement and impact.

Knowledge Exchange and Societal Impact. An essential outcome of this initiative is the reciprocal knowledge exchange between students, community members, and project partners. Student reflections highlight how their understanding of community dynamics evolved through immersive participation:

> *"What stood out was, irrespective of the evident poverty and the lack of basic infrastructure, there is an atmosphere of community spirit and resourcefulness among the residents. We realised that there is an ongoing effort to improve living conditions and access to basic services. We believe that projects such as this will enable us to work towards inclusive and sustainable economic development." (G4)*

While the full impact from the community's perspective is still unfolding, early indications suggest that the quality and relevance of student-led solutions improve each year due to increased community engagement. Students consistently highlight this engagement as one of the most valuable aspects of their learning experience. The iterative nature of this project ensures that both students and community members benefit from an evolving, collaborative, and impactful approach to sustainable development.

7.2 Government Helix

The Government Helix within the QH framework underscores the role of government in enabling, supporting, and sustaining projects that drive socio-economic and environmental transformation. In this initiative, collaboration with local government has been instrumental in shaping student projects, aligning them with municipal policy objectives, and ensuring their long-term relevance.

Alignment with Local Policy. Since the 2023 project iteration, local officials have actively contributed through guest lectures, site visits, and student feedback. This collaboration formed part of the Cape Higher Education Consortium – City of Cape Town Annual Research Programme, which funded the initial iteration and supported the dissemination of student work through the City's Urban Planning and Design Department. Dunoon, identified as a priority intervention area, presents complex socio-economic and environmental challenges. Due to resource constraints, the City relies on external academic contributions, as echoed by a local government representative:

> *"Dunoon is a priority area...But because the City cannot prioritise it all at the same time, it is very important to make use of external assistance...We therefore fully support and appreciate the work that the students and their lecturers do in this area through the academic institutions' programmes". (LK CoCT, 2024)*

The City also provided strategic policy documents, including the Municipal Spatial Development Framework and Environmental Strategy, enabling students to anchor their work within a broader planning framework.

Funding and Institutional Support. Financial support through the Consortium further demonstrated the City's investment in higher education partnerships. The project aligns with local development goals such as "Resilience for Inclusive Development, Infrastructure and Sustainability, and Citizenship and Democracy", focusing on innovation, environmental justice, and community voice. However, to sustain the initiative beyond early-stage funding, deeper integration into municipal processes is needed. Embedding student-developed solutions into planning mechanisms and enabling pilot implementations would help realise their long-term value.

Long-Term Viability and Challenges. While the project has benefited from City support, its long-term viability will depend on deeper collaboration, such as integrating student solutions into municipal planning processes and facilitating pilot implementations. One major challenge in government-community collaboration is the power imbalance between local government and civil society, often shaped by political influences. This dynamic, exacerbated by South Africa's apartheid legacy, has created mistrust among community members, making engagement efforts more complex. As noted in student reflections, access to community members willing to participate in the project was at times difficult.

> *"On-site, we sometimes experienced challenges in gaining access to community members...due to political influences that create mistrust between the community and outsiders". (G5)*

To address this, the project engages trusted community champions (e.g. NGOs) who facilitate communication and foster inclusion. Students also critically explored broader governance questions, especially around the informal economy's role in cities like Dunoon. Their reflections raised key provocations: How can formality be introduced without compromising flexibility? Who advocates for informal workers, and how can collaboration foster meaningful change?

These questions underscore the need for inclusive governance that supports grassroots entrepreneurship rather than stifling it. Informality should be recognised as an adaptive solution to gaps in state capacity. Municipal frameworks must accommodate this by offering flexible permits, integrated planning, and regulatory environments that protect informal livelihoods.

Sustained collaboration between local government, academia, and communities will be vital in translating student innovations into actionable solutions that advance inclusive urban development.

Moving forward, continued engagement with municipal structures and expanded government collaboration will be critical in translating academic work into actionable urban solutions that benefit both the local government and the communities they serve.

7.3 Industry Helix

While this project has successfully engaged governmental actors and community stakeholders, industry participation has been limited. The current economic climate and negative forecast in South Africa resulted in a lack of appetite from industry partners to venture into the risky student innovation space. The limited active industry involvement constrains the potential for sustainable-smart innovations to be commercialised, scaled, and integrated into existing economic structures. Industry engagement within the helix framework is essential for achieving practical relevance and co-creation to ensure that the innovations are aligned with real-world economic and technological needs. Furthermore, industry involvement can enhance the potential for solutions to be commercialised and sustained beyond the project lifecycle and provide students with professional skills, increasing their employability and entrepreneurial potential.

Currently, industry engagement in the project is limited and primarily takes the form of advisory contributions, such as guest lectures, feedback on student projects, and occasional input from local entrepreneurs based in the target community. Several barriers hinder more active and sustained involvement. These include limited recognition of the commercial potential of student-driven innovations, concerns about the risks of engaging in politically sensitive and informal economic contexts, and the absence of structured mechanisms to support long-term industry collaboration. At present, industry engagement is largely confined to advisory roles, such as guest lectures, project reviews by industry representatives and participation from local entrepreneurs operating within the project's geographical focus. The barriers to deeper engagement include limited awareness of the commercial viability of student-led innovations. The risks are roles than others associated with engagement in politically complex and informal economic settings, and a lack of structured engagement mechanisms to facilitate sustained industry participation.

The absence of robust industry engagement represents a gap in the project's holistic impact, necessitating a structured approach to industry collaboration. Integrating the Industry Helix into the project's existing framework is essential to ensure the long-term sustainability and impact of student-led innovations. By shifting from passive advisory roles to active co-creation and implementation, industry stakeholders can contribute meaningfully to inclusive economic development. The inclusion of a co-creation workshop with selected partners from industry is planned for the 2025 iteration. Project partners are also in discussion with venture capitalists to explore the commercialisation of selected solutions and consider options for developing the prototypes to a stage closer to commercialisation, with the assistance of the Technology Transfer Office at one of the universities.

7.4 Academic Helix

This helix emphasises the importance of academic research and knowledge transfer in driving innovation. In the review of the Academic Helix evidence of the learning outcomes, student engagement and research and innovation are presented to determine the strengths and current limitations.

The overarching learning objective was to equip students with valuable skills, knowledge, and mindset shifts to address complex community challenges, navigate uncertainty, and contribute to sustainable development through digital social innovations. The design of the project featured six learning outcomes:

- Interdisciplinary Collaboration: As discussed, the students worked in diverse teams to leverage multidisciplinary expertise. The outcome of their collaboration and learning was assessed through team meeting records, reflection questionnaires, blogs, and peer assessments.
- Embedding sustainability in the design and interpreting the complexity of wicked problems within the informal sector. Their understanding of complexity was evaluated through literature reviews, site visit videos, and project presentations to partners.
- Creative Thinking and Problem-Solving: Using design thinking and human-centred design approaches, students demonstrated empathy and incorporated community perspectives into problem definition and solution development. This was measured through project documentation, prototype testing, decision matrices, and reflective questionnaires. The design of the final prototypes was also scrutinised to ensure that students understood the users and their unique requirements.
- Developing Digital and Technological Skills: Students utilised various digital tools and technologies throughout the project, including prototype development. Their proficiency was assessed based on the quality of outputs in each project phase.
- Practical Application of Interdisciplinary Knowledge: Students translated theoretical concepts into practical, contextually relevant solutions with tangible social impact. The quality and relevance of prototypes served as a key measure of success.
- Reflective and Ethical Practices: Students demonstrated a commitment to social and environmental justice principles. Ethical practices were evaluated through project presentations and adherence to a Team Code of Conduct document.

The lecturers from the three universities reviewed the outcomes and found that the collaboration successfully enhanced the educational experience for students from all participating universities. Participants reported high levels of satisfaction with the shared resources and expertise, the quality and diversity of educational materials and tools and the exchange of knowledge and best practices, fostering a culture of continuous improvement.

The focus of our review was more on the limitations identified to improve future iterations. Limitations included aspects such as the challenges in reconciling conflicting disciplinary approaches, leading to delays in decision-making. The imbalances in contribution, with some students taking on more leadership roles than others. The cultural and language barriers within diverse teams occasionally hinder effective communication. We also identified that some groups struggled to fully grasp the interconnectedness of sustainability challenges, leading to oversimplified solutions. Some prototypes also lacked feasibility due to resource constraints or limited understanding of the community's technical capabilities. A few groups struggled to balance creativity with practicality, resulting in solutions that were innovative but not implementable. Some of the solutions were overly reliant on technology, neglecting low-tech alternatives that might have been more appropriate.

Research and Innovation. The results from the projects have been published in journal publications and conference proceedings by the researchers, including publications with students. These outputs are contributing to knowledge on the impact of inter and transdisciplinary projects situated in marginalised settings that apply concepts such as digital social innovation, SDGs, local knowledge and collaborative partnerships. It has also contributed to collaboration with other institutions and researchers working in similar settings. However, the outputs are still largely academic and more collaboration between academia, industry, and community stakeholders is required to bridge the gap between research and implementation. We are currently working on actions to deepen community involvement through more targeted workshops with partners in the informal economy and securing funding for pilot projects. Some of the solutions developed are being tested further in the community at present, as illustrated in Fig. 4.

7.5 Natural Environment Helix

The fifth helix of the QH framework focuses on bringing knowledge from the natural environment into innovation projects. This helix is the most vulnerable of the helices and requires special care [32]. This helix represents ecological actors that typically serve as resource bases for both production and daily survival. In this project, nature was centralised by framing the community challenges in the context of sustainability. The challenge that was put to student groups was to translate the global SDGs into actionable, locally relevant objectives applicable to their specific project theme.

Because of the complex nature of the natural environment within not only urban settings but especially informal settings, student groups had to be guided by both global and local sustainability frameworks. The SDGs with their associated targets were prominent in this project, with students tasked with relating primary and secondary SDGs to

Fig. 4. Prototypes being tested further with community partners

their specific informal economy challenge at both the problem exploration and solution development stages.

By focusing on the SDGs, students were made aware of their role as custodians of the natural environment and that this responsibility will become ever more important as pressure increases on natural resources such as clean, fresh water, quality food and breathable air. All of these life-supporting elements are directly impacted by human activity in general and specifically by economic activities.

As mentioned above, economic activities have harmed life-supporting environmental systems primarily through unsustainable practices that deplete resources and increase pollutants [33]. At a local scale, the same can be said about the informal economy that is characterised by excessive litter, dumping of excess products and the associated human health threats [34]. The lack of sufficient waste management practices was a major concern for student groups, as many focused their attention on developing a response to this challenge. Sustainable-smart innovations such as a water drone to clean debris from the informal traders that end up in the local river, recycling and upcycling apps and sensors to monitor the closest communal waste dumpster and alert the local authorities when it should be emptied, are some responsive solutions (Fig. 5).

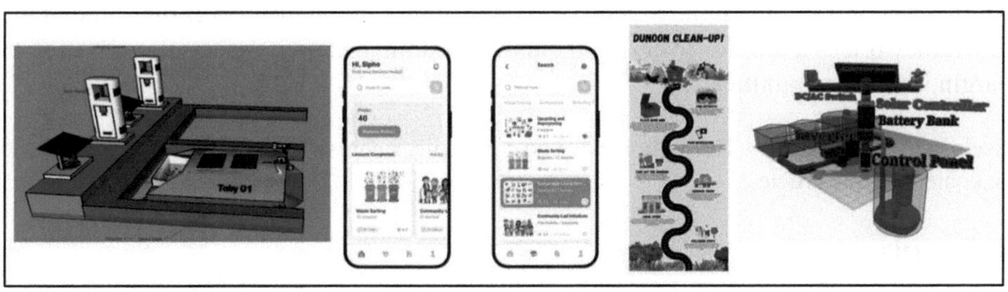

Fig. 5. Water drone and low-data recycling/upcycling application.

A further concern that both community members and student groups recognised was the resource usage in the community. Resource optimisation strategies were found to be limited but did exist in the form of recycling and repurposing initiatives such as the retreading of used tyres and the reselling of second-hand clothing. Unfortunately, very few creative recycling outputs were found and there might be a potential for upskilling community members in culturally-appropriate arts and crafts for the tourist markets.

By embedding the sustainability principles within every aspect of this student project, we sensitised students, as future leaders, to concepts such as the SDGs, sustainable-smart cities and Society 5.0. Further, as the environment is usually the most vulnerable stakeholder in the QH, the solutions that groups co-developed had to illustrate both the short-term and long-term environmental footprint.

In future project iterations, this helix will continue to be prominent in the interdisciplinary student project as it provides an opportunity to consider the natural environment not only as a provider (resources) and receiver (pollutants) of human activities but also as an active contributor to new knowledge which is desperately needed in the current ecological instability we are experiencing.

8 Conclusion

This paper has demonstrated the potential of the QH framework to guide transdisciplinary student projects in addressing complex sustainability challenges within the informal economy. By integrating academia, industry, government, civil society, and the natural environment, the project in Dunoon, Cape Town, has highlighted the importance of collaborative knowledge co-creation in fostering sustainable-smart innovations. The findings reveal that active community engagement, interdisciplinary collaboration, and alignment with sustainability principles are critical to developing contextually relevant solutions to real-world challenges. However, the study also identifies key limitations, such as the lack of robust industry involvement and the challenges of translating prototypes into implemented solutions.

To enhance the impact of such initiatives, future iterations should focus on deepening partnerships with industry stakeholders, securing funding for pilot projects, and fostering long-term community engagement. Additionally, greater emphasis should be placed on scaling and commercialising student-led innovations to ensure their sustainability beyond the academic context. By addressing these gaps, transdisciplinary projects can play a transformative role in empowering informal economy actors, driving digital innovation, and contributing to the SDGs. Ultimately, this study underscores the value of the QH framework as a tool for fostering inclusive, sustainable, and impactful innovation in marginalised communities.

Disclosure of Interests. The authors have no competing interests to declare that are relevant to the content of this article.

References

1. Etim, E., Daramola, O.: The informal sector and economic growth of South Africa and Nigeria: a comparative systematic review. J. Open Innov. Technol. Mark. Complex. **6**(4), 1–26 (2020). https://doi.org/10.3390/joitmc6040134

2. Smit, S.: Connecting the urban informal settlement to the city: a systems approach. Ph.D. dissertation, Stellenbosch (2019). https://doi.org/10.32964/tj18.4
3. Mkulisi, S.N., Susuman, A.S.: Examining the influence of socio-economic and demographic transformation on employment in the informal sector from 2017 to 2020. J. Asian Afr. Stud. (2024). https://doi.org/10.1177/00219096241296125
4. Carayannis, E.G., Campbell, D.F.J.: Triple helix, quadruple helix and quintuple helix and how do knowledge, innovation and the environment relate to each other? A proposed framework for a trans-disciplinary analysis of sustainable development and social ecology. Int. J. Soc. Ecol. Sustain. Dev. **1**(1), 41–69 (2010). https://doi.org/10.4018/jsesd.2010010105
5. Etzkowitz, H., Leydesdorff, L.: The dynamics of innovation: from national systems and 'mode 2' to a triple helix of university–industry–government relations. Res. Policy **29**(2), 109–123 (2000). https://doi.org/10.1016/S0048-7333(99)00055-4
6. Carayannis, E.G., Campbell, D.F.J.: 'Mode 3' and 'quadruple helix': toward a 21st century fractal innovation ecosystem. Int. J. Technol. Manag. **46**(3–4), 201–234 (2009). https://doi.org/10.1504/ijtm.2009.023374
7. Bartoloni, S., et al.: Towards designing Society 5.0 solutions: the new quintuple helix – design thinking approach to technology. Technovation **113**, 102413 (2022). https://doi.org/10.1016/j.technovation.2021.102413
8. Carayannis, E.G., Campbell, D.F.J.: Towards an emerging unified theory of helix architectures (EUTOHA): focus on the quintuple innovation helix framework as the integrative device. Triple Helix **6**(3), 1–11 (2022). https://doi.org/10.1163/21971927-bja10028
9. Pappas, I.O., Mikalef, P., Dwivedi, Y.K., Jaccheri, L., Krogstie, J.: Responsible digital transformation for a sustainable society. Inf. Syst. Front. **25**(3), 945–953 (2023). https://doi.org/10.1007/s10796-023-10406-5
10. Carayannis, E.G., Barth, T.D., Campbell, D.F.: The quintuple helix innovation model: global warming as a challenge and driver for innovation. J. Innov. Entrep. **1**(1), 2 (2012). https://doi.org/10.1186/2192-5372-1-2
11. Petersen, L.M., Charman, A.J.E.: The scope and scale of the informal food economy of South African urban residential townships: results of a small-area micro-enterprise census. Dev. South. Afr. **35**(1), 1–23 (2018). https://doi.org/10.1080/0376835X.2017.1363643
12. Musara, M., Nieuwenhuizen, C.: Informal sector entrepreneurship, individual entrepreneurial orientation and the emergence of entrepreneurial leadership. Afr. J. Manag. **6**(2), 194–213 (2020). https://doi.org/10.1080/23322373.2020.1777817
13. Ebrahim, A.Q., van den Berg, C.L.: The barriers to technology adoption among businesses in the informal economy in Cape Town. S. Afr. J. Inf. Manag. **26**(1), 1–13 (2024). https://doi.org/10.4102/sajim.v26i1.1872
14. Daramola, O., Etim, E.: Affordances of digital platforms in sub-Saharan Africa: an analytical review. Electron. J. Inf. Syst. Dev. Ctries. **88**(4), 1–21 (2022). https://doi.org/10.1002/isd2.12213
15. Mramba, N., Rumanyika, J., Apiola, M., Suhonen, J.: ICT for informal workers in sub-Saharan Africa: systematic review and analysis. In: 2017 IEEE AFRICON: Science, Technology and Innovation for Africa (AFRICON 2017), pp. 486–491. IEEE (2017). https://doi.org/10.1109/AFRCON.2017.8095530
16. Nguimkeu, P., Okou, C.: A tale of Africa today: balancing the lives and livelihoods of informal workers during the COVID-19 pandemic. World Bank Rep. **1**, 1–8 (2020). https://doi.org/10.1596/34582
17. Sousa, M.J., Rocha, Á.: Digital learning: developing skills for digital transformation of organizations. Future Gener. Comput. Syst. **91**, 327–334 (2019). https://doi.org/10.1016/j.future.2018.08.048
18. Girollet, D.: Digital inclusion and performance of informal firms in sub-Saharan Africa. Doctoral thesis, Université de Bordeaux (2023)

19. Heeks, R.: Digital inequality beyond the digital divide: conceptualizing adverse digital incorporation in the global South. Inf. Technol. Dev. **28**(4), 688–704 (2022). https://doi.org/10.1080/02681102.2022.2068492
20. Chen, M.A.: Technology, informal workers and cities: insights from Ahmedabad (India), Durban (South Africa) and Lima (Peru). Environ. Urban. **28**(2), 405–422 (2016). https://doi.org/10.1177/0956247816655986
21. Serpa, S., Ferreira, C.M.: Society 5.0 and sustainability digital innovations: a social process. J. Organ. Cult. Commun. Confl. **23**(1), 1–14 (2019)
22. Fukuyama, B.M.: Society 5.0: aiming for a new human-centered society. Japan Spotlight **27**(5), 47–50 (2018)
23. Mishra, P., Thakur, P., Singh, G.: Sustainable smart city to Society 5.0: state-of-the-art and research challenges. S. Afr. Inst. Electr. Eng. J. **113**(4), 152–164 (2022)
24. Rosak-Szyrocka, J., Apostu, S.A., Turi, J.A., Tanveer, A.: University 4.0 sustainable development in the way of Society 5.0. Sustainability **14**(23), 1–17 (2022). https://doi.org/10.3390/su142316043
25. Leal Filho, W., et al.: A framework for the implementation of the Sustainable Development Goals in university programmes. J. Clean. Prod. **299**, 126915 (2021). https://doi.org/10.1016/j.jclepro.2021.126915
26. Kotlarsky, J., Oshri, I., Sekulic, N.: Digital sustainability in information systems research: conceptual foundations and future directions. J. Assoc. Inf. Syst. **24**(4), 936–952 (2023). https://doi.org/10.17705/1jais.00825
27. United Nations Development Programme: The SDGs in action (2025). https://www.undp.org/sustainable-development-goals. Accessed 13 Feb 2025
28. Horn, A., Scheffelaar, A., Urias, E., Zweekhorst, M.B.M.: Training students for complex sustainability issues: a literature review on the design of inter- and transdisciplinary higher education. Int. J. Sustain. High. Educ. **24**(1), 1–27 (2023). https://doi.org/10.1108/IJSHE-03-2021-0111
29. Burns, D., Howard, J., Lopez-Franco, E., Shahrokh, T., Wheeler, J.: Work with us: how people and organisations can catalyse sustainable change. IDS Report (2013). https://hdl.handle.net/20.500.12413/13763
30. Kroeze, J.H.: Digital coloniality: an Ubuntu perspective. Scand. J. Inf. Syst. **36**(2), 175–216 (2024)
31. McKenney, S., Reeves, T.C.: Educational design research: portraying, conducting, and enhancing productive scholarship. Med. Educ. **55**(1), 82–92 (2021). https://doi.org/10.1111/medu.14280
32. Donati, L., Stefani, G., Bellandi, M.: The evolutionary emergence of quintuple helix coalitions: a case study of place-based sustainability transition. Triple Helix **3**(3), 1–31 (2023). https://doi.org/10.1163/21971927-12340010
33. Folke, C., et al.: Our future in the Anthropocene biosphere. Ambio **50**(4), 834–869 (2021). https://doi.org/10.1007/s13280-021-01544-8
34. Grangxabe, X.S., et al.: The escalation of informal settlement and the high levels of illegal dumping post-apartheid: systematic review. Challenges **14**(3), 38 (2023). https://doi.org/10.3390/challe14030038

Evaluating AI-Generated C# Code in Computing Education: Implications for Academic Integrity

Adewuyi Adetayo Adegbite(✉) and Eduan Kotzé

Department of Computer Science and Informatics, University of the Free State, Bloemfontein, South Africa
adewuyi.adegbite@aaua.edu.ng, KotzeJE@ufs.ac.za

Abstract. The rapid integration of Generative Artificial Intelligence (GenAI) tools, such as ChatGPT, Blackbox.AI, and Microsoft Copilot, into computing education has transformed how students learn programming languages like C#. These tools enhance learning by offering immediate code generation and support; however, they challenge academic integrity by facilitating potential misuse, such as submitting AI-generated code as original work. This study explores the use of Generative Artificial Intelligence (GenAI) in C# programming courses through four research questions, utilising a mixed-methods approach with 368 questionnaire responses, code examination, and grade comparisons. Results reveal that ease of use drives model preference, with ChatGPT being the most favoured. Generative Artificial Intelligence (GenAI) code exhibits detectable structures, and grading analysis shows it consistently outperforms human-written code, with Blackbox.AI leading, followed by ChatGPT and Microsoft Copilot. However, Generative Artificial Intelligence (GenAI) accessibility poses integrity risks, necessitating robust detection and assessment strategies. This research contributes to computing education by thoroughly examining Generative Artificial Intelligence (GenAI) C# code and proposing practical measures, such as code interviews and process documentation, to balance Generative Artificial Intelligence (GenAI) benefits with equitable evaluation, ensuring students develop authentic programming skills. These findings offer actionable insights for educators adapting to AI-driven education landscapes.

Keywords: Generative AI · Academic Integrity · C# Programming · Grading Analysis · Student Perceptions · Computing Education

1 Introduction

The emergence of Generative Artificial Intelligence (GenAI) tools, such as ChatGPT, Microsoft Copilot, Gemini, Blackbox.AI, Codex and DeepMind's AlphaCode, has profoundly transformed computing education by equipping students

L. Nel et al. (Eds.): SACLA 2025, CCIS 2770, pp. 119–136, 2026.
https://doi.org/10.1007/978-3-032-12457-9_8

with advanced resources for code generation, debugging, and real-time problem-solving [14,17]. These tools enhance learning efficiency, provide immediate feedback, and support novice programmers struggling with syntax, logic, and complex programming concepts [9,25]. In C# programming courses, widely used in education and industry, students can leverage Generative Artificial Intelligence (GenAI) to quickly produce functional code, reducing cognitive load and accelerating their understanding of foundational principles [4]. However, this advancement poses significant challenges to maintaining academic integrity, as the ease of generating AI-assisted code fuels concerns about plagiarism, over-reliance on automated solutions, and misrepresentation of students' true programming capabilities [26,32]. In computing education, where code submissions are critical for assessing learning outcomes, distinguishing between AI-generated and human-written code has become an urgent ethical issue.

The rise of Generative Artificial Intelligence (GenAI) in education mirrors broader trends in artificial intelligence's influence, positioning computing education at the forefront of this shift. These tools allow students to focus on higher-level problem-solving rather than low-level syntax errors, boosting coding efficiency and comprehension [8,17]. Yet, this accessibility introduces ethical dilemmas, including a growing risk of dependency that may weaken independent critical thinking [32]. The sophistication of AI models further complicates efforts to maintain integrity, as tools like Turnitin and MOSS fail to detect AI-generated content, necessitating new evaluation strategies [16,30]. This is especially evident in C# undergraduate programming modules, where assignments double as learning and assessment tools [1]. Universities struggle to adapt assessment frameworks, grappling with questions of authorship, responsibility, and the purpose of programming education [10]. Submitting AI-generated code without understanding its logic bypasses learning, sparking debates about AI's role as a co-learning tool versus its restriction in assessments [6]. Institutions are responding with process-oriented evaluations, AI literacy training, and transparent AI-use policies to balance innovation and integrity [29]. Despite the growing adoption of Generative Artificial Intelligence (GenAI), research on its specific impact on computing education, particularly for C# programming language usage, remains limited [1,3,20,31].

The article is structured as follows. First, a presentation of the research questions and their sub-questions is provided, followed by an overview of previous research related to Artificial Intelligence in computing education and prior studies concerning AI-generated code. The methods followed in the current study are discussed next, after which the results are presented and discussed. The article concludes with final remarks and recommendations for further research.

2 Research Questions

To address the identified gap, this study investigates the following research questions (RQs), with sub-questions (SRQs) added where necessary to clarify the scope:

1. **RQ1:** Why do students prefer one language model over another for generating programming code?
2. **RQ2:** What stylistic, structural, and functional features distinguish AI-generated C# code from human-written code?
3. **RQ3:** Is there a correlation between the grades of AI-generated and human-written code, and what factors influence this correlation?
   - **RQ3a:** Is there a correlation between grades awarded to AI-generated C# code and human-written code?
   - **RQ3b:** What factors influence the strength and direction of this correlation?
4. **RQ4:** How does the use of AI-generated code affect academic integrity in programming courses, and what measures can ensure fair assessment?
   - **RQ4a:** How does the use of AI-generated C# code affect academic integrity in undergraduate programming courses?
   - **RQ4b:** What strategies or measures can promote fair and ethical assessment in the presence of AI-generated code?

3 Related Work

This section discusses prior research on AI-generated code in computing education, identifying key findings, existing methodologies, and research gaps relevant to programming code, grade correlation, and academic integrity.

3.1 AI in Computing Education

AI tools have revolutionised programming education by enabling students to generate working code efficiently, and have been integrated into educational settings, raising debates on their ethical use. Studies indicate that AI can support learning but also enable plagiarism. However, concerns regarding originality, comprehension, and assessment fairness persist [25]. The increasing adoption of AI in education has transformed how students engage with programming. AI-powered tools, such as ChatGPT, Microsoft Copilot, and Blackbox.AI assist learners in writing, debugging, and optimising code [17]. These tools have enhanced efficiency and learning speed, allowing students to grasp programming concepts with minimal effort. However, concerns remain regarding their impact on student engagement and independent problem-solving skills [32].

Benefits and Challenges of AI in Programming Education. AI-driven code generation tools enhance learning efficiency by offering real-time feedback [25] and reducing syntax errors, allowing students to focus on logic and problem-solving [4]. Additionally, they optimise code by generating efficient solutions and suggesting best practices [8]. While AI-generated code enhances learning, it also introduces challenges, such as dependency on AI, which causes over-reliance on AI and may reduce students' ability to write code independently [30]. There are plagiarism risks as AI-generated solutions may be submitted as original work, raising academic integrity concerns [10]. AI-generated code may cause a loss of creativity and also often lacks the problem-solving approaches inherent in human-written solutions [29].

3.2 Student Preferences for AI-Generated Code

Considering the first research question of this study (see RQ1), students' preferences for specific large language models (LLMs) in programming tasks are shaped by factors such as ease of use, accuracy, debugging support, and seamless integration with their workflows. Research shows that ChatGPT is favoured for its conversational interface and ability to explain code, making it particularly appealing to beginners learning C# [15,23]. In contrast, Microsoft Copilot is preferred by students working in integrated development environments (IDEs) like Visual Studio, owing to its real-time code suggestions and compatibility with C# development [24]. Additional studies highlight that accuracy in generating syntactically correct solutions, ease of use via intuitive interfaces, and adaptability to diverse coding styles further influence preferences [6,22,27]. For instance, ChatGPT-4 outperforms earlier models in producing readable, high-quality C# code, reducing debugging time and enhancing learning efficiency [13,23]. However, the literature lacks specific investigations into why students choose particular LLMs for C# over other languages, a gap critical to tailoring educational tools and policies as GenAI becomes ubiquitous in programming courses.

3.3 AI-Generated vs. Human-Written Code

Considering the second research question (see RQ2), distinct stylistic and structural differences between AI-generated and human-written code offer insights into their implications for education. AI-generated code, such as that from ChatGPT or Copilot, typically exhibits uniform indentation, generic variable names, and extensive, well-structured comments, reflecting adherence to standard conventions [4,7,17]. Human-written code, however, displays greater variability, with idiosyncratic problem-solving approaches, context-specific annotations, and diverse logic, reflecting individual understanding [8,18]. By analysing these patterns, machine learning models can detect AI-generated code with up to 85% accuracy [28]. In teaching and learning, these differences are significant. AI-generated C# code often provides functional, optimised solutions but may lack the creativity, optimisation, or contextual depth instructors seek to foster [29]. Key differences between AI-generated and human-written code encompass aspects of syntax, structure, logic diversity, readability, and originality. Few studies, however, explore these features specifically in C# or their direct impact on pedagogical outcomes, leaving a gap in understanding how detection can inform teaching strategies.

3.4 Correlation Between Grades of AI and Human-Written Code

The third research question (see RQ3) focuses on the correlation of grades. Evidence on grade correlations between AI-generated and human-written code is mixed but suggestive. AI-generated code often earns high marks for syntactic correctness, functionality, and adherence to best practices, particularly in straightforward C# assignments [11,17]. However, it may underperform in tasks requiring innovative thinking, optimisation, or complex design decisions, where human-written code excels due to its reflection of deeper understanding [8].

Factors influencing this correlation include task complexity, the specificity of prompts given to AI models, and students' ability to refine AI outputs [17,29]. A simple task might yield similar grades, while a project demanding architectural decisions could favour human efforts. Many existing studies have compared AI-generated and human-written code in terms of correctness, complexity, security flaws, coding standards, and code quality [12]. Despite these preliminary findings, no studies have systematically correlated grades in computing education, isolated factors like rubric design or assignment type, or examined AI-generated marked and human-written code to correlate and focus on grades. This highlights the need for empirical research to ensure fair assessment in the GenAI era.

3.5 Academic Integrity Concerns

The fourth research question (see RQ4) examines how AI-generated code affects academic integrity in programming courses and what measures can ensure fair assessment. Educators face challenges in detecting AI-assisted plagiarism as existing traditional tools like MOSS [21] and Turnitin [19] have limitations in detecting AI-generated code due to the sophisticated, unique outputs of modern LLMs [30]. This necessitates the adoption of improved evaluation strategies [30].

The use of AI-generated code in programming courses, especially C#, poses significant academic integrity challenges. Submitting AI-generated work as one's own is widely viewed as plagiarism, misrepresenting students' abilities and undermining learning goals [10,13]. This issue is especially pronounced in C# courses, where assignments are integral to both learning and evaluation. Proposed mitigation strategies include process-based assessments (e.g., oral code reviews or documented coding processes), AI-detection tools to flag generated content, and transparent AI-use policies requiring disclosure of assistance [2,6,17,23]. Institutions are also integrating AI literacy into curricula to promote ethical usage [32]. While promising, these measures lack empirical validation particularly in C#-specific contexts, highlighting the need for research to develop robust and fair assessment frameworks.

3.6 Motivation for the Study

Drawing from the reviewed literature, this study is conceptually grounded in four core themes: (1) student preferences for GenAI tools, (2) the stylistic and structural differences between AI-generated and human-written code, (3) grade correlations and grading fairness, and (4) academic integrity in the context of GenAI-assisted assessments. These themes map directly to the four research questions and inform the study's mixed-methods design, which integrates questionnaire data (student perceptions) with empirical code analysis and grade comparisons. By structuring the investigation along these dimensions, the study bridges existing literature gaps and offers a novel framework for understanding the impact of GenAI in C# programming education.

4 Methodology

This section outlines the methodology employed in the study, organised into five sub-sections for clarity. Subsection 4.1 presents the research design, detailing the mixed-methods approach integrating qualitative and quantitative data. Subsection 4.2 outlines the programming problems employed in the study. Subsection 4.3 describes the data collection procedures, including questionnaires administered to students and code sample compilation. Subsection 4.4 explains the data analysis techniques, encompassing thematic analysis for qualitative data and statistical methods for quantitative data. Finally, Subsect. 4.5 addresses ethical considerations, ensuring compliance with institutional guidelines and participant anonymity.

4.1 Research Design

A mixed-methods approach was employed, analysing student-generated C# code samples, conducting surveys, and collecting instructor evaluations. This study employs a mixed-methods research design to investigate the impact of AI-generated C# code on academic integrity. The approach integrates both qualitative and quantitative methodologies to provide a comprehensive understanding of students' use of generative AI in programming education. The research design involves three core components: (1) a questionnaire administered to students, (2) an assessment of grading patterns to evaluate potential disparities in academic performance, and (3) an analysis of AI-generated and human-written code.

4.2 Programming Problems

The programming problems in this study were designed for first-year undergraduate students in an introductory C# programming course. They targeted fundamental concepts, including variables, data types, control structures (e.g., conditionals and loops), functions, and basic object-oriented programming (e.g., classes and objects). The difficulty was tailored to students with no or minimal prior programming experience. Example tasks included: writing a program to compute the average of a set of numbers, implementing a function to reverse a string, and creating a class to model a simple shopping mall transaction. Each problem included a specification and test cases and was completed within supervised lab sessions adhering to coding standards.

4.3 Data Collection

A questionnaire was administered to students to understand AI model preferences and perceived usefulness. Additionally, code analysis was done for comparative evaluation of AI-generated and human-written C# code. Code grading was analysed to gain insights into grading AI-generated assignments and issues related to academic honesty.

Questionnaire. A structured questionnaire was distributed among undergraduate first-year students in the Department of Computer Science and Informatics at the University of the Free State, Bloemfontein, South Africa to assess their preferences for AI-generated code, frequency of use, perceived effectiveness, and ethical concerns. The questionnaire included Likert-scale, ranking, and open-ended questions. Students were asked to rate the ease of use of LLMs; list other LLMs used, rate these LLMs on their usage, list other LLMs commonly used in generating code, average time to generate and run instruction, and provide additional comments.

It is important to note that students were not involved in evaluating the quality or correctness of the code samples. All code analyses, including syntactic, structural, and grading evaluations, were conducted by the researchers. The students' role was limited to providing subjective feedback on tool usability and preferences via the questionnaire.

Grading Pattern Assessment. To examine academic performance trends, student grades were analysed for assignments completed with and without AI assistance. Statistical methods, including Pearson's correlation coefficient, were employed to determine relationships between AI usage and student performance. Additionally, rubrics used for assessing AI-generated and human-written code were compared to identify potential biases in grading methodologies.

Code Sample Analysis. A dataset consisting of AI-generated and human-written C# code submissions was compiled from targeted experiments and university first-year programming assignments, respectively. AI-generated code was sourced from ChatGPT, Microsoft Copilot, and Blackbox.AI, while human-written code was gathered from student submissions completed under supervision without the use of AI. Each code sample was analysed and evaluated based on structure, syntax, lexical analysis, error handling, and logical flow.

4.4 Data Analysis

Statistical analysis was applied to identify patterns in grading discrepancies and AI detection reliability. A mixed-methods approach was adopted, analysing student-generated C# code samples, questionnaire responses, and grades. Thematic analysis was applied for the qualitative analysis of student questionnaire responses and grades to identify recurring themes related to AI reliance, ethical considerations, and learning outcomes. Descriptive and inferential statistical techniques were employed to analyse questionnaire results and grading patterns for quantitative analysis. T-tests and ANOVA were conducted to assess statistical differences in academic performance between AI-generated and human-written code.

4.5 Ethical Clearance

Ethical approval for this study was obtained from the General/Human Research Ethics Committee of the university, with ethical clearance number UFS-HSD2024/0601. Participants were informed of the study's purpose and provided with a consent form prior to participating in the questionnaire. Anonymisation techniques were applied to protect student identities. The study aligns with the ethical guidelines for AI research in education, emphasising transparency, informed consent, and responsible data handling [5].

5 Results and Discussion

This section analyses 368 questionnaire responses from students regarding their interactions with AI-generated code in a C# programming course. The dataset includes difficulty rankings, tool preferences, code generation times, problem-solving outcomes, and qualitative feedback - all specific to AI-generated code produced by ChatGPT, Microsoft Copilot, and Blackbox.AI. The analysis employs descriptive statistics, preference tallies, time efficiency metrics, problem-solving frequencies, and thematic analysis of comments to explore student experiences and their implications for computing education.

5.1 Perceived Difficulty of AI-Generated Code

The frequency distributions were computed for perceived difficulty of AI-generated code from 360 valid responses (8 were missing) across four categories: *Very Easy*, *Easy*, *Difficult*, and *Very Difficult*, as shown in Table 1.

Table 1. Result of Perceived Difficulty of AI-Generated Code

Category	Number of Students	Percentage
Very Easy	124	34.4%
Easy	198	55.0%
Difficult	36	10.0%
Very Difficult	2	0.6%
Total	360	100.0%

A significant 89.4% (322 out of 360) of participants found AI-generated code either *Easy* or *Very Easy* to work with, reflecting its accessibility for C# tasks. The 10.6% who rated it *Difficult* or *Very Difficult* often cited issues like "logical errors" or "unclear instructions" in their comments. The high ease of use (89.4%) suggests AI tools effectively support students with C# syntax and basic logic generation. However, the 10.6% difficulty rate indicates occasional challenges, such as error-prone outputs, underscoring the need for students to develop critical debugging skills.

5.2 Student Preferences for AI Tools

Preferences were assessed by analysing top ease-of-use rankings (1 = easiest) for ChatGPT, Copilot, and Blackbox.AI from 342 valid responses (26 missing full rankings), complemented by qualitative ease-of-use feedback, as shown in Table 2.

Table 2. Student Preferences for AI Tools

AI Tool	Students (n, %)	Average Ranking	Feedback
ChatGPT	168 (49.1%)	1.6	"Fast, under 10 s," but "sometimes incomplete."
Microsoft Copilot	94 (27.5%)	2.1	"Input limits make it harder."
Blackbox.AI	80 (23.4%)	2.3	"Word limit issues."

ChatGPT emerged as the preferred tool, with 49.1% of students selecting it as their top choice and an average ranking of 1.6, attributed to its speed, ease of use, and clarity. Copilot (27.5%, 2.1 ranking) and Blackbox.AI (23.4%, 2.3 ranking) followed, with students citing usability constraints such as input restrictions. ChatGPT's dominance underscores its effectiveness for C# learners, though concerns remain regarding incomplete outputs. The lower rankings of Copilot and Blackbox.AI suggest that interface design significantly influences adoption, highlighting the need for educators to guide students in prioritising output quality over mere convenience.

5.3 Time Efficiency of AI Code Generation

Code generation time from 364 valid responses was standardised to minutes (e.g., "*15MIN - 30MIN*" = 22.5) and analysed for average duration and variability by difficulty level. The 10.24-min average indicates rapid code generation, though longer times (e.g., 150 min) correlate with error correction efforts (e.g., "had to fix error"). Shorter times align with easier tasks, while the *Very Difficult* outliers suggest dismissive or anomalous entries. AI's speed enhances productivity for simple C# tasks, but increased time with higher difficulty reflects debugging demands. This suggests AI is most effective for routine assignments, requiring oversight for complex ones. The box plot in Fig. 1 illustrates the distribution of time taken (in minutes) to generate code across different difficulty levels and the four boxes show the median, quartiles, and potential outliers for time taken per difficulty level.

5.4 Problem-Solving Effectiveness

Frequencies of problems solved (labelled 1 through 9) were tabulated from the responses to gauge AI's utility across different C# tasks. Problems 2 (138) and 3 (134) were most frequently solved and often rated *Easy*, indicating AI's strength in standard C# tasks. Problem 8 (72) had the lowest frequency and was often rated *Difficult*, pointing to potential complexity or AI limitations. AI excels in

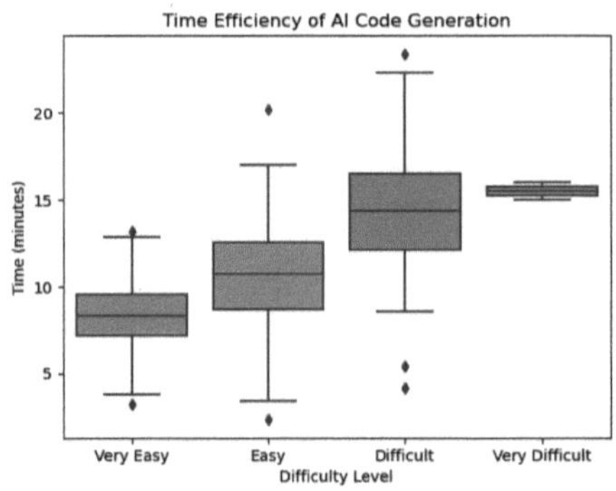

Fig. 1. Time Efficiency of AI Code Generation

routine problem-solving but falters with more intricate tasks. This suggests educators design assignments that leverage AI for basics while challenging students to tackle advanced problems manually. Problems 1 to 9 have 110, 138, 134, 100, 94, 94, 90, 72, and 80 students who successfully solved each problem using AI tools, respectively, as shown in Table 3.

Table 3. Frequencies of Problems Solved

Problem	1	2	3	4	5	6	7	8	9
Frequency	110	138	134	100	94	94	90	72	80

5.5 Qualitative Insights

Thematic analysis of student comments identified recurring themes related to AI-generated code, as shown in Table 4. Students noted consistent syntax but frequent errors in AI outputs, praised usability despite flaws, appreciated learning benefits, and expressed concerns about over-reliance. AI's predictable structure aids error detection, while its learning benefits and dependency risks highlight the need for balanced pedagogy that fosters critical thinking alongside tool use. Table 4 displays the frequency of key themes mentioned in student comments about AI-generated code. Code quality is clearly important, as seen from the qualitative insights, and the errors in AI-generated code reveal the need for students to refine their AI input to achieve the desired output. The comment, "*it breaks down code*", shows how GenAI can support understanding programming segments.

5.6 Correlation Between AI-Generated and Human-Written Code Grades

Grades were analysed for each of the three LLMs used to generate C# code namely ChatGPT, Blackbox.AI, and Microsoft Copilot, as well as for human-written C# code. As shown in Table 5, AI-generated C# code achieved an average score between 88 and 92, significantly higher than the human average of 62.81. Additionally, AI-generated grades exhibited less variability (standard deviation: 14–17) compared to human grades (standard deviation: 23.77). The higher standard deviation in human grades indicates greater variability among students' performance. Generative AI-produced C# code was more consistent, with Blackbox.AI frequently scoring 100% and showing lower variability in some problems. This suggests that Blackbox.AI outperforms ChatGPT and Microsoft Copilot in grading accuracy and could lead to higher student scores.

Table 4. Qualitative Insights

Category	Examples	Mentions
Code Quality	"Logical errors" and "similar across LLMs"	20
Usability	"Copilot is slow" and "fun to use"	10
Learning Impact	"Enhances skills" and "breaks down code"	6
Dependency	"Replaces programmers" and "confuses without understanding"	6

Table 6 shows the mean grades for each problem across the LLMs and the human-written code. Human grades are consistently lower across all problems, with noticeable drops in Problems 4, 5, 8, and 9 due to their higher difficulty. Problems with higher difficulty had lower grades for AI-generated C# code. The highest human grades were for Problem 6 (average grade: 73.93) and Problem 2

Table 5. Descriptive Statistics for AI Vs. Human C# Code Grades

LLMs Vs. Humans	Mean	Median	Std Dev	Min	Max	N
ChatGPT	88.95	96	15.45	6	100	1,237
Blackbox.AI	92.14	100	14.93	13	100	1,162
CoPilot	88.23	96	16.68	14	100	1,179
Human	62.81	65	23.77	0	100	1,257

(average grade: 73.31), while the lowest were for Problem 8 (average grade: 47.41) and Problem 9 (average grade: 55.38), both of which are difficult problems.

The average differences between AI scores and human scores were calculated: ChatGPT had an average difference of 25.88, Blackbox.AI had 28.91, and Microsoft Copilot had 25.29. This suggests that Copilot's grades are slightly closer to human performance compared to ChatGPT and Blackbox.AI. Problems 2 and 6 appear to be easier, as indicated by higher human grades and smaller gaps between AI and human scores. In contrast, Problems 4, 8, and 9 are more difficult, as shown by lower human grades and larger gaps.

Statistical analysis using Pearson's correlation with human grades on paired complete data shows that ChatGPT has a correlation coefficient of 0.36, Blackbox.AI has 0.25, and Microsoft Copilot has 0.34. These values indicate a moderate positive correlation, with ChatGPT and Copilot aligning slightly more with human grades than Blackbox.AI.

Table 6. Mean Grades by Problem

Problem	ChatGPT	Blackbox	CoPilot	Human	N
1	86.52	94.74	88.94	64.77	141
2	96.31	97.72	98.72	73.31	141
3	91.49	93.23	83.23	67.09	141
4	96.74	96.83	95.83	58.45	141
5	86.06	85.71	85.11	56.83	141
6	92.58	88.49	96.93	73.93	139
7	85.71	87.77	86.33	61.15	139
8	88.53	83.33	95.37	47.41	135
9	86.54	90.63	83.65	55.38	130

5.7 Distinguishing Features of AI-Generated and Human-Written Code

Analysis of code submissions revealed several key differences between AI-generated and human-written code. The first C# code sample from each problem was selected for ChatGPT, Blackbox.AI, Copilot and human-written code, resulting in a total of 36 code samples examined. Comments were not analysed as they could be removed or modified by users, making it difficult to determine whether the code was generated by GenAI or humans.

The analysis focused on syntax, lexical structure, error handling, output formatting, and code logic. The **syntax** aspect examined the use of loops, conditionals, and methods in the C# construct. **Lexical analysis** focused on naming conventions, variable names, and code readability. **Error handling** considered approaches to input validation and exception management, while **output formatting** assessed how results were presented to the user. Lastly, **code logic** examined the algorithmic approach and structural efficiency.

Summarising the observations:

- **ChatGPT-generated code** was found to be modular, descriptive, with robust validation and polished output formatting.
- **Blackbox.AI code** was consistent, procedural, using basic naming conventions and more decorative output elements.
- **Copilot-generated code** appeared practical and visually appealing, often using inline logic, and showed less consistent error handling.

Table 7. Distinct Features of GenAI Vs. Human Code

Feature	AI-Generated Code	Human-Written Code
Syntax	Consistent use of modern C# features (e.g., string interpolation, TryParse), reflecting up-to-date programming practices. Structured with loops and conditionals optimised for task efficiency (e.g., ChatGPT's while with TryParse in Calculator)	Relies on basic constructs (e.g., Console.WriteLine without interpolation), less leveraging of modern C# features
Lexical Structure	Standardised naming (e.g., totalBeforeTax, pricePerHoodie), adhering to C# conventions, unlike human's prefixed variables.	Unique, often prefixed naming (e.g., iNum, sMsg), deviating from standard conventions
Error Handling	Robust with try-catch or TryParse, ensuring program continuity (e.g., Blackbox's loop reset, ChatGPT's validation). More proactive than human's reactive, minimal error handling	Minimal or flawed (e.g., HCF's infinite loop attempt), lacking AI's robustness
Output Formatting	Polished with formatted strings (e.g., string.Format, "$"), enhancing readability compared to human's concatenation	Crude, manual string building (e.g., "Total:" + value), less visually appealing
Code Logic	Algorithmically sound (e.g., Euclidean HCF in all AI versions), avoiding human's logical missteps	Prone to errors or incomplete logic (e.g., Car Sale Decision's misplaced conditions), reflecting less systematic design

- **Human-written code** was idiosyncratic and error-prone, with verbose variable naming and basic formatting.

As shown in Table 7, human-written code is less polished, more individualistic, and more prone to logical flaws compared to GenAI code. AI-generated code was more structured and featured more robust error handling. As detailed in Appendix A, human-written code uses prefixes like "i" for integers and "s" for strings in variable names, whereas GenAI code favours descriptive names without prefixes.

Extracting the code from Problem 6 and comparing the ChatGPT-, Blackbox.AI-, Copilot- generated code and human-written code revealed the following differences:

- **ChatGPT** used descriptive variables such as *multiplier* and *continueChoice*, employed string interpolation alongside *String.Format*, and allowed the program to continue on error and restart the loop.
- **Blackbox.AI** used a *do-while* loop for repetition, generic variable name, number and *string.Format* for its output, and exited with *Console.ReadKey()*.
- **Microsoft Copilot** featured decorative prompts for the multiplication table, inline logic, exited on error with the use of return, and a mix of formatting.
- **Human-written code** used prefixed naming such as *iNum*, *sMsg*, and *cGenerate*. It also used raw concatenation with basic *String.Format*, no error handling, and redundant prompts.

5.8 Impact on Academic Integrity and Measures for Fair Assessment

The use of AI-generated code in programming courses raises notable concerns for academic integrity, driven by its accessibility (89.4% of students found it easy to use) and efficiency (average generation time of 10.24 min). These attributes heighten risks of plagiarism and over-reliance, potentially misrepresenting students' coding skills. Existing detection tools, such as MOSS and Turnitin, struggle to identify AI-generated content due to its advanced nature [30]. To ensure fair assessment, educators can adopt process-based evaluations, like oral code reviews or documented coding processes, to confirm students' understanding [6]. Furthermore, embedding AI literacy into the curriculum, as suggested by Zviel-Girshin [32], can promote ethical AI use. These strategies address RQ4 by balancing AI benefits with authentic skill assessment.

6 Limitations of the Study

The work focused only on first-year programming students at a single university, and only C# was considered. Generalisation should thus be approached with caution. Nevertheless, the study still provides valuable insights into the use of GenAI in C# programming language code.

The use of first-year students, who may have limited programming experience, does not impact code evaluations as they only report usage preference and perceptions while the code quality assessment and evaluations were conducted by the researchers. Future studies may involve senior students to gather more technically informed perceptions of GenAI tools.

7 Conclusion and Future Research

GenAI tools like ChatGPT, Blackbox.AI, and Microsoft Copilot into C# programming education will enhance learning efficiency as 89.4% found AI code easy to use and rapid code generation as the results showed an average of 10.24 min. However, it also poses significant challenges to academic integrity. Our findings align with Silva et al. [25], who noted that AI tools reduce syntax errors but risk over-reliance, which will in turn reduce problem-solving skills. Similarly, Pan et al. [17] found that AI-generated code often outperforms human-written code, which is consistent with our grade analysis showing AI scores (88–92) surpassing human averages (62.81).

However, our study uniquely emphasises C# specific patterns such as AI's syntax versus human code logic, extending Xu et al.'s work [30] on detecting AI-generated code through contrastive learning. This reinforces the case for tailored detection strategies in C# programming education.

Furthermore, to balance GenAI's benefits and risks, educators need to adopt process-based assessments, such as oral code reviews, and integrate AI literacy into curricula, echoing Zviel-Girshin's [32] call for ethical AI education. Future work could explore cross-language generalisability by comparing C# with Python and Java, building on Ariza et al.'s [3] review. Additionally, text mining techniques such as deep learning and fine tuning codeLLMs as suggested by Adegbite and Kotze [1], could enhance AI-generated code detection across diverse datasets. Finally, investigating adaptive assessment frameworks that reward creativity over uniformity is important and could ensure GenAI supports authentic skill development while maintaining academic integrity in an AI-driven educational space.

Acknowledgement. The efforts of C# programming instructors, Ms. Reba Phuthi and Mr. Jay Vieira who assisted in administering the questionnaires, and Mr. Tiaan de Lange, who contributed to marking the GenAI C# code, are greatly appreciated.

Disclosure of Interests. The authors have no competing interests to declare that are relevant to the content of this article.

Appendix I: Variable Names Across LLMs & Human-Written Code

Problem	ChatGPT Variables	Blackbox Variables	CoPilot Variables	Human Variables
Car Selling	modelYear, odometerReading, currentYear, carAge	modelYear, odometerReading, sellCar	modelYear, odometerReading, currentYear, carAge	iModelYear, dOdometer, iAge, iCurrentYear
Food Ordering	choice, price, ex, prompt, input, result, quantity, costPerMeal, totalPrice	menuItem, ex	choice, price, ex, prompt, quantity, costPerMeal, total	iquantity, input, ivalue, quantitymeal, costpermeal, mTotal
Hoodie Invoice	PRICE_PER_HOODIE, VAT_RATE, customerName, addressLine1, addressLine2, city, postalCode, numberOfHoodies, totalBeforeTax, tax, totalDue	customerName, streetAddress, suburb, city, postalCode, numberOfHoodies, pricePerHoodie, vatRate, totalBeforeTax, tax, totalWithVat	pricePerHoodie, vatRate, customerName, addressLine1, addressLine2, city, postalCode, numberOfHoodies, totalBeforeTax, taxAmount, totalAmountDue	sName, sAddress, sCity, sProvince, sPostalcode, sAmount, iAmount, sDeliveryAddress, value, mTotalBefore, mVAT, mFinalTotal
Calculator	operation, prompt, number, count, sum, i, num1, num2	operation, prompt, input, number, count, sum, i, num1, num2, product, dividend, divisor, quotient	choice, count, sum, i, num1, num2, prompt, number	UserChoice, choice, iCount, sum, i, number, iFirstNumber, iSecondNumber, IfirstNumber, iProduct, dividend, divisor, quotient
Multiplication Table	number, continueChoice, multiplier	number, response, i	number, response, i	iNum, cGenerate, iSum, iCounter, sMsg
Money Composition	amount, cents, prompt, count, response, input	amount, cents, repeat, prompt, units, unitValue, input	amount, cents, prompt, units, unitValue, response, input	sAmount, cReply, dRand, dCents, dRem, iUV
HCF Calculator	m, n, remainder	m, n, temp, hcf	m, n, originalM, originalN, temp, remainder	im1, in2, iHCF, iRemainder

References

1. Adegbite, A.A., Kotze, E.: Detection of genai-produced and student-written c# code: a comparative study of classifier algorithms and code stylometry features. Afr. J. Inf. Commun. **35**, 1–20 (2025)
2. Ahdi, P.: Harnessing AI for policy and documentation standardization in education: benefits and mitigation of drawbacks. In: The 5th International Conference on Teacher Education and Professional Development (InCoTEPD), pp. 862–867 (2024)

3. Ariza, J.A., Restrepo, M.B., Hernández, C.H.: Generative AI in engineering and computing education: a scoping review of empirical studies and educational practices. IEEE Access **3**, 30789–30810 (2025)
4. Buscemi, A.: A comparative study of code generation using ChatGPT 3.5 across 10 programming languages. arXiv preprint arXiv:2308.04477 (2023)
5. Floridi, L., Cowls, J., King, T.C., Taddeo, M.: How to design AI for social good: seven essential factors. In: Ethics, Governance, and Policies in Artificial Intelligence, vol. 144, pp. 125–151 (2021)
6. Gagich, M.: Using process-based pedagogical assessment practices to challenge generative AI in the writing classroom. In: Educational Assessments in the Age of Generative AI, pp. 1–32. IGI Global Scientific Publishing (2025)
7. Gurioli, A., Gabbrielli, M., Zacchiroli, S.: Is this you, LLM? Recognizing AI-written programs with multilingual code stylometry. arXiv preprint arXiv:2412.14611 (2024)
8. Horvath, M., Bubenkova, L., Pietrikova, E.: Exploring GPT-generated variations in C programming assignments. In: 2025 IEEE 23rd World Symposium on Applied Machine Intelligence and Informatics (SAMI), pp. 331–336. IEEE, Slovakia (2025)
9. Kazemitabaar, M., Chow, J., Ma, C.K.T., Ericson, B.J., Weintrop, D., Grossman, T.: Studying the effect of AI code generators on supporting novice learners in introductory programming. In: Proceedings of the 2023 CHI Conference on Human Factors in Computing Systems, pp. 1–23 (2023)
10. Khreisat, M.N., Khilani, D., Rusho, M.A., Karkkulainen, E.A., Tabuena, A.C., Uberas, A.D.: Ethical implications of AI integration in educational decision making: systematic review. Educ. Adm.: Theory Pract. **30**(5), 8521–8527 (2024)
11. Li, S., Cheng, Y., Chen, J., Xuan, J., He, S., Shang, W.: Assessing the performance of AI-generated code: a case study on github copilot. In: 2024 IEEE 35th International Symposium on Software Reliability Engineering (ISSRE), pp. 216–227. IEEE, Japan (2024)
12. Licorish, S.A., Bajpai, A., Arora, C., Wang, F., Tantithamthavorn, K.: Comparing human and LLM generated code: the jury is still out! arXiv preprint arXiv:2501.16857 (2025)
13. Mijwil, M.M., Hiran, K.K., Doshi, R., Dadhich, M., Al-Mistarehi, A.H., Bala, I.: ChatGPT and the future of academic integrity in the artificial intelligence era: a new frontier. Al-Salam J. Eng. Technol. **2**(2), 116–127 (2023)
14. Mittal, U., Sai, S., Chamola, V.: A comprehensive review on generative AI for education. IEEE Access **12**, 142733–142759 (2024)
15. Nizamudeen, F., Gatti, L., Bouali, N., Ahmed, F.: Investigating the impact of code generation tools (ChatGPT & github copilot) on programming education. In: 16th International Conference on Computer Supported Education. CSEDU 2024, pp. 221–229. Science and Technology Publications, Lda (2024)
16. Ogwueleka, F.N.: Plagiarism detection in the age of artificial intelligence: current technologies and future directions. In: AI and Ethics, Academic Integrity and the Future of Quality Assurance in Higher Education, vol. 3, pp. 120–129 (2025)
17. Pan, W.H., et al.: Assessing AI detectors in identifying AI-generated code: implications for education. In: Proceedings of the 46th International Conference on Software Engineering: Software Engineering Education and Training, pp. 1–11 (2024)
18. Patel, A., Sultana, K.Z., Samanthula, B.K.: A comparative analysis between AI generated code and human written code: a preliminary study. In: 2024 IEEE International Conference on Big Data (BigData), pp. 7521–7529. IEEE, USA (2024)
19. Pinzolits, R.: Ai in academia: an overview of selected tools and their areas of application. MAP Educ. Humanit. **4**, 37–50 (2024)

20. Prather, J., et al.: Beyond the hype: a comprehensive review of current trends in generative AI research, teaching practices, and tools. In: 2024 Working Group Reports on Innovation and Technology in Computer Science Education, pp. 300–338 (2025)
21. Pudasaini, S., Miralles-Pechuán, L., Lillis, D., Llorens Salvador, M.: Survey on AI-generated plagiarism detection: the impact of large language models on academic integrity. J. Acad. Ethics, 1–34 (2024)
22. Reunanen, T., Nieminen, N.: Artificial intelligence as a catalyst: a case study on adaptive learning in programming education. In: Human Factors, Business Management and Society, p. 135 (2024)
23. Rodrigues, M., Silva, R., Borges, A.P., Franco, M., Oliveira, C.: Artificial intelligence: threat or asset to academic integrity? A bibliometric analysis. In: Kybernetes (2024)
24. Shah, A., Chernova, A., Tomson, E., Porter, L., Griswold, W.G., et al.: Students' use of github copilot for working with large code bases. In: Proceedings of the 56th ACM Technical Symposium on Computer Science Education V. 1, pp. 1050–1056 (2025)
25. Silva, C.A.G.D., Ramos, F.N., De Moraes, R.V., Santos, E.L.D.: ChatGPT: challenges and benefits in software programming for higher education. Sustainability **16**(3), 1245 (2024)
26. Tang, C.M., Ng, V.S., Leung, H.M., Yuen, J.C.: AI-generated programming solutions: impacts on academic integrity and good practices. Anglia Ruskin Research Online (ARRO). Conference Contribution (2023)
27. Wang, R., Cheng, R., Ford, D., Zimmermann, T.: Investigating and designing for trust in ai-powered code generation tools. In: Proceedings of the 2024 ACM Conference on Fairness, Accountability, and Transparency, pp. 1475–1493 (2024)
28. Wang, Y.: Survey for detecting AI-generated content. Adv. Eng. Technol. Res. **11**(1), 643 (2024)
29. Xiaodan, X., et al.: Distinguishing LLM-generated from human-written code by contrastive learning. ACM Trans. Softw. Eng. Methodol. (2025). Just Accepted
30. Xu, X., et al.: Distinguishing LLM-generated from human-written code by contrastive learning. ACM Trans. Softw. Eng. Methodol. (2024)
31. Zimmermann, M., Janetzko, H., Haymond, B.: Integrating generative AI methods in computer science education: perspectives, strategies, and outcomes. In: EDULEARN24 Proceedings, pp. 10358–10365. IATED, Spain (2024)
32. Zviel-Girshin, R.: The good and bad of AI tools in novice programming education. Educ. Sci. **14**(10), 1089–1091 (2024)

Overcoming Debugging Challenges: Expert Strategies for Novice Programmers

Tipson Maleti[1,2] and Liezel Nel[1](✉)

[1] Department of Computer Science and Informatics, University of the Free State, Bloemfontein, South Africa
maletit@solusi.ac.zw, nell@ufs.ac.za
[2] University of Solusi, Bulawayo, Zimbabwe

Abstract. Debugging is a critical yet challenging programming skill, particularly for novice programmers who often rely on ineffective trial-and-error approaches. This study applied Steps 2 and 3 of the Decoding the Disciplines (DtD) framework to address a major debugging bottleneck: novices' inability to plan and execute structured debugging strategies. Through decoding interviews, structured interviews, and think-aloud exercises with six expert debuggers, we uncovered the implicit mental processes that guide expert debugging. Data analysis by means of a Narrative Data Analysis Framework (NDAF) revealed seven systematic steps that experts follow when locating and resolving program errors. These steps were synthesized into a structured debugging model that can be used for instructional purposes, offering novices a clear and replicable process for approaching debugging tasks. The study also demonstrated how experts' self-theories influence their debugging practices, with growth-oriented experts showing greater adaptability and persistence. By making expert strategies explicit, this research contributes a practical model for teaching debugging, with the potential to improve novices' problem-solving skills and foster growth-oriented approaches to programming challenges.

Keywords: Debugging · Novice programmers · Expert strategies · Self-theories · Mental processes · Decoding the Disciplines

1 Introduction

Debugging is a fundamental aspect of computer programming and is widely regarded as an essential skill for students to master [4, 25]. It involves systematically identifying and fixing errors within computer programs, a process that is often challenging, especially for novice programmers who are studying introductory programming courses [13, 22]. In contrast, experienced programmers typically debug more effectively due to their developed skills, strategies, and familiarity with the debugging process [25, 27].

For novices, debugging difficulties often arise from a combination of limited programming knowledge and ineffective problem-solving skills. They struggle particularly with semantic and logical errors, which, unlike syntax errors, do not result in immediate compiler feedback and thus require a deeper level of program comprehension and

L. Nel et al. (Eds.): SACLA 2025, CCIS 2770, pp. 137–152, 2026.
https://doi.org/10.1007/978-3-032-12457-9_9

structured problem-solving approaches [1, 2, 5]. Without effective debugging strategies, novices tend to rely on unstructured and inefficient trial-and-error approaches, often exacerbating their confusion and frustration [14].

This study addresses a significant research gap identified in a previous research phase: Novice programmers' inability to plan and use structured debugging strategies to locate and fix program errors was identified as a major debugging challenge experienced by novice programmers. This article reports on a follow-up phase employing Steps 2 and 3 of the Decoding the Disciplines (DtD) framework [16, 17] to directly address this bottleneck. The primary objective of this phase was to uncover and document the explicit mental processes and structured debugging strategies employed by expert debuggers. Furthermore, we investigated the relationship between experts' self-theories (fixed versus growth mindsets) and their debugging success. Ultimately, this work aims to inform instructional strategies that can be utilized to explicitly teach effective debugging processes to novices, promoting both improved debugging skills and positive self-theories towards programming challenges.

The remainder of the paper is structured as follows: Sect. 2 provides a background discussion, elaborating on debugging strategies, self-theories, and the DtD framework. Section 3 describes the research method, including details on participant selection, data collection methods, and data analysis techniques. Section 4 presents the findings and discussion, focusing on the decoded mental processes used by expert debuggers and the relationship between their self-theories and debugging success. Specifically, we will present the seven distinct mental steps identified in expert debugging processes. Section 5 concludes the paper by summarizing the key findings and discussing their implications for teaching debugging to novice programmers.

2 Background

This section outlines the theoretical and conceptual foundations for the study. The first part contrasts the strategies typically used by novice programmers with those of experts and highlights the importance of adopting structured debugging approaches. The discussion then considers the role of self-theories in shaping how individuals respond to programming challenges. The section concludes by introducing the DtD framework, which provides the pedagogical basis for the study's design and application.

2.1 Debugging Strategies: Comparing Expert and Novice Debuggers

Novice programmers typically approach debugging in an unstructured, trial-and-error manner, often without a clear strategy. They often handle errors in a disorganized manner by randomly modifying code and repeatedly executing the program to locate and correct issues [14]. This unsystematic approach can inadvertently introduce new errors and result in inefficient use of time and effort, leading to frustration and discouragement [14].

In contrast, expert programmers tend to employ structured and systematic strategies for debugging. They typically use forward (top-down) or backward (bottom-up) reasoning, systematically analyzing code to hypothesize and test potential error causes [25, 27]. Their extensive experience allows them to prioritize underlying causes rather than surface symptoms, making debugging more efficient and effective. Experts rarely rely solely on guesswork [27].

2.2 Concept of Self-theories and Their Relation to Debugging

Self-theories, also known as mindsets, refer to individuals' beliefs about intelligence and their learning capabilities [9]. These beliefs exist along a continuum from fixed to growth mindsets [8, 18, 20]. Individuals with a fixed mindset perceive their intelligence and abilities as inherent and static, attributing their successes or failures to innate capabilities. Those with a growth mindset see intelligence as malleable, developed through effort and learning.

In the context of debugging, mindset significantly influences responses to challenges. Students with fixed mindsets often become discouraged by difficult debugging tasks and view persistent challenges as a reflection of their limited abilities. This mindset may result in helpless behaviours, such as abandoning tasks or avoiding challenging problems [18]. On the other hand, students with growth mindsets approach debugging difficulties as learning opportunities, demonstrating resilience and persistence. They are more likely to engage in structured problem-solving behaviours, seek assistance, and adapt their strategies when encountering difficulties [8].

2.3 The Decoding the Disciplines (DtD) Framework

The Decoding the Disciplines (DtD) framework is a structured pedagogical approach developed to help students overcome learning bottlenecks by explicitly modelling discipline-specific expert thinking [16, 17]. The framework involves seven iterative steps: (1) identifying common learning bottlenecks; (2) uncovering the mental operations experts use to address these bottlenecks; (3) modelling these processes explicitly for students; (4) creating structured opportunities for students to practice the modelled processes; (5) providing feedback to support and motivate students as they refine these practices; (6) assessing changes in student learning to evaluate effectiveness; and (7) sharing the insights with colleagues to improve disciplinary teaching more broadly [16, 17, 21].

In the context of DtD, an expert is defined not by formal credentials but by their ability to successfully perform the disciplinary thinking or practice that students are expected to learn. This individual, often a lecturer, researcher, or advanced student, executes these complex mental operations fluently and often unconsciously. The decoding process seeks to make these expert moves explicit, so they can be systematically taught to novices who struggle at key bottlenecks in learning [17].

This cycle ensures that decoding is not only about identifying and articulating expert practices, but also about integrating them into teaching and sustaining their impact through assessment and dissemination. Figure 1 provides an overview of the seven-step DtD framework.

In the present study, the DtD framework was applied to address the identified debugging bottleneck: *Novices' inability to plan and use structured debugging strategies to effectively locate and resolve program errors.* While the investigation concentrated on

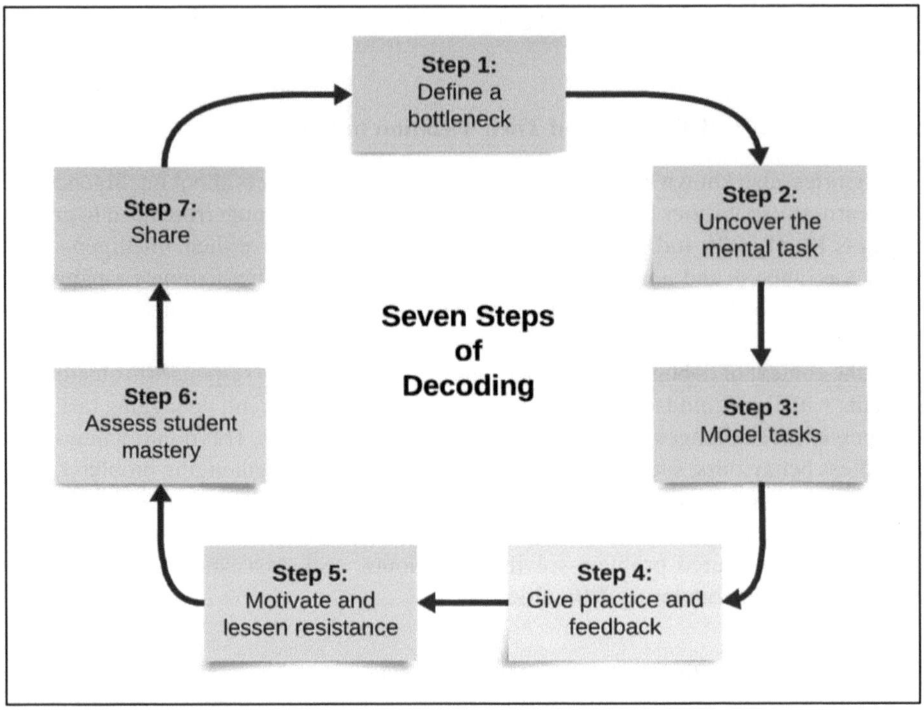

Fig. 1. The seven-step Decoding the Disciplines (DtD) framework (adapted from Middendorf and Shopkow [17])

Steps 2 and 3 – decoding experts' debugging processes and modelling them to novices – these steps are situated within the broader DtD cycle that connects diagnosis, instruction, feedback, and disciplinary dialogue.

3 Research Method

Within a DtD-informed research design, this study adhered to a mixed-methods approach based on Plowright's [23] Frameworks for an Integrated Methodology (FraIM). The FraIM emphasizes coherent integration, allowing for the combination of multiple research approaches within a single study. The data management strategy was an experiment designed to gather detailed information from a small group of participants (programming lecturers). The researchers maintained a high degree of control through structured questioning, audio recording, and direct observation. This provided in-depth exploration and rich data collection [23].

3.1 Population and Sampling

The research population comprised 17 programming lecturers from three Zimbabwean higher education institutions. These lecturers had completed the Dweck Mindset Instrument (DMI) questionnaire in an earlier phase of the study. The DMI comprises 16 items derived from Dweck's [8] Mindset Scale. This psychological assessment tool is used to evaluate individuals' beliefs about the nature of intelligence and talent. It aims to determine whether a person holds a growth, fixed, or undecided mindset. These 17 lecturers were categorized as having either a definitive fixed or growth mindset. Six participants (three with fixed mindsets and three with growth mindsets) were randomly selected [6] for this experiment. The decision to focus on six participants was guided by both conceptual and practical considerations. Conceptually, including an equal number of growth- and fixed-mindset participants ensured that contrasting perspectives could be explored in depth. Practically, the decoding interview and think-aloud protocol are time-intensive, generating large volumes of narrative data for analysis. Limiting the sample to six participants allowed for rich, detailed accounts to be collected and analysed while still capturing variation across the two mindset categories. This approach is consistent with qualitative research designs that prioritise depth of insight over breadth of coverage.

The six selected participants were regarded as expert debuggers since they had at least three years' experience in teaching programming or actual experience as real-world programmers. Each participant was assigned a unique code upon recruitment: Participants P1, P2, and P3 had growth mindsets, while participants P4, P5, and P6 had fixed mindsets.

3.2 Data Collection Methods

For this experiment, asking questions and observations [23] were used to collect data from the six expert debuggers. As part of the asking-questions data-collection method, data were collected by means of decoding interviews [16], structured interviews [23], and think-aloud [27] debugging exercises. (Note: Four of the experts were interviewed virtually due to COVID-19 restrictions imposed by the Zimbabwean government at the time.)

The decoding interviews aimed to uncover the debugging strategies and the implicit mental processes (steps) that expert debuggers would go through during the debugging process. In a decoding interview, two or more interviewers normally conduct the interview [21]. They verbalize their views, pose questions to the respondents, and provide an abstract summary of their thinking to the interviewees [17]. Given the structure of the decoding interview, two minds would be more equipped to guide the interviewing process toward completion than a single interviewer, who might become mired in the intricacies and get lost in the interview details [17]. For this reason, Middendorf and Pace [16] consider the decoding interview to be the most cognitively taxing of all the DtD phases.

The structured interviews aimed to determine if there was a relationship between the expert debuggers' self-theories and debugging success or failure. This interview was structured in the sense that the experts had to answer specific questions within a specific time slot [23]. The questions were formulated based on the characteristics of individuals with fixed and growth mindsets [8, 18, 20].

Participants engaged in one-hour think-aloud protocols while debugging three C++ programs, explaining their strategies. Interviewers asked clarifying questions and observed participants' behaviors and strategy implementation.

3.3 Data-Collection Procedure

After participants completed an informed consent form, the principal interviewer (Author 1) explained the ground rules and instructions to all the participants.

During the decoding interview, the participants were first asked to describe their general debugging strategy in as much detail as possible. Where necessary, any one of the interviewers would intervene with a probing question. This was done to encourage the participants to provide more explicit details in cases where they did not clearly verbalize all their mental processes.

Immediately after the decoding interview, each participant took part in a structured interview. The participants were asked to describe in general how they perceived their own intelligence. More so, they were also asked to describe how their intelligence influenced their debugging successes or failures. Where necessary, any one of the interviewers could interpose with probing questions to prompt the participants to provide more details. This was done to reveal the relationship, if any, between the participants' self-theory (growth or fixed) and their debugging success or failure.

Lastly, the participants participated in a one-hour think-aloud protocol while debugging three C++ programs or questions. They were asked to illustrate and verbally explain the debugging strategies they described during the decoding interview. Where actions or explanations were not clear, any one of the interviewers could ask probing questions. The participants had to explicitly explain their debugging strategies by giving more details and examples. The debugging exercises were done to enable the researchers to observe the expert debuggers' implementation or execution of the debugging strategy (as described during decoding interview) during an actual debugging exercise.

All proceedings during the data collection were video and audio recorded with the participants' permission.

3.4 Data Analysis

The narrative data collected during the decoding interview sessions were analyzed thematically based on an adapted version of Creswell and Creswell's [6] Narrative Data Analysis Framework (NADF). The NDAF is particularly suited for systematically analyzing qualitative data collected through interviews, observations, and think-aloud protocols, as was the case in this experiment. The analysis followed a structured, iterative process of data reduction, display, and interpretation to identify key themes, patterns, and categories related to expert debugging strategies.

Initially, audio-recorded interviews and observational data were transcribed verbatim and reviewed multiple times to achieve thorough familiarity. Next, the six validated and verified transcripts were loaded for coding and additional analysis into NVivo 12 Professional for Microsoft Windows. Codes (nodes) were created by highlighting portions (paragraphs, sentences, keywords) that contain mental processes that could be extracted. Subsequently, specific themes began to emerge that provided crucial details about the dataset. As a result of carrying out this process further, recurring themes emerged. Lastly, frequencies of occurrence for each of the developed themes were generated using NVivo. During the analysis, the researchers were specifically looking for data that articulated the experts' implicit mental processes, self-theories, debugging strategies, experiences, motivations, and opinions during the debugging process.

4 Discussion and Findings

This section presents and interprets the findings of the study. The first subsection describes the seven mental processes followed by expert debuggers, identified from interviews and think-aloud exercises. The focus then shifts to the specific strategies experts employed and the relationship between their self-theories and debugging success. Together, these findings inform the development of a structured debugging model and point to its potential instructional value.

4.1 Mental Processes Followed by the Experts During Debugging

Analysis of the narrative data collected during the interviews and debugging exercises revealed seven explicit mental processes (steps) that expert debuggers go through during the debugging process (in relation to the identified bottleneck). Mental or cognitive processes refer to tasks or activities that human brains do continuously to process all the information received from the surrounding environment into easily manageable cognitive tasks [19]. The seven identified mental steps are discussed in more detail in the following sub-sections.

Step 1: Identify the Program Objective(s). The first step involves understanding the objective(s) of the program; i.e., knowing what the program is trying to achieve [26]. Four participants (P1, P2, P4, and P5) started their debugging with this step. P1 and P2 echoed that the first step in debugging is to know what the program is trying to achieve; i.e., understanding the objective of the program. P2 explained further: "*Look at the output of the program vis-à-vis what you intend it to do.*" P5 emphasized that the debugger must "*keep in mind the objective of the program during the debugging process.*" During the think-aloud debugging exercise, it was also observed that all the participants endeavored to understand each program's objective.

Step 2: Familiarize Yourself with the Program Before Problem Determination. This step involves discovering what the program is doing by reading through parts of the code [26]. P1 supported this step by remarking: "*I check the compliance of the program to the general C++ program structure. I check if all components are available and well presented.*" P5 elaborated by saying: "*I check the pre-processor directives, then the global declarations, then the local declarations, the int main() and statements that make up the main(), until the last statement return 0;.*" To best achieve this step, P1 and P5 reiterated that there is a need to understand the programming language's fundamental concepts on variables, data types, operators, expressions, control structures, arrays, functions, structures, data input, and data output.

During the debugging exercises it was observed that most participants walked through the code line by line (executing just like a computer) and explained what the line does, as well as its effect on the whole program. Where P1, P2, and P3 could not understand some sections of the code, they searched the Internet and watched YouTube video tutorials as a way of familiarizing themselves with the program.

Step 3: Localize (Spot) the Program Error(s). During the decoding interviews, all the participants alluded that they used debugging tools (e.g., debuggers) to detect or find program errors. P6 summarized his process as follows: "*I use debugging tools [IDE Debugger] to identify all types of errors, whether it's a syntax error or semantic error or logical error.*" He further remarked: "*C++ debugger identifies and highlights the errors and give descriptions of each identified error.*" In the same vein, P1 stated that "*the IDE Debugger should show me where the syntax errors are because it will not run if there are syntax errors.*" P1 also mentioned that he used JUnit testing to localize errors in Java programs, while P6 mentioned using the Partial Dependence Plot toolbox (an interactive source code debugger) to locate errors in Python programs. P6 further highlighted how he used break points to identify errors: "*I come up with 'break points' when debugging to make sure that at each break point the program is running quite well until I reach that line that has an error.*"

During the decoding exercise, it was observed that P2, P3, P4, and P5 used the Code::Blocks open-source cross platform IDE to build and run the debugging exercises. The IDE Debugger identified some syntax errors and displayed logs. However, P1 used the Online C++ Compiler, which neither detected program errors nor displayed logs.

It should be noted here that P6 decided to withdraw from attempting the debugging exercises when he reached the point where he had to start identifying the program errors. As the reason for his withdrawal, he indicated that it has been a long time since he used C++. P6's withdrawal may be an indication of his fixed mindset. Individuals with such a mindset typically withdraw or give up when they encounter a difficult problem [10].

Step 4: Classify the Program Error(s). Program errors are classified as syntax errors, semantic errors, and logical errors [1]. As the expert debuggers started finding errors, they classified them for easy handling starting with syntax errors, then semantic, and lastly logical errors [2]. Since syntax errors prevent a program from successful compilation [12], it was observed during the debugging exercises that the participants first attempted to fix these errors so that they could start executing the program. In this regard, P2 remarked: "*Once the code becomes valid, it is going to compile and run.*" He explained further that the next thing is to ask is whether the program is doing what it is supposed to do. This is normally the debugging of semantic errors where a program compiles but causes abnormal termination at runtime and logical errors where a program compiles and runs successfully, but produces incorrect results [2, 15].

Step 5: Determine the Actual Cause (Understanding the Bug). During the decoding interview, all the participants indicated that they go online to determine the actual cause and possibly find a solution or a clue on how to solve the program error [26]. Some participants visited the Stack Overflow website, which provided more information about the bug. P1 remarked: "*Stack Overflow is like following a blog where people who had similar problems will post on how to solve the bug encountered.*" P2 echoed in the same vein: "*Normally I read through logs, books [manuals], searching the Internet through Google, and asking people who had the similar problem on how to fix the bugs.*" He further stated: "*The objective is to have a conceptual understanding of the bug at hand.*" P3 added: "*So having the information resource is important to allow me to get to where the problem is.*" He remarked further that "*the C++ language documentation is the guide which enables me to understand the bug.*"

During the debugging exercise, the researchers observed that P1, P2, and P3 visited the Stack Overflow website especially regarding the declaration of the constant in Question 1 and removing the semantic error in Question 2. P4 and P5 searched the Internet to get clues on the syntax of some keywords and functions in Questions 1 and 2. It was also observed that P1, P2, P3, P4, and P5 used the dry-run approach (manually working through their code to trace the value of variables) to understand the cause of the logical error in Question 3.

Step 6: Repair/Fix the Program Error. This is the climax of the debugging process, which is in line with what the participants said during the decoding interview. P2 remarked: "*I change one thing [code] at a time; I don't change all the code. I change one particular element at a time.*" He went on to explain that "*you change the line of code where you suspect most is blocking you from reaching your goal ... the most critical line of code that will get closer to your goal is the one you change first.*" P5 also emphasized why it is crucial to debug one error at a time: "*Don't debug all errors at once because you might create more errors and to see where you have created the error, it becomes a web of the problems altogether.*"

P3 explained the order in which he would fix errors as follows: "*The first step is I try to fix those I can fix on my own by inspection identification, then from there I move on to the debugger.*" For P5, the order in which errors are fixed is especially important: "*For example, given Error 1, Error 2, Error 3, Error 4, and Error 5. Sort out that fifth error... If you have done it correctly, you will find you have solved the error and now you have four errors, then you go to the fourth error and debug and go to the third one until you are done.*"

P6 highlighted the importance of considering the compiler error messages: "*Even C++ compiler highlights the error and gives a description of the error to help the programmer on how to correct the error. So what you need to do is to go to that particular line and see how to fix the program error.*"

During the think-aloud debugging exercise it was observed that five participants (P1, P2, P3, P4, and P5) applied a repair and fixed one error at a time [26]. When all syntax errors were fixed and the program was executing, the participants would repair and fix semantic errors, and lastly logical errors. From the observations it also seemed that P1, P2, and P3 seemed to fix program errors more easily than P4 and P5. This could be because they relied on online resources to get hints on how to repair and fix the program errors highlighted by the IDE Debugger.

Step 7: Re-test the program. This step comes immediately after repairing each bug. The debugger re-tests the program by rebuilding and running (re-testing) the program until the program performs as intended [26]. During the decoding interview, P2 stated: "*It is important that you rebuild and re-run the program after making some changes, until all program errors are fixed.*"

Furthermore, it was observed during the debugging exercise that all the participants, except P6, who did not participate, re-compiled and re-ran the program after debugging each program error (bug). P2 used Microsoft Visual C++, a GUI debugger that allows interactive debugging from within the IDE through the editor window.

Expert Debuggers' Mental Processes Model. Based on these uncovered mental steps, Fig. 2 presents the seven-step expert debuggers' mental process model. This simplified flowchart can be utilized by instructors (as part of Step 3 of the DtD framework) to model the explicit debugging steps taken by experts to novices. Figure 3 outlines the more precise sub-activities for each step as derived from the discussed expert debuggers' debugging strategies.

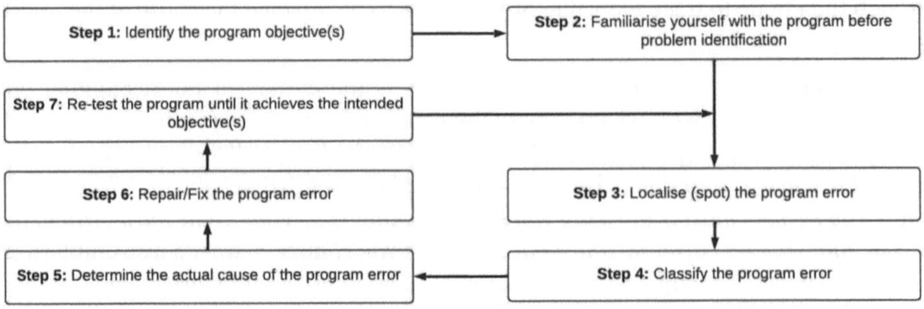

Fig. 2. Expert Debuggers' Mental Processes Model

4.2 Expert Debuggers' Actual Debugging Strategies

According to Katz and Anderson [11], bug-finding strategies can be classified broadly into forward reasoning and backward reasoning. Expert debuggers usually apply both these strategies during the debugging process [4, 24]. Forward reasoning is applied to understand a program's objective and its current status, while backward reasoning is used to search and look for hints from the program's outputs [4]. Furthermore, they use previous debugging experiences to solve current program errors. During the decoding interviews, P1, P2, P3 (with growth mindsets), and P6 (with a fixed mindset) mostly used forward reasoning debugging strategies [24] in a top-down incremental approach. P1 explained his preference for the top-down incremental approach as follows: "*I will start right at the top of the program going down... Sometimes I may need to refer back to the top part that I might have gone through earlier on. For instance, if I am to encounter a variable, I might need to check if that variable was initially declared or a constant to check if it was initially declared, or even a structure to see if it was initially declared. So basically, I call it a top-down incremental approach.*"

In the same vein, P2 viewed a program as a system: "*I look at inputs one at a time, then processing one at a time, then output one at a time ... I walk through each and every line in a program detecting and fixing errors.*" P3 had this to say: "Then I will start looking at the code from top to bottom."

.Only participant P5 (with a fixed mindset) indicated that he typically used backward reasoning debugging strategies. He commented during the decoding interview: "*I always prefer bottom-up; i.e., starting from where I want the results going upwards. ... I start from where the major errors are being highlighted by the debugger and then I go up to where I finally want to be at the end of the day.*" However, during the debugging exercises, it was observed that P5 debugged the programs line-by-line from top to bottom on all syntax errors.

1. Identify the program objective(s):
   a. Scan through the program
   b. Visualize what the program is trying to achieve
   c. Keep in mind or write down the objective(s)
2. Familiarize yourself with the program before problem identification:
   a. Read through the program line by line
   b. Check fundamental C++ concepts
   c. Check pre-processor directives
   d. Check global and local declarations
   e. Check statements within the main()
3. Localize (spot) the program error:
   a. Build, compile, and run the program using C++ Debugger
   b. Use break points to reach lines with errors
   c. Check each line by line-locating error
   d. Locate (spot) the program error located by the C++ compiler
4. Classify the program error:
   a. Is the syntax correct?
   b. Are the semantics correct?
   c. Is the logic correct?
5. Determine the actual cause of the program error (understand the program error):
   a. Read through error logs, descriptions, and suggested solutions from the IDE Debugger
   b. If you cannot understand the program error:
      - Read through language manuals, textbooks, and tutorials
      - Research on the Internet (e.g., visit Stack Overflow and YouTube to obtain more information about the bug)
      - Ask someone who had similar problem(s)
   c. Dry-run the code (manually tracing values of variables)
6. Repair/fix the program error:
   a. If the error is syntax, then:
      Fix the syntax error and go to Step 7
   b. If the error is semantic, then:
      Fix the semantic error and go to Step 7
   c. If the error is logical, then:
      Fix the logical error and go to Step 7
7. Re-test the program until it achieves the intended objective(s)
   a. Rebuild and re-run the program
   b. Repeat Step 3

Fig. 3. Sub-activities for Expert Debuggers' Mental Processes Model

The data analysis revealed that the five expert debuggers who participated in all the debugging exercises (three with growth mindsets and two fixed mindsets) used forward reasoning strategies to find and fix syntax errors in Question 1. This corresponds with McCauley et al.'s [15] observation that experts are more likely to use a forward reasoning approach when debugging someone else's code. However, it was observed that all the participants switched to backward reasoning when debugging semantic and logical errors in Questions 2 and 3 respectively. This is because clues on program errors are easily identified from program output [4].

4.3 Relationships Between the Experts' Self-theories and Their Debugging Success

Self-theories played a central role in how participants approached the debugging tasks. They shaped persistence, adaptability, and reactions to setbacks, with clear differences between growth-oriented and fixed-oriented mindsets. Growth-mindset participants tended to view difficulties as challenges that could be overcome through effort and strategy, while fixed-mindset participants were more likely to disengage or persist with unproductive approaches. The following analysis illustrates how these contrasting orientations influenced the debugging process.

Expert Debuggers' Self-theories (Growth and Fixed Mindsets). Analysis of data collected during the structured interviews, confirmed that P1, P2, and P3 had growth mindsets and P4, P5, and P6 had fixed mindsets, which corresponded with the DMI results (from an earlier research phase). P1 remarked: "*I wouldn't say my intelligence is inborn, it's something that I gradually have through learning ... So I really need to learn and acquire the skills and concepts.*" In the same vein, P2 remarked: "*I classify myself as an average person and a constant learner, which helps me a lot when it comes to programming.*" P1 and P2's remarks correspond with Dweck's [8] assertion that people with a growth mindset believe that through effort and learning, they can become smarter or more talented. P3 said: "*It is more of through continuous hard working, practicing, and persistence that I will eventual become good in debugging.*"

P1, P2, and P3's remarks correspond with Dweck's [8] assertion that people with a growth mindset regard their success as a result of learning, hard work, and persistence [8, 18].

On the other hand, P4, P5, and P6 viewed intelligence as inborn [9] and as something that cannot change [3]. P4 remarked: *"It is inborn because even from the younger ages, I would know that this is what I am able to do, even mathematics."* P5 concurred: *"I am inborn, because the field of computing is mathematically driven and that has always been my strong point since a small child. Where others would be struggling, I would not be struggling."* P6 remarked: *"Of course it is inborn because I can easily identify the problem and solve the issue at hand without even going to the other resources ... My parents and peers confirmed that as I was growing up. Even now my workmates can actually confirm that."*

P4, P5, and P6's views of intelligence correspond well with Dweck's [8] assertion that people with fixed mindsets believe that if someone has ability, they do not need to put in effort because things come easily.

Intelligence in Debugging. During the structured interviews, P1, P2, P3, and P6 perceived that their intelligence in debugging was influenced by learning, hard work, and continuous practice [8, 18]. P1 remarked: "*I cannot run away from the aspect of learning. Like I said, I need to learn to consolidate the knowledge and also the skills.*" P2 added: "*I think I get there through hard working ... more of continuous work and practice.*" In the same vein, P3 noted: "*As I spend more time working with various problems, I discovered* *that I now know most of the common errors.*" P6 (with a fixed mindset) asserted: "*I still need to learn and acquire knowledge to complement my inborn intelligence.*"

Participants with fixed mindsets attributed their intelligence in debugging to experience and inborn intelligence [10]. P5 echoed: "*It boils down to experience. I have a number of years of experience supervising and checking work [codes] done by others ... this is in addition to the inborn intelligence I have.*" Similarly, P4 remarked: "*I take debugging to be more of problem solving, which is in line with my inborn intelligence ... I have to solve any debugging problem.*"

The structured interview data analysis revealed that five participants (P1, P2, P3, P5, and P6) attributed their intelligence in debugging to learning, hard work, persistence, continuous practice, experience, and understanding the syntax of the language [8–10].

Interpretation of Debugging Success. Debugging is an elevated way of coding [7]. P1 echoed this by stating: "*Debugging is the highest level of coding, which requires paying attention to detail and hav[ing] a feeling that you can achieve... This drives and motivates [me] in debugging successfully... [Debugging needs] a lot of effort, dedication, and determination to go through a long list of statements.*" P2 attributed his debugging success to "*continuous learning... I always approach debugging as a learner.*" P3 added that he "*solve[s] a challenging bug with a lot [of] persistence, studying, hard work, and always overcoming resistance.*" The experiment therefore revealed that experts with growth self-theories attribute their debugging success to continuous learning, dedication, determination, hard work, persistence, and challenging the program error [8].

However, P4 took debugging to be "*more of problem solving, which requires inborn intelligence with an element of persistence.*" However, he remarked: "*Persistence is not what helps in solving of the problem, because I will be solving the problem in the back of my mind, coming up with some solutions and strategies of solving that particular problem.*" This aligns with the fixed mindset theory, which suggests that intelligence is an innate trait that resides within people and is unchangeable [3].

On a scale of 1 to 10, P5 rated himself 7 or 8 on debugging success. He remarked: "*I have always debugged successfully and where I have not been successful, it is due to lack of time or lack of appreciation of the original problem.*" On the other hand, P6 stated: "*When I fail to debug, it gives me hope to say I am still learning the language and I still have to learn and acquire a particular knowledge to complement my inborn intelligence.*" He will therefore research and acquire more knowledge about the new concept and skills in debugging.

Participants with fixed mindsets attribute their debugging success to be influenced by their innate or natural intelligence that is complemented by acquired new knowledge [9, 18].

Response to Debugging Setbacks. People with a malleable mindset mostly focus on learning while continuing to apply effective debugging strategies [18]. In this regard, P1 stated: "*When I encounter a bug, I calm down, look at the error code, and peruse the code again and again. Then I put all my effort to resolve the bug.*" In the same vein, P2 commented: "*As soon as I reach debugging setbacks, I change my focus, and work until I produce the results.*" Similarly, P3 concurred: "*I continue working and look at the program errors from a different perspective until I fix all of them.*"

On the other hand, people with a fixed mindset easily get frustrated, take breaks, and are less likely to accept help from others when they encounter debugging setbacks [9, 18]. P4 stated: "*I get frustrated ... I leave it, do something else. Later I will start thinking about it, visualizing how maybe that was supposed to be done and how I should have approached it ... I don't seek help from others, no, I won't!... Later, I will try it when I feel I am now able to concentrate or to focus.*" Similarly, P5 remarked: "*Normally when I am not making any headway, I don't force things, I stop there, do other things unrelated to the problem... I will come back refreshed, normally I solve the bug within a short space of time. I don't seek help from others, remember, the assumption that I have is that I am intelligent ... I always tell myself that I am intelligent ... I am supposed to solve this bug.*"

However, P6, who had a fixed mindset, seemed to have attributes of a malleable mindset, who normally seek help from others [18]. He remarked: "*When I get a setback, I don't get frustrated or get angry because there are so many people in this industry. I feel challenged and read more about that particular problem or I share with my colleagues whom I exchange notes [with] whenever we encounter coding and debugging challenges ... If we still have challenges, we keep on reading trying to discover the area we will be having challenges on in the program until a problem is solved.*"

The responses to debugging setbacks suggest that fostering a growth-oriented mindset among novice programmers could significantly enhance their persistence, adaptability, and overall debugging effectiveness.

The influence of self-theories on expert debugging highlights the need to incorporate this dimension into the structured debugging model so that novices are better supported in sustaining effort and flexibility when they face debugging challenges.

5 Conclusion

This study applied Steps 2 and 3 of the DtD framework [16] to decode and document the explicit mental processes and structured debugging strategies used by expert debuggers. By revealing the systematic and structured ways expert programmers approach debugging, seven distinct mental steps were uncovered. These steps provide a detailed understanding of the cognitive processes involved in effectively identifying and resolving programming errors. The results further highlight differences in debugging approaches influenced by experts' self-theories. The experts who were classified as having growth mindsets, demonstrated how this self-theory facilitates adaptive and resilient debugging behaviours.

The explicit debugging model and detailed sub-activities developed through this research have practical implications for teaching debugging to novices. By explicitly modelling expert debugging strategies, educators can equip novice programmers with systematic approaches, enhancing their capacity to resolve errors efficiently. Additionally, fostering a growth-oriented mindset [8, 20] may further amplify these positive outcomes by increasing students' persistence and adaptability in debugging tasks. Future research could focus on assessing the effectiveness of instructional interventions based on this model, further validating its potential to significantly improve novice programmers' debugging skills.

Furthermore, future research could explore the development and implementation of targeted motivational and feedback strategies, aligning closely with Steps 4 and 5 of the DtD framework. Step 4 involves explicitly modelling expert strategies for students, while Step 5 emphasizes providing structured opportunities for practice with ongoing formative feedback. Such DtD-aligned interventions, designed specifically to assist novice programmers with fixed mindsets in transitioning towards growth-oriented beliefs, may not only enhance their resilience during debugging tasks but also support sustained motivation, persistence, and ultimately, improved programming proficiency.

Acknowledgements. This paper is based on research conducted under the supervision of Prof. L. Nel, in fulfilment of the requirements for the Doctoral Degree in Computer Information Systems in the Department of Computer Science and Informatics, in the Faculty of Natural and Agricultural Sciences at the University of the Free State, and is published with the necessary approval.

Statement on Ethics. Ethical approval for this study was obtained from the General/Human Research Ethics Committee of the University of the Free State (Reference number: UFS-HSD2019/0114/1504/21).

References

1. Ahmadzadeh, M., Elliman, D., Higgins, C.: An analysis of patterns of debugging among novice computer science students. ACM SIGCSE Bull. **37**(3), 84–88 (2005). https://doi.org/10.1145/1151954.1067472
2. Alqadi, B.S., Maletic, J.I.: An empirical study of debugging patterns among novice programmers. In: Proceedings of the 2017 ACM SIGCSE Technical Symposium on Computer Science Education, pp. 15–20. ACM, New York (2017). https://doi.org/10.1145/3017680.3017761
3. Bandura, M., Dweck, C.S.: Self-conceptions and motivation: conceptions of intelligence, choice of achievement goals, and patterns of cognition, affect, and behavior. Unpublished manuscript, Harvard University (1985)
4. Chiu, C.-F., Huang, H.-Y.: Guided debugging practices of game-based programming for novice programmers. Int. J. Inf. Educ. Technol. **5**(5), 343–347 (2015). https://doi.org/10.7763/IJIET.2015.V5.527
5. Cook, S.W., Bjerkeset, O.-C.: Common mistakes made by novice programmers: a comparison between Java and Python. Master's thesis, Norwegian University of Science and Technology (2023)
6. Creswell, J.W., Creswell, J.D.: Research Design: Qualitative, Quantitative, and Mixed Methods Approaches, 5th edn. Sage, Thousand Oaks (2017)
7. Deitz, S., Buy, U.: From video games to debugging code. In: Proceedings of the 5th International Workshop on Games and Software Engineering, pp. 37–41. ACM, New York (2016). https://doi.org/10.1145/2896958.2896964
8. Dweck, C.S.: Self-Theories: Their Role in Motivation, Personality, and Development. Taylor & Francis/Psychology Press, New York (2000)
9. Dweck, C.S., Grant, H.: Self-theories, goals, and meaning. In: Shah, J.Y., Gardner, W.L. (eds.) Handbook of Motivation Science, pp. 405–416. Guilford Press, New York (2008)
10. Kaijanaho, A.-J., Tirronen, V.: Fixed versus growth mindset does not seem to matter much: a prospective observational study in two late bachelor-level computer science courses. In: Proceedings of the 2018 ACM Conference on International Computing Education Research, pp. 11–20. ACM, New York (2018). https://doi.org/10.1145/3230977.3230982

11. Katz, I.R., Anderson, J.R.: Debugging: an analysis of bug location strategies. Hum.-Comput. Interact. **3**(4), 351–399 (1987)
12. Ko, A.J., Myers, B.A.: A framework and methodology for studying the causes of software errors in programming systems. J. Vis. Lang. Comput. **16**(1–2), 41–84 (2005). https://doi.org/10.1016/j.jvlc.2004.08.003
13. Lahtinen, E., Ala-Mutka, K., Järvinen, H.-M.: A study of the difficulties of novice programmers. ACM SIGCSE Bull. **37**(3), 14–18 (2005). https://doi.org/10.1145/1151954.1067453
14. Mase, M.B., Nel, L.: Common code writing errors made by novice programmers: implications for the teaching of introductory programming. In: Leung, W.S., Coetzee, M., Coulter, D., Cotterrell, D. (eds.) SACLA 2021. CCIS, vol. 1461, pp. 1–16. Springer, Cham (2022). https://doi.org/10.1007/978-3-030-95003-3_7
15. McCauley, R., et al.: Debugging: a review of the literature from an educational perspective. Comput. Sci. Educ. **18**(2), 67–92 (2008). https://doi.org/10.1080/08993400802114581
16. Middendorf, J., Pace, D.: Decoding the disciplines: a model for helping students learn disciplinary ways of thinking. New Dir. Teach. Learn. **98**, 1–12 (2004). https://doi.org/10.1002/tl.142
17. Middendorf, J., Shopkow, L.: Overcoming Student Learning Bottlenecks: Decode the Critical Thinking of Your Discipline. Taylor & Francis, New York (2018)
18. Murphy, L., Thomas, L.: Dangers of a fixed mindset: implications of self-theories research for computer science education. ACM SIGCSE Bull. **40**(3), 271–275 (2008). https://doi.org/10.1145/1597849.1384344
19. Newen, A.: What are cognitive processes? An example-based approach. Synthese **194**, 4251–4268 (2017). https://doi.org/10.1007/s11229-015-0812-3
20. O'Dell, D.H.: The debugging mindset: understanding the psychology of learning strategies leads to effective problem-solving skills. Commun. ACM **60**(6), 40–45 (2017). https://doi.org/10.1145/3052939
21. Pace, D.: The Decoding the Disciplines Paradigm: Seven Steps to Increased Student Learning. Indiana University Press, Bloomington (2017)
22. Panorkou, N., York, T., Germia, E.: Using debugging as a platform for transdisciplinary learning. Cogn. Instr. **42**(1), 124–158 (2024). https://doi.org/10.1080/07370008.2023.2270094
23. Plowright, D.: Using Mixed Methods: Frameworks for an Integrated Methodology. Sage, London (2011)
24. Romero, P., Du Boulay, B., Cox, R., Lutz, R., Bryant, S.: Debugging strategies and tactics in a multi-representation software environment. Int. J. Hum.-Comput. Stud. **65**(12), 992–1009 (2007). https://doi.org/10.1016/j.ijhcs.2007.07.005
25. Tsan, J., Weintrop, D., Franklin, D.: An analysis of middle grade teachers' debugging pedagogical content knowledge. In: Proceedings of the 27th ACM Conference on Innovation and Technology in Computer Science Education, vol. 1, pp. 533–539. ACM, New York (2022). https://doi.org/10.1145/3502718.3524770
26. Vessey, I.: Expertise in debugging computer programs: a process analysis. Int. J. Man-Mach. Stud. **23**(5), 459–494 (1985). https://doi.org/10.1016/S0020-7373(85)80054-7
27. Whalley, J., Settle, A., Luxton-Reilly, A.: A think-aloud study of novice debugging. ACM Trans. Comput. Educ. **23**(2), 1–38 (2023). https://doi.org/10.1145/3589004

Author Index

A
Adegbite, Adewuyi Adetayo 119

D
de Wet, Lizette 84

F
Fouché, Rouxan C. 51

G
Greeff, Japie 69

K
Kandjimi, Herman 33
Kotzé, Eduan 119

L
Levin, Marc 33
Lotriet, Hugo 17

M
Maleti, Tipson 137
Moonsamy, Wesley 17
Muller, Jacqui 69

N
Naidoo, Rennie 1
Nel, Liezel 137

S
Safla, Aslam 33

V
van den Berg, Carolien 102
Venter, Marisa 84
Verster, Belinda 102

L. Nel et al. (Eds.): SACLA 2025, CCIS 2770, p. 153, 2026.
https://doi.org/10.1007/978-3-032-12457-9

MIX
Papier aus verantwortungsvollen Quellen
Paper from responsible sources
FSC® C105338

If you have any concerns about our products,
you can contact us on
ProductSafety@springernature.com

In case Publisher is established outside the EU,
the EU authorized representative is:
Springer Nature Customer Service Center GmbH
Europaplatz 3, 69115 Heidelberg, Germany

Printed by Libri Plureos GmbH
in Hamburg, Germany